9(5)

Edward H. Schludermann

EVANGELICALS TODAY

EVANGELICALS TODAY

13 Stock-taking essays

edited by
John C. King

LUTTERWORTH PRESS · GUILDFORD AND LONDON

First published 1973
Copyright © 1973 Lutterworth Press

ISBN 0 7188 1982 9

Printed in Great Britain by
Ebenezer Baylis and Son Limited
The Trinity Press
Worcester, and London

CONTENTS

CONTRIBUTORS

NORMAN ANDERSON is Director of the Institute of Advanced Legal Studies and Professor of Oriental Laws in the University of London; Chairman of the House of Laity of the General Synod of the Church of England.

COLIN BUCHANAN is Registrar of St John's College, Nottingham, and a member of the Church of England Liturgical Commission (since 1964).

PETER COUSINS is Principal Lecturer in Religious Studies, Gipsy Hill College of Education and Editor of *Spectrum*.

GERVASE DUFFIELD is Editor of *News Extra*, and until recently of *The Churchman*, chairman of Marcham Manor and Sutton Courtenay Presses, and a member of the Standing Committee of the General Synod.

BRYAN ELLIS is Vicar of St Agnes, Leeds.

MICHAEL GREEN is Principal of St John's College, Nottingham, Canon-Theologian of Coventry Cathedral, and a member of the Church of England Doctrine Commission.

GORDON LANDRETH is General Secretary of the Evangelical Alliance.

SIR JOHN LAWRENCE is Editor of *Frontier*, and a member of the General Synod.

ALEC MOTYER is Principal of Trinity College, Bristol.

JIM PACKER is Associate-Principal of Trinity College, Bristol.

CONTRIBUTORS

ROB PEARMAN is arts critic for the *Christian Weekly Newspaper Group*, and until recently worked for Scripture Union's Modern Communications Unit.

JOHN STOTT is Rector of All Souls, Langham Place, W1, and Joint Honorary Secretary of the Evangelical Fellowship in the Anglican Communion.

1

A TIME FOR STOCK-TAKING

JOHN C. KING

It may perhaps gain a readier welcome for this book if I say at the outset that the idea for it was not mine. I merely took up a suggestion made by Dr Cecil Northcott and assembled a team of contributors to take stock of the position of Evangelicals—more particularly Church of England Evangelicals—today; contacted likely contributors, asking them what they thought of the idea, and suggesting topics which seemed to need their expert attention.

As the contributions rolled in, I found my enthusiasm growing. Not because my contributors showed infinite respect for deadlines (they did not). The enthusiasm grew from a realization that my team—and I hope readers will agree that it is reasonably representative—were not making safe statements and treading delicately so as to let sleeping dogs lie; instead they were looking questions in the eye and setting out to answer them in plain language.

The result is a book that by no stretch of the imagination could be described as sweetly harmonious; as well as producing incidental discords it may seem that some performers are following a quite different score from that being followed by some of their colleagues. For me this is immensely rewarding, for it seems that in this book there is an honest reflection of what is called—for want of a better word—evangelicalism. And evangelicalism today is a tumultuous, surging, youthful, inquiring phenomenon.

The chapters that follow provide a cumulative indication of a readiness on the part of Evangelicals to revalue themselves, to make a new assessment of questions that were thought to be open and shut. The book amounts to an acknowledgement that, good as the old ways were, they can no longer be considered good enough. The significance of the book, as I see it, is that it represents a determined effort on the part of Evangelicals to recognize that traditional evangelicalism is something less than Biblical, and to bring old customs and conventions under fresh examination. After all, if it is true to its own determining principle, evangelicalism must be prepared to reshape itself in the light of fresh truth from God's Word. In their own way the contributors are seeking a better, more Biblical pattern of evangelicalism than has been customary hitherto. It is my sure belief that the contributors are not alone in this search.

Just over seventy years ago H. C. G. Moule published his charming little book *The Evangelical School in the Church of England*. He set out to deal with the Evangelicals during the nineteenth century and confined himself to Evangelicals within the Church of England. Inevitably he recognized the impossibility of providing a sharp and unfailing distinction between Evangelicals and others, and he made generous allowance for the mutual influence which members of different groups within the Church of England exercise upon each other. 'In such a period,' he wrote, 'we shall trace abundant differences between one generation of Evangelicals and another, on the surface, although the interior continuity of main convictions, and of the ruling and informing spirit, has been, as I believe, unbroken.'

Anybody who reckons himself a member of the continuing school of Evangelicals can recognize the continuity to which Dr Moule was referring. What may not be so clear is the manner in which those convictions break surface; life today is too subtle, too complex, too full of rich variety to admit of all-embracing accepted judgments and canned slogans. Where the nineteenth-century Evangelical could afford to make certain assumptions about the Church, about society, and about moral values, today's Evangelical must cope with a bewildering array of thoughtful attempts to deal adequately with issues that were—in the nineteenth century—decisively closed as far as churchmen were concerned.

I happen to have in my possession a curious book entitled *Evangelicalism*, published in 1925. Edited by the Rev J. Russell Howden, who was then Vicar of St Peter's, Southborough, Tunbridge Wells, the book is a symposium 'mostly written without any opportunity for mutual consultation, and the responsibility of each writer is to be understood as strictly limited to his own contribution'. What is most noticeable to the present-day reader of this 1925 volume is the narrow range of its interests. Incarnation, resurrection, atonement, justification, and so on—these were the points considered determinative in those days. By comparison, the statement produced by the National Anglican Evangelical Congress in 1967 has a sweep and a scope that are staggering. Noticeable too in the 1925 volume is the defensive frame of mind suggested by the editor's preface, particularly his reference to 'the proposals which are now being earnestly debated for the revision of the Prayer Book'.

This book from nearly half a century ago is a vintage expression of a type of evangelicalism which has all but passed away. Whether old-fashioned Evangelicals like it or not, evangelicalism today is a horse of a different colour, and not least of the changes is a switch of interest. Evangelicals today are not interested in the same issues as their fathers and grandfathers; without ceasing to have strong convictions about the incarnation, the resurrection, the atonement, justification by faith alone, etc., they are much more concerned about the impact of the Gospel on the secular society that surrounds them.

More recently a booklet *What is an Evangelical?* by T. C. Hammond put the position as it was seen by a stalwart Evangelical leader in 1956. Archdeacon Hammond's exposition moved from a brief description of the rise of evangelicalism, through justification by faith, etc., to the practical consequences of being an Evangelical—which, as far as the booklet was concerned, meant the kind of dress worn at Holy Communion, the error of genuflecting to the Holy Table, and the misleading nature of the eastward position. Evangelicals today would not greatly disagree with any of this; they would, if anything, be rather bored by it. Other things are more important.

It is still possible, of course, to find Evangelical churches as Victorian in outlook as they are in their furnishings. Long reiterative sermons, a complacent and tenacious grasp of elementary articles of dogma, a simplistic and usually condemnatory approach to creative movements—there is no need to enlarge on the kind of thing I mean; I have described it sufficiently elsewhere.

It is now possible, however, to find quite different features characterizing Evangelicals and their churches. Perhaps the most salutary is a spirit of patient inquiry. Whereas at one time Evangelicals took the view that most of the important issues in life were susceptible of a yes/no answer, and that Evangelicals had been granted an answer of unimpeachable authority, it is now beginning to emerge that many of the primary issues of life are vexed and frustrating and that any two thoughtful people— even two convinced Evangelicals—will most probably arrive at conflicting answers.

If, indeed, Evangelicals are 'taking stock' the reader will expect there to be in this book some signs of definite thought about specific questions that come immediately to mind. On the fundamental subject of the authority of Scripture, for example, a reader may expect to find consideration of objections to infallibility that occur to every person who takes an intelligent interest in religious matters. When all has been said about the theological and philosophical arguments for accepting the Bible as God's undoubted Word to man, there must be an attempt to grapple with the inescapable problems of authorship (in the case of Isaiah, for example) and historical conundrums (Quirinius, Theudas, and so on). Anybody who asserts the divine authority of the Scriptures must be prepared for a verse-by-verse contest in which he must not too easily fall back on one improbable explanation after another to defend his thesis. One incidental problem in this field is that Evangelical congregations (i.e. congregations in the care of an Evangelical incumbent) are simply not accustomed to any rigorous examination of the composition of the book of Isaiah (or for that matter of the Gospels). Inquiry into such matters is, in practice, a costly business. The inquirer finds he cannot rest content with general statements, but directly he begins his inquiries he finds that whatever detailed and specific conclusions he comes to, they are unacceptable to many of his fellow-Evangelicals. This of course is but one example of the general principle that evangelical unity is much more ostensible than actual, and rests upon an eagerness to get on with the work in hand rather than a persevering attempt to discover truth.

The reader may also approach this book looking for evidence that Evangelicals have something sensible to say about the arts and creative activity. I believe myself that in this field there is a vital contest to be resolved. Descending as it does from a number of sources—the Puritans, the Methodist Revival, Charles Simeon —evangelicalism can expect to betray numerous inconsistencies. In one field, however, it has been remarkably coherent; it has declined to regard music, the theatre or literature as interests which a redeemed man should properly concern himself with. The time is too short. Other things must be given priority. The result has of course been an open invitation to triviality, ugliness, and insensitivity. The days of complacent deprivation, however, may be numbered—or, if that is claiming too much, then it may be true to say that a decisive contest is to be joined between, on the one hand, those who believe that a thankful and creative approach to God's world is appropriate and, on the other hand, those who believe that response to the Gospel requires an immediate and total renunciation of the interests and activities of a fallen world.

On these two matters I hope that the reader of this book may find signs of something better than a flat-footed and wearisome defence of the indefensible. When I first approached the contributors I expressed the hope that the book would prove to be an invitation to readers to identify themselves with the views expressed so that steps towards practical and coherent policies would be possible. Whether the invitation is in fact accepted is a matter for the reader; I hope that, whether accepted or not, the invitation will prove to be an opportunity for lucid, realistic and Biblical discussion of matters that are too important to be categorized as settled for good and all.

I hope too that this book will be regarded as an indication of Evangelical willingness to come into the open and discuss matters reasonably with others. So infuriating has been the evangelical habit of disinheriting fellow-Christians because they do not measure up to the Evangelical's own private understanding of appropriate response to the Gospel, that the non-Evangelical has found it impracticable to do anything other than get on with his work, as though the Evangelical did not exist. The Evangelical has brought this upon himself by choosing to elevate questions of his own creation: e.g., 'What is a Christian?', into decisive categories of thought and refusing to have anything to do with those who choose, what are to him, disagreeable answers. But a new spirit is abroad and the responsible positions occupied by contributors to this book are evidence of a new readiness to participate in the larger life of the Church.

I should like to thank my contributors—busy men, all of them—for the ready way in which they agreed to take part in this project. Occasionally there was need for a spot of pleading and arm-twisting, but I knew my men, most of them, from the days when I was twisting their arms to write for the *Church of England Newspaper*. They have shown exemplary patience with my badgering and I am grateful to each of them.

Only Gervase Duffield and Gordon Landreth have seen any contribution other than their own; it was agreed at an early stage that they should have the opportunity of exchanging typescripts before finally submitting their respective chapters.

Each contributor expresses his own understanding of the matter before him; indeed the fact that a contributor has agreed to write in no sense carries the implication that he supports a view expressed by any other contributor.

2

TAKING STOCK IN THEOLOGY

JAMES PACKER

Stance

The National Evangelical Anglican Congress at Keele was a milestone in twentieth-century evangelical history, for it broke with a long-prevalent pietist and sectarian mood.

Pietism (the name comes from the German Lutheran movement which borrowed from Puritanism and fertilized Wesleyanism) signifies any view, which, in concentrating on personal faith and soul-culture, retreats from questions of theology and church structures, and from the challenges of secular thought and culture. It is in these respects less than piety and falls short of full-orbed Christianity.[1] *Sectarianism*, as described by Troeltsch and later sociologists of religion,[2] is a label for movements which, in concentrating on the development of a close-knit community with clear standards, high morale and a fully mobilized membership, become isolated and exclusive in their relation to the rest of the Christian world. *Ecclesiola in ecclesia* (the little church within the church, the inner ring, the 'keenites' meeting separately from the 'not-so-keenites') is the typical pietist structure, and its sectarian tendency is obvious. Now it is an unfortunate fact that, for half a century before Keele, Anglican evangelicalism had occasionally shown symptoms of both diseases, and had in consequence acquired a public image in which intense devotion and missionary zeal were linked with archaic theology, spiritual conceit, ecclesiastical isolationism, social unconcern, pessimism about

---

[1] Cf. J. I. Packer in *Guidelines: Anglican Evangelicals Face the Future* (a pre-Keele study book), Falcon Books, 1967, pp. 25–8.

[2] E. Troeltsch, *Social Teachings of the Christian Churches*, Allen and Unwin, 1931; W. Stark, *The Sociology of Religion*, vol. II, Routledge, 1967; Bryan Wilson, *Religion in Secular Society*, Penguin Books, 1969, pp. 207 ff.; etc.

both the world and the Church, an old-fashioned life-style, and a cultural philistinism only too keen to plead guilty to G. K. Chesterton's indictment of Protestantism as Manichean to the core. This image, however, Keele swept away—in intention, at any rate, even if not yet fully in achievement.

It must be said at once that there was ample reason for evangelical recessiveness in pre-Keele days. A series of blows had shattered morale. Anglican Evangelicals, numbering perhaps a quarter of the church, had entered the twentieth century in a confident and outgoing mood,[1] and in 1909 an editorial in the *Guardian* (a now-defunct Church paper, seen in its lifetime as the ecclesiastical equivalent of *The Times*, which bishops and other top people were thought to read) had declared: 'A new Evangelical party is in process of evolution . . . We believe that the new Evangelicalism will have to be reckoned with, not only by other schools of thought within the Church, but by those who stand without it . . . There are many signs . . . that the new type of Evangelical is full of life and energy . . . He is eager to take a full share in Church life, and to develop it, if he can, on his own lines. He studies, writes, publishes books, even popular booklets, of great ability and wide range . . . He believes in Church order, in discipline; he is imbued with the conviction that he is a member of a real Divine Society. For a movement with such ideals there is a future.'[2] But Anglo-Catholic dominance during the inter-war years, plus repeated experiences of division and defection in the evangelical camp due to the inroads of 'liberal' thought, turned hopefulness and enterprise into a pessimism that showed itself by widespread withdrawal into adventist speculation, while it was left to 'liberal evangelicals' to think about the rôle and future of the Church in a changing world. Victory in the Prayer Book debates of 1927–28 was in a deeper sense defeat, for it made the evangelical name 'mud' in the Church for many years. Indeed, it was thought by many that evangelicalism in its non-liberal form was on the way out.

The Keele statement, however, testified to resurgent life.[3] It

---

[1] Cf. H. C. G. Moule, *The Evangelical School in the Church of England*, Nisbet, 1901; G. R. Balleine, *A History of the Evangelical Party in the Church of England*, 3rd ed., Longmans, 1911, pp. 205 ff., 211 ff.

[2] *The Guardian*, Dec. 15, 1909.

[3] *Keele 1967*, ed. Philip Crowe, Falcon Books, 1967.

could fairly be described as a return to the stance of 1909, a shift back in outlook from isolationism to involvement. Each of its six sections (the Church and its Message, its Mission, the World; the Church and its Structures, its Worship, its Unity) is in a very obvious way the product of attention paid to present-day debates in the wider Church. The statement was indeed addressed to these debates, and was among other things the expression of a will to join responsibly and constructively in the ongoing discussion. Since Keele, further concrete proofs of this willingness have been forthcoming.[1]

To some Evangelicals, both in and outside the Church of England, this change of stance has been unwelcome, and it has been heavily criticized as compromising the claim to finality which has historically been made on behalf of evangelical faith. The usual line of criticism has been this: Keele committed Evangelicals to ecumenical dialogue. ('The initial task for divided Christians is dialogue, at all levels and across all barriers. We desire to enter this ecumenical dialogue fully.')[2] But ecumenical dialogue is intrinsically compromising, for it proceeds on the basis that, whatever surface differences there may appear to be, deep down everybody's positive convictions are right; and the purpose of dialogue is, in the last analysis, to adumbrate a synthesis of them all. But such a programme reflects either cynical unconcern about truth or a relativist view of its nature, and in either case obliterates the antithesis between revealed truth and man-made error which is basic to New Testament Christianity. Also, any comprehensiveness which the church achieves through dialogue will embody, not the virtue of tolerating different views on secondary issues on the basis of clear agreement on essentials (which was what comprehensiveness meant in Reformation times), but the vice of retreating from the light of Scripture into an intellectual murk where no outlines are clear, all cats are grey, and syncretism is the prescribed task.

[1] E.g. Latimer Monographs dealing with liturgical revision (*Baptism and Confirmation*, ed. R. T. Beckwith, C. O. Buchanan, K. F. W. Prior, Marcham, 1967; *Holy Communion*, ed. R. T. Beckwith with J. Tiller, Marcham, 1972); *Growing into Union*, a joint Evangelical-Catholic work by C. O. Buchanan, E. L. Mascall, J. I. Packer and the Bishop of Willesden, SPCK, 1970; the combination parish magazine inset, *News Extra* (Evangelical) and *News Plus* (Catholic); etc.

[2] Sec. 83.

2

Thus dialogue launches you down the slippery slope which ends in total theological ruin.

The answer commonly, and, it would seem, rightly given to this begins by agreeing that comprehensiveness based on a relativizing synthesis of truth and error would be just as disastrous as the objectors make out; but, the answer continues, it is a mistake to think that the practice of ecumenical dialogue either commits anyone to aim at this or makes it unavoidable in the event. Keele defined dialogue as 'conversation in which each party is serious in his approach both to the subject and to the other person, and desires to listen and learn as well as to speak and instruct'.[1] Dialogue, as such, is neither more nor less than this: neither a tool for syncretism nor an instrument of diplomacy, but a technique of understanding by mutual interrogation, so that points of agreement and difference may be precisely defined. As the first policy statement of the Roman Catholic Secretariat for Non-believers pointed out,[2] there are three types of dialogue, distinguishable according to their aim. Dialogue one aims simply at achieving mutual understanding and respect; dialogue two seeks to understand truth which the other man is thought to hold; dialogue three has in view the establishing of a basis for collaboration and united action. Dialogue with unbelievers (Marxists or humanists, for instance) will not necessarily go beyond dialogue one, and the same is true of dialogue with Christians representing persuasions different from our own, though naturally one hopes that the outcome will be a recognition and an enhanced understanding of truth which the other holds. What must determine whether we accept his positions as truth, however, is not his holding them, but the Bible's endorsing them, and if Biblical endorsement is lacking, the dialogue should end in respectful disagreement and thus lead in to courteous controversy.

As for Keele's statement that in dialogue 'we may hope to learn truths held by others to which we have hitherto been blind, as well as to impart to others truths held by us and overlooked by them'[3]—another statement that has been much criticized— this does not in any way abandon the claim to finality for those

[1] Loc. cit.
[2] Printed in Herder Correspondence, Dec. 1968, pp. 367 ff.
[3] Sec. 84.

Gospel truths for which the New Testament itself claims finality (i.e. the sufficiency of Christ, and free grace, and faith apart from works, for a full saving knowledge of God); it only says that none may suppose his present grasp of revealed truth in its totality to be so complete that nothing remains for other professing Christians to teach him. (Here again, it is assumed that Scripture must judge what he and they say, and indeed must judge whether they may regard each other as Christians in the full New Testament sense.) Certainly, the New Testament does not suggest that intellectual error on some things argues lack of understanding of everything else (else where would any of us be?); and help on particular issues of faith is often available in quite unlikely quarters. Thus, dialogue between Christians of different theological backgrounds and denominational stripes is in its place a duty, not only to remove misunderstandings but also to enlarge the grasp of truth on both sides.

So far, perhaps, so good; but at the same time it must be admitted that the Keele-type, 1909-type evangelicalism faces major theological obstacles in the present-day Church of England, obstacles which it would be unrealistic to ignore, and which those who doubt the viability of the Keele stance are fairly entitled to point out. It is true that Anglicanism, being tradition-conscious (stuck in the mud, some might say), has not on the whole welcomed theological subjectivism, iconoclasm and innovation during the past decades as some bodies have. Nonetheless, current Anglican trends regarding the Bible and the problem of authority are quite discouraging. Whereas the Reformers believed in a Bible which was a God-given, self-interpreting theological whole, capable of speaking decisively on issues of faith and life; and whereas Richard Hooker, while stressing that reason and tradition had their place in the Christian principle of authority, insisted also that where Scripture speaks its teaching must be accepted without question; the Lambeth Conference of 1968 declared that authority for Anglicans belongs to their multiple inheritance of faith, patristic, Reformation and post-Reformation—an inheritance within which different Anglicans differently estimate different strands, and make different selections of what they think significant.[1] This amounts to saying that what the Anglican conscience is captive to is not the mind of

[1] *The Lambeth Conference 1968*, SPCK, 1968, pp. 82 ff.

God as learned from the Bible by direct exegesis and exposition, but the mind of the Church as variously expressed down the ages and now evaluated by our critical intelligence. The formula is in fact a loose amalgam of the traditionalist and subjectivist principles of authority.[1] What the bishops seem to have forgotten is that the Bible speaks for itself, and that what Scripture says God says, so that what men say in the Church must be tested and evaluated by what God is found to say in the Scriptures. The bishops also said that assent and subscription to the Thirty-nine Articles 'should be regarded as an expression of a determination to be loyal to our multiple inheritance of faith'[2]—but it would be better and truer to say that subscription should express a determination to be subject to the teaching of 'God's Word written' in the way that Articles 6 and 20 direct.[3] Lambeth opinions have no legislative force, but they usually reflect the general Anglican state of mind—which shows that Evangelicals face a situation in which other Anglicans will certainly wish to relativize, as strands in the great tradition, Biblical positions which Evangelicals regard as being absolute and final. If Evangelicals do not challenge this relativism, they will be living in a fool's paradise and will fail to be faithful to their God; but if they do challenge it, they need not expect to be popular in the present-day Anglican Church.

Structure

We have spoken of evangelical theology as both in dialogue

---

[1] Cf. J. I. Packer, *Fundamentalism and the Word of God*, IVF, 1958, ch. III.

[2] P. 83.

[3] Cf. J. I. Packer, *The Thirty-nine Articles*, Falcon Books, 1961, pp. 19, 45 f. It should be stated that while the bishops evidently thought that in taking their line they were following the lead of the Doctrine Commission's report, *Subscription and Assent to the Thirty-nine Articles*, SPCK, 1968, they were in fact abandoning it; for their paragraphs have the effect of closing a question which the report explicitly left open (see secs. 19–21), namely, the question whether the historic evangelical view of the nature of Scripture and its proper authority in the church is true or not. There is a world of difference between saying, as the report does in its proposed new form of assent, that *the Christian faith in God* is 'uniquely shown forth in the Holy Scriptures', and saying, as the bishops do, that *the multiple Anglican inheritance of faith* is uniquely shown forth there. The former statement points to Scripture as a norm; the latter allows it only to be a source.

with and in opposition to other versions of Christian belief. But what is it in terms of itself?

Here, of course, opinions necessarily differ, but the Evangelical's own view is that it is the authentic New Testament faith, the doctrine of God's free and sovereign grace to sinners, angled as the apostles angled it against all the manifold forms of pride, self-assertion and self-righteousness before God that fallen human nature can devise. From this standpoint, Paul against the Judaizers, Augustine against Pelagius, Luther against the 'free will' sponsored by Erasmus, and Calvin against the natural theology of the Scholastics, are characteristic Evangelical theologians. The God of Evangelical faith is a God who speaks to men verbally (the ministry of the incarnate Son, to look no further, shows that), and Evangelical theology is not a verbalizing of Christian 'feeling', as Schleiermacher thought, but an echoing and spelling out of truth which the eternal God has told. The key-features of Evangelical theology may be listed as follows:

First, *a Biblical perspective*. Evangelical theology receives the canonical Scriptures as God's instruction (*doctrina Dei*, in Calvin's phrase): clear, coherent, true, trustworthy. The Holy Spirit is acknowledged as their inspirer (the one who, in a mystery for which the Incarnation provides the only analogy, caused the verbal witness of man to God and of God to himself to coincide); as their identifier (the one who has enabled the Church to recognize the divine source and authority of these sixty-six books, as forming together the God-given *canon* or rule for faith); and as their interpreter (the one who enlightens Christians so that they see how the elements of the divine-human message, the word of Christ, bear on their lives). The thinking of the Biblical writers about the works and ways of God is taken as both source and control for ours; the Bible is enthroned as Christ's royal proclamation whereby he declares himself; and reformation— that is, correction and renewal—by the word of God (meaning by that the total message of Holy Scripture) is embraced as the only principle of spiritual life for churches or individuals.

Second, *a Trinitarian shape*. In evangelical theology, 'God' means the triune Yahweh, Father, Son and Holy Spirit; and saving grace (the central reality of Scripture) means the holy Three working in unity to fulfil the eternal plan whereby the

Son redeems and the Spirit renews sinners whom the Father chose. Basic to the shape of Evangelical theology are the relations between the three persons—the Father loving and sending the Son; the Son loving and serving the Father by making satisfaction for our sins on the cross; the Son sending the Spirit from the Father; the Spirit witnessing to the Son, and through that witness bringing the redeemed to know the Father. Together these relationships spell out that salvation, first to last, is God's sovereign gift, just as the principles about Scripture, stated above, spell out that all our knowledge of God is his sovereign gift also.

Third, *a radical view of sin and grace*. Evangelical theology, with Augustine, insists that fallen human nature fails through badness, not just weakness, and our renewal in Christ necessitates the straightening out of moral and spiritual perversity at every point. Paul's description of the mind of the flesh as 'enmity against God' (Rom. 8: 7) is taken most seriously. Any 'natural' goodness or right thinking about God in non-Christians is diagnosed as being in reality far from natural; it is a gift of God in common grace, not what would have resulted had it been nature that led them. For our natural fallen state is one of total *depravity* (total in extent, of course, not necessarily in degree), and consequently of total *inability* to respond or behave rightly to God in any way at all. All our thoughts and ways are naturally infected, more or less, with anti-God perversity. Thus, salvation, which is by grace only through Christ only and is received by faith only, presupposes nothing in man save total need. God's giving of faith, and of justification and sonship and freedom through faith, together with what Paul calls 'new creation' (2 Cor. 5: 17; Gal. 6: 15) and living in the Spirit, is a complex work of grace involving a complete re-setting of personalities which, so far as God is concerned, are radically disoriented and disordered. In these terms, Evangelicals interpret the conversion experience, correlating it with the Holy Spirit's work of regeneration (though at the same time remembering that convertedness as a condition matters more than conversion as an experience, and also that, as Richard Baxter put it, 'God breaketh not all men's hearts alike'). Evangelical theology is at war with all views which graft salvation on to natural goodness or revelation on to natural knowledge, on the grounds that such views fail to grasp both the sinfulness of sin and the graciousness of grace. The truth is that, as no theology takes a lower view of the natural man, so none takes a higher view of the present riches of saving grace, or of the substance of the hope of glory.

Fourth, *a spiritual view of the Church*—a view embodied in the Reformers' description of the Church is *invisible*. The adjective sounds bizarre, but what is meant is this. The Church is essentially a community of believers, chosen in Christ and united to him by the Spirit through faith, and now sharing a life 'hid with Christ in God' (Col. 3: 3). Now since neither Christ, nor faith, nor the Spirit, can be made objects of sight, no man can see the Church as it really is—that is, as God sees and knows it—and what is visible, namely, the worshipping community in each place, while it is a sure sign of the Church's reality there, may in certain respects mislead. Thus, congregations may be out of communion with each other, yet God sees the Church as one. Ministerial and sacramental forms vary, yet the Spirit of God makes the reality of ministry and sacraments to be the same everywhere. The congregations of the baptized contain some who are unregenerate, whose deficiency men may not know, but whom the Lord does not acknowledge. These optical illusions, if we may call them that, make it improper to identify the Church with what we see: the Church is always more a mystery of faith than an object of sight. Holding this, Evangelicals decline to view the Church as either a voluntary human association, like a club which Christians are free to join or not to join, as they wish, or as a divinely accredited institution for dispensing saving sacraments, like an embassy dispensing valid visas. The Church is believing people in fellowship with Christ, and in Christ with each other.

These are the main structural features of Evangelical theology, from which its evangelism, spirituality, pastoral care, and view of mission, have sprung. Though expressed at different times with differences of accent, emphasis, and detail, they remain constant. Undeniably they have the Bible backing them and the Spirit's power confirming them. They are not, of course, exclusive to Anglican evangelicalism; Evangelicals everywhere share them. Nor are they at every point exclusive to Evangelicals; much of what Evangelicals hold about revelation, the Godhead, sin and grace, and God's people, is the common property of all who maintain Christian supernaturalism in any form. But the Evangelical finds himself thinking that, on the points of belief, behaviour and spirituality, where he and his brother supernaturalists differ, his own position is closer to the Scriptures; which is why he continues to hold it.[1]

Substance

To make a stock-taking survey of Evangelical theology in the Church of England today is not easy, particularly in a brief space. This is an era of rapid theological change, and the situation is complex. Perhaps the most useful course is quickly to review some of the main areas of debate in which Evangelical beliefs have been implicitly or explicitly challenged, and note what kind of response has been forthcoming. At no point in recent debates have Evangelicals held the initiative, but a review of their responses will show something of their vitality, and also the direction in which they are at present going.

Take first the debate about *God*. During the past decade self-styled radicals have announced 'the end of theism' and 'the death of God'; they have told us that 'our image of God must go', and we must embrace 'the gospel of Christian atheism' and look for 'God beyond God'; they have turned God into our 'ultimate concern', and sentenced him (or, from their own standpoint, promoted him) to walk incognito through the secular city.[2] How have Evangelicals reacted to these ideas? Not favourably. The trouble, in their view, lies with the presuppositions and method from which radical theology has derived. The radicals follow the liberal method, which Schleiermacher pioneered, of commending religion to its 'cultured despisers'[3] by compelling it to speak

---

[1] For confirmation of the structural significance of these four key themes in evangelical theology the reader may like to examine side by side Calvin's *Institutes of the Christian Religion* and sections 1–17 of the Keele statement ('The Church and its Message').

[2] Authors represented in this selection of slogans include J. A. T. Robinson, T. J. J. Altizer, Gabriel Vahanian, Paul Tillich, and Harvey Cox. For a good introduction to this debate, see David Jenkins, *Guide to the Debate about God*, Lutterworth, 1966; for a more technical treatment of the debaters, see Heinz Zahrnt, *The Question of God*, Collins, 1969.

[3] The phrase comes from the title of Schleiermacher's first book, published in 1797: *On Religion—Speeches to its Cultured Despisers*.

their language and think their thoughts;[1] and this method has led the radicals to put their intellectual eggs into the basket of existentialism, the Smerdyakov of Kant's philosophical family, in its atheistic form of development.

On this basis 'God' has to be defined in terms, not of revelation given (in the accepted sense, there is on this view none), but rather of decisions made—God becomes the pressure that prompts the decision. But is that all he is? Evangelicals cannot forget that the God of the Bible is a God who is 'there', sovereign and vocal. 'God, even God, the Lord, hath spoken, and called the earth . . .' (Ps. 50:1). Paul, evangelizing pagan Athens, saw need to start with Christian theism—God acknowledged as creator of all and lord of history, God both transcendent and immanent, God who made man for himself and now calls man back to himself, God who raised Jesus from the dead and will one day judge the world (see Acts 17:24-31).

Today, too, it has to be said that thoughts of God can never be right unless they operate within a theistic frame. For theism, as defined, is the *paradigm* of Christian theology—that is, the basic conceptual structure in terms of which all particular views of doctrine should be formed and focused. Views that reflect a different paradigm may be interesting, but they cannot be fully Christian. Now, in theology, as in the sciences (or perhaps we should say, in theology as in the other sciences), the paradigm, being the presupposition of all 'proofs' within the system, cannot itself be 'proved': it can, however, be 'justified' (i.e., vindicated) by showing how many facts it fits, how few even appear to go against it, and how much more coherent it is than any alternative; and this is what Evangelical apologetics today are increasingly concerned to do. In this they follow the line marked out a century ago by the Dutch genius Abraham Kuyper and developed by a Dutch-American School of thought including

[1] Cf. the comment of the sociologist Peter L. Berger: 'The theological novelties which have dominated the Protestant scene in the last two decades all seem basically to take up where the older liberalism left off. This is certainly, and in these cases biographically, the case with Paul Tillich and Rudolf Bultmann . . . The various recent movements of "radical" or "secular" theology have returned even more unambiguously to the older liberalism, whether the "cultured despisers" being cognitively embraced are psychoanalysts, sociologists, existentialists, or language analysts' (*A Rumour of Angels*, Penguin Books, 1971, p. 25).

Herman Dooyeweerd, Cornelius Van Til and, at more popular level and with some modifications, Francis Schaeffer.[1] Thus existentialist theology and other such undersized products of liaisons between faith and modern philosophy are undercut and outflanked.

Take next the debate about *Scripture*. For over a century the historic Christian and Biblical notion that Scripture is inspired in the sense of being essentially God's own instruction (*doctrina Dei*), as the prophets' oracles claimed to be, has been under attack for failing to take seriously the Bible's humanity. It is argued that by not allowing for the fallibility, unevenness, and sometimes idealization and tendentiousness, of Holy Scripture, and by not accepting critical theories of the this-is-a-bit-of-a-spoof type, we sentence ourselves to miss much of its meaning and message. Whole expositions of Old and New Testament theology have been put together on this basis, while the categorization of Biblical material as myth, contrary to the beliefs of its own human authors, has become a commonplace in the schools. How do Evangelicals today react to all this?

First, they maintain the old belief in Biblical inspiration unflinchingly, accepting the Bible as true and trustworthy, *not* because this can at every point be proved (though, as they are quick to point out, it cannot at any point be disproved either), *but* because this was demonstrably Jesus' own view of the nature of Scripture; and Jesus' teaching on this, as on all other matters, should (so they believe) be taken as from God.[2] Awareness that this is a faith-position is stronger and more clear-headed than it was; rarely these days are young Evangelicals, or old ones for that matter, thrown off balance when critical scholars produce their lists of alleged discrepancies of detail in the text. Moreover, English Evangelical scholarship, with Anglicans, be it said, in the van, having accepted the propriety of critical enquiry into the

[1] For an introduction to Dooyeweerd, see William Young in *Creative Minds in Contemporary Theology*, Eerdmans, 1966, pp. 270–305; for useful comments on Van Til and Schaeffer, see Colin Brown, *Philosophy and the Christian Faith*, Tyndale Press, 1969, pp. 245 ff., 260 ff.

[2] Evangelicals regard Jesus' view of Scripture as of decisive importance in this debate: cf. J. W. Wenham, *Our Lord's View of the Old Testament*, Tyndale Press, 1953; *Christ and the Bible*, Tyndale Press, 1972; J. I. Packer, '*Fundamentalism*' *and the Word of God*, ch. III.

human origins and character of Biblical books, now claims as its own the exegetical dividends of modern study and produces scholarly work whose quality impressively vindicates the presupposition on which it rests, namely, that the Bible is *both* human *and* divine.[1] If Evangelicals are still short of top-grade Biblical scholars, they are not as short as they were, and are indeed at this point in a stronger position than at any time in the twentieth century.

Take third the debate about the *world*. Here all Christendom is rethinking in face of massive drift from the faith, and many for reasons good, bad and indifferent, are attempting to exhibit the declension as in truth a triumph of grace, by revaluing secular culture, urban life, revolutionary politics, non-Christian religions, and the prospects of the unbeliever, in terms of the axiom that 'God's in his heaven, all's right with the world'. Evangelicals perhaps needed to rethink these things more than any, for evangelicalism had long been in the grip of a cultural negativism which saw worldliness in all the fine arts; a social conservatism which resisted all change as disrupting God's order; and a blanket pessimism about all other religions as being realms of unrelieved demonic darkness. While more discriminating, and, in the present writer's view, more Scriptural judgments now get a fair crack of the whip in evangelical debate, it can hardly be said that all the needed rethinking has yet been done. Moreover, Evangelicals have a reason for moving slowly. They still see worldliness, anarchy, syncretism and universalism, as evils; they still hold a more radical view of sin than most others do; naturally, therefore, they show caution when confronted with optimistic naïveté, and look long and hard at the proposed revaluations offered by others lest acceptance of them would let in the above-mentioned evils.

The Keele statement indicated accurately how far present-day Evangelicals will go in rethinking their inherited negativeness about the world, and where they feel bound to draw the line.

[1] The key body sponsoring this development has been the Tyndale Fellowship for Biblical Research within the IVF. Examples of recent evangelical work are the Tyndale Commentaries on the New Testament, and some books of the Old; the many books and commentaries of Professor F. F. Bruce; *The New Bible Dictionary*, ed. J. D. Douglas, *et al.*, IVF, 1962.

Christian redemption, said the statement, 'results in the active renewal both of the individual, physically, mentally and spiritually, and also of society, in terms of love and justice'. Here was a broadening of interest beyond the bounds of conventional pietism. However, the social task retains an evangelistic dimension, for 'the longing for human dignity and decency which lies behind many present-day forms of cultural revolt, needs the gospel message of sin and grace, with its summons to self-denial and bond-service to Jesus Christ. This is the only foundation for true humanism.'[1]

On other religions, the statement said: 'We welcome sympathetic dialogue with their adherents, but we reject as misleading the statement that Christ is already present in other Faiths. We cannot regard those true insights which non-Christian religions contain as constituting a way of salvation.'[2] And furthermore: 'Whereas God in the gospel commands all men to repent and believe, and offers salvation freely to all who do, not all men accept his grace. Scripture has no place for a universal salvation, or for the possibility of a further successful probation in a future life for those who reject Christ in this. A persistent and deliberate rejection of Jesus Christ condemns men to hell.'[3]

Within these limits, evangelical reflection on our attitude to the world, and our task in it, proceeds—reflection which on the one hand is informed by knowledge that God made the creation good, that man has been made its manager (this appears from the so-called 'cultural mandate' of Gen. 1: 28), and that 'God so loved the world that he gave . . . ' (John 3:16), and which on the other hand bears in mind that creation is fallen, and 'the whole world lieth in the wicked one'. (1 John 5: 19). A new interest in social ethics is abroad,[4] and evangelical readiness and capacity to identify with the problems of the human community, as such, seems to be on the increase. So under God we may hope it will continue.

Take finally the debate about the *Church*, and its renewal.

It was once thought that the Evangelical view of the Church as

---

[1] Secs. 8, 13.
[2] Sec. 28.
[3] Sec. 11.
[4] Cf., e.g. J. N. D. Anderson's important little work, *Into the World*, Falcon Books, 1968.

invisible effectively forbade any positive concern for improving the Church's visible aspect; and certainly for two centuries Anglican Evangelicals showed remarkable unconcern about the Church's outward structures and forms of worship. (In fact, they valued an unchanging Prayer Book as a bulwark against Rome and the Romanizers in their own camp.) To be sure, this is only half the story; the other half is that as Anglican evangelicalism was born, or reborn, in revival under Whitefield and those who followed him, so evangelical concern for renewal has historically taken the form of seeking spiritual awakening. But unhappily this went with an attitude which made almost a fetish of dowdy worship, and which became articulate in a polarizing polemic against ritualists as follows: '*we* put spiritual life first, and so are content with plainness in worship; *you* go in for outward gorgeousness, and so show that you are not concerned about spiritual life.' One can be thankful, however, that today this sort of thing is hardly heard, and instead Anglican Evangelicals, with Keele, display an enlarged concern embracing *both* the Church's need of revival *and* the quest for its renewal in worship, structures, and unity—which involves seeking local rapprochements of separated denominational groups.[1] This double-aspect vision of renewal is in fact broader and more comprehensive than that of any other body of opinion, and this breadth, together with the regular Evangelical insistence on a full and clear doctrinal platform as a basis for Church union,[2] is perhaps the main contribution to ecumenical thinking that Evangelicals have to make.

The Anglican Evangelical record in theology is, no doubt, spotty. 'The Anglican Evangelicals have had a far more distinguished record in theology than is apt to be recognized', wrote J. K. Mozley,[3] and one is grateful for the comment. When they are read today, however, the narrowness of their range of themes (Reformation re-statement, anti-Catholic polemic, and issues of personal piety) is obtrusive and a little depressing, though their concentration on the person and work of Jesus Christ is much to be praised. If the Evangelical theology of our

---

[1] Cf. *All in Each Place*, ed. J. I. Packer, Marcham, 1965, ch. I.
[2] Cf. R. T. Beckwith in *All in Each Place*, pp. 112–147; Buchanan, Mascall, Packer, Willesden, *Growing into Union*, pp. 98–109.
[3] J. K. Mozley, *Some Tendencies in British Theology*, SPCK, 1951, p. 26.

time, while keeping God's grace in Christ as its centrepiece, and the Bible as its touchstone, can continue to speak to present-day issues as Keele began to do, it will render good service. The signs seem quietly hopeful.

3

EVANGELICALS, HONESTY AND NEW TESTAMENT STUDY

MICHAEL GREEN

Evangelicals ought to be the last people who could be arraigned for intellectual dishonesty. We dare to believe that truth matters. It matters so much that it has become incarnate. At a particular period in history, at a particular place on the map, the ultimate has become observable, the ideal real. In the life and death of Jesus of Nazareth we believe we have final truth about God, man, and the world. Not all the truth that there is: he does not exhaust the deity. But truth all the same, truth unmixed with error. When Pilate asked Jesus scornfully 'What is truth?' he got no answer in words: the answer was staring him in the face in the person of the one who on another occasion said, 'I am the truth'.

Now nobody ought to be able to believe that easily. The incarnation of ultimate reality into the person of Jesus of Nazareth is a claim of breath-taking magnitude. But if a man does come to believe it, he is thereby released from petty-mindedness and obscurantism. Such a man has no right to live in a cosy world of make-believe, where the chill winds of criticism cannot blow. He claims to have the truth. Not to know it all, mind you, for there are many aspects of Jesus to which I am, alas, blinded by my prejudices or my background or my partial understanding; not to know it all, but to have it. To have, in Jesus Christ, God's final word about himself, about ourselves, about what it means to be human, about what it means to love and to forgive and to sacrifice. Such a belief is liberating. It means that I shall never be afraid of the truth, wherever I find it. It means that the truth cannot possibly harm me. Whatever is true in science or art, in music or painting, in human love or natural beauty, sheds some light, some further precious light, upon the quintessence of truth,

Jesus Christ, and is in itself illuminated by him. Away, then, with
phobias, to which Evangelicals have too long been prone! The
God who has given us minds to search after truth has given us
truth to satisfy them, and this truth stands before us concentrated and self-validating, in the Man of Nazareth. Indeed, our
claim verges on the insane. With St Paul we would want to claim
that 'in him dwells all the fullness of the Godhead in bodily
form', that 'all things were created through him and for him.
He holds the sovereignty over all things, and through his agency
all things hold together.' We believe that 'God who spoke in
many and various ways to our fathers through the prophets,
has in these last days spoken to us in the person of his Son', who is
the creator of all things, the goal of all things, no less. Such is our
Christology. It is not blindly accepted. There are excellent
reasons for our belief in the full deity of Jesus Christ, but this is
not the place to deploy them. Suffice it to say that if we do believe
these things about Jesus Christ we ought to have our minds as
capable of enlargement as the universe itself. We ought to think
big, not small. There ought to be no trace of obscurantism about
us.

Very well, then. If Jesus is what we claim him to be, what are
we to make of the New Testament? We cannot allow it a venera-
tion of the sort accorded by Muslims to the Koran. It is not in
itself a holy book, descended from heaven for our adulation. Its
authority is a derived authority, for the place of final truth is not
held for us by any book: it is occupied by a Person, and what a
thrilling thing that is—to know that in this perplexing and often
sub-personal world final truth is personal! The New Testament,
therefore, is testimony to a person whom we believe to enshrine
all the truth about God and man that we need to know in order
to get right with God. What sort of testimony is it?

It is very human testimony, to be sure. Mark's Greek is appal-
ling, the grammar of the Apocalypse is non-existent, the voca-
bulary of St John small. Paul gets so carried away that he sometimes does not finish his sentences, and on other occasions goes on
for fifteen verses without a main verb—before coining a form of
word which is unique and probably a howler! Very human
stuff: the treasure is in earthen vessels all right. But it is precious
all the same. Because it is testimony from the first generation of
Christians to God's supreme word to man, Jesus Christ. That is

what makes the Bible, in the words of the Coronation Service, 'the most precious thing this world affords'.

It is well known that Evangelicals accord the supreme place, under Christ, to the Scriptures. I want, in the space I have, to look at two aspects of this position. Why, in the first place, do Evangelicals get so excited about the Scriptures? And then, how do they face the problems in belief and practice to which this adherence to Scripture exposes them?

Presuppositions

Evangelicals believe that the New Testament is supreme over all other Christian writing, for the simple reason that it is the witness of the eyewitness generation to Jesus Christ, the Word of God. The New Testament documents emanate from the apostolic circle, though by no means all from the apostles themselves. They enshrine the testimony of those who had known Jesus or had known his immediate followers. By definition, therefore, that stage is unrepeatable. We cannot get back *behind* the testimony about Jesus given to us in the New Testament. There is no independent access to the mind of Christ. We know him through the New Testament witness or not at all. That is why, as early as the New Testament itself, the apostolic circle is seen as the foundation layer of the building of the Church (Eph. 2: 20, 3:5, 1 Pet. 1:11, 12, Rev. 21:14). Any gospel which by-passes or contradicts the apostolic gospel is no gospel at all (Gal. 1: 6–8; 2 Thess. 3: 6–15; 2 John 10; Rev. 22: 18ff). That is why in the second century the canon of Scripture recognized what proceeded from the apostolic circle but rejected Christian writings which, like 1 Clement and Ignatius, were orthodox but sub-apostolic, or works like the Gospel of Peter, which were pseudonymous. What was required by Christian people was the unrepeatable first generation witness to Jesus Christ. The purest water is found near the source of the river: the risk of pollution is too great if you drink from further down the mountain.

Evangelicals believe not only that Scripture is the only window we have into Jesus Christ, but that its writers were inspired by the Spirit of God to bear true testimony to Christ. Jesus himself seems to have envisaged this. In passages such as John 16: 12–14 he promises them the Holy Spirit who would equip them to interpret his person and significance, just as in the Old Testa-

3

ment God not only acted redemptively for Israel but inspired men to interpret that redemption. Jesus sends his disciples out clothed with his own authority—'He who receives you receives me', and 'As my Father has sent me, even so send I you' (Matt. 10 : 40 ; John 20 : 21). So much so that in the great commission of Matt. 28 : 18f, Jesus can say: 'All authority in heaven and earth is committed unto *me* . . . *Go you* therefore, and lo, I am with you always, even to the end of the age.' The apostles are clothed with the authority of Christ as they bear witness to him.

They certainly claimed this inspiration. St Peter claims that the same Spirit who inspired the prophets is at work inspiring the apostles (1 Pet. 1 : 11, 12). 2 Peter puts 'the words which were spoken previously by the holy prophets', and 'the command-ments of us the apostles of the Lord', on the same level. This need not surprise us. For Peter proceeds to give perhaps the clearest indication of the nature of inspiration to be found in the whole Bible (2 Pet. 1 : 21). What characterizes 'scripture' is that holy men spoke from God as they were carried along by the Holy Spirit. There is a co-operation in the writing of Scripture. Man does it, in his own style and against his own cultural background. But it is the Holy Spirit of God who directs his hand, so that what emerges is not distorted by the human agency but is God's message incarnated, so to speak, in that author's way of putting things. We find basically the same claim in John's repudiation of anyone who does not hold the apostolic doctrine (2 John 10), confident as he is of the rightness of his own inter-pretation of the Word made flesh, because he has seen, known and touched him (1 John 1 : 1–4). St Paul made breathtaking claims to inspiration by the Spirit of God for his writings; see 1 Thess. 2 : 13; Gal. 1 : 6–12; 2 Thess. 3 : 14; 1 Cor. 2 : 16 and 7 : 17. Perhaps the most shattering claim he gives comes at the end of his treatment of men who were very conscious of the Holy Spirit at work in them. As an apostle of the Lord he can say, 'If anyone thinks that he is a prophet or spiritual he should acknowledge that what I am writing to you is a command of the Lord. If anyone does not recognize this *he is not recognized*' (1 Cor. 14 : 37f RSV). It is interesting to note that this was too strong meat for many scribes, who altered the *agnoeitai* to *agnoeitō* with the banal meaning: 'If anyone does not recognize it . . . well, let him not recognize it!'—which is certainly not what the apostle wrote!

Because the New Testament writings claim to be divinely inspired (a claim, incidentally, gladly acknowledged by the leaders of the sub-apostolic era who readily and clearly distinguished between their own authority and that of the apostles: e.g., Ignatius's 'I do not command you as Peter and Paul did. They were apostles'), we Evangelicals recognize them as having a binding authority over us in both what we believe and how we behave. New Testament teaching is decisive for belief and ethics. The word 'infallibility' is sometimes used to describe this normative quality of the Scriptures. At its very least it means that if you follow it you will not go astray. Some Evangelicals would want to go further and maintain that there is no possibility of any particle of error in the Scriptures, and that if there were it would jeopardize the reliability of the whole. This seems to me an unduly defensive piece of *a priori* argument and by no means necessary to upholding the New Testament's claims for itself. What all Evangelicals would agree is that if you show them a doctrine that is undoubtedly taught in the New Testament they will credit it and teach it, however little they may like it. If you show them a command that is clearly taught in the New Testament they will seek to let it guide their lives, however difficult it is. In other words, Evangelicals agree to take the New Testament as decisive for their faith and conduct. For it contains the gospel of salvation by grace through what Jesus has done. It interprets and discloses to us his person and the significance of his achievement, and is inspired by the Spirit of God. That is why Evangelicals give Scripture the regard they do. They are not oddities in so doing. They are merely following the indications of the Bible itself. They believe, yes, really believe, what most of the Churches profess to believe in their confessional and credal statements. Thus, the Council of Trent wrote: 'The Synod, following the example of the orthodox fathers, receives and venerates all the books of the Old and New Testament, seeing that one God is the author of both.' The Lutheran Formula of Concord says: 'The Holy Scriptures alone remain the only judge, rule and standard according to which all dogmas shall be discerned and judged'; and the Church of England in its Thirty-nine Articles puts it thus: 'Holy Scripture containeth all things necessary to salvation: so that whatsoever is not read therein nor may be proved thereby is not to be required of any man that it should be believed as an article of the faith.' Indeed, the Church of England goes much further. It demands of all ordinands to the priesthood: 'Are you persuaded that the holy Scriptures contain sufficiently all doctrine required of necessity for eternal salvation through faith in Jesus Christ? And are you determined out of the said Scriptures to instruct the people committed to your charge and to teach nothing (as required of necessity to eternal salvation) but that which you shall be persuaded may be concluded and proved by Scripture?' The 'oddity' of the Evangelical's presuppositions and practice is that he believes just that and tries to practise just that.

Problems

But it is high time to turn to some of the problems which beset a man who takes this attitude towards Scripture. How does he go about facing the difficulties adduced by modern critical study of the New Testament?

How does this Stone Age attitude of 'Back to Jesus and the apostles!' square with the assured results of modern criticism?

Well, of course, it does not always square with modern theories. For one thing, the assured results of modern criticism are by no means assured. Not long ago the pseudonymity of 2 Thessalonians, the priority of Mark, the existence of a unified Greek or Aramaic document known as 'Q', and the lateness of the Fourth Gospel, were all unassailed bastions of critical orthodoxy. Now all that has changed. Indeed, recent study has shown that the whole basis of the generally accepted solution to the Synoptic Problem is in grave doubt. The Evangelical notices this. He reads Ronnie Knox's *Essays in Satire*, and he glances casually at the piles of unsaleable theological rubbish in second-hand bookshops that was once the latest thing off the presses. Can we blame him for being just the tiniest bit unpersuaded that the latest heterodox Ph.D. thesis is the answer?

But another reason why the position of the Evangelicals may not always square with modern theories is that their respective presuppositions may be quite different. Many theologians will honestly acknowledge their presupposition that the Bible is entirely governed by the laws which obtain in secular literature, and is nothing more than any secular document apart from the fact that it is all about God. The Evangelical, persuaded both by the testimony of Jesus and the experience in his own life of the power of the Bible, that there is a divine authorship as well as a human to this book, is bound to come at it a different way. He will not rule out the possibility of a predictive element in prophecy, for instance. He will not deem it impossible that the Holy Spirit did bring things to the remembrance of the disciples. He will not rule out the possibility that Paul really had, as he claimed, the mind of Christ in his teaching rôle.

But when this has been said, it must not be supposed that the Evangelical is blind to the work of modern critical study. He is committed to it. He is committed to *textual* criticism, because the very importance he assigns to Scripture drives him to ascertain, as far as he can, which among variant readings is the correct one. Gone is the day, if it ever existed, when obscurantists claiming to be Evangelicals said, in effect: 'The Authorized Version was good enough for St Paul. It is good enough for me.' Significantly enough, some of the most distinguished work on the text of the New Testament in recent years has been done by Evangelicals, men like Tasker in Britain and Metzger in the States.

The Evangelical is equally committed to *source criticism*. The more seriously he takes the significance of the Gospels, the more intrigued he will be by the inter-relationship of the first three. Was Mark's the first to have been written? Or was there, perhaps, a primitive pattern which they all, Mark included, incorporated? And did Luke and Matthew depend on it? Is the sayings material common to Matthew and Luke (known as 'Q') a document which is otherwise unknown? Or does it represent oral tradition which they both reproduce? If it is oral, how come that much of it is word for word? If written, how come that much of it is so diverse? These are questions which will exercise the ingenuity, the patient study, the imagination, and the hard work of the Evangelical, just as much as any other New Testament scholar — perhaps even more, for the motivation is all the greater, when the scholar approaches the problem humbly seeking the truth, whatever it may be, and uncommitted either to the tradition of the Evangelical elders or the theological band-wagon of the moment.

Perhaps this is the moment to digress a little on this question of sources. It need not be supposed that the Evangelical will be in the least disturbed if, say, 'Q' should turn out to be a lost document, partly preserved in Matthew and Luke. He will rejoice to have so early a testimony to the teaching of Jesus, as old as Mark's, if not older. Likewise, Evangelicals have no antipathy to hypotheses which postulate a source 'M' behind St Matthew's Gospel, nor any stake in maintaining that Matthew the tax-gatherer wrote it. It does not claim to be by Matthew the tax-gatherer; it does not seem to be, for the evidence continues to point to the probability that the author used Mark, and that would be a very odd thing for an apostle and eyewitness to do. In point of fact, all the Gospels are anonymous, and their authorship is an open question. It is no more 'Evangelical' to suppose that the Fourth Gospel was written by the Son of Zebedee than to assign it to John the Elder, if that shadowy character really existed. I do not mind who wrote the Fourth Gospel. I do not mind what sources, be they never so numerous, lay behind the Synoptic Gospels. But I do receive those Gospels as four shafts of bright light on the person of Jesus, that enable me to understand something of his person, his achievement and his will for human life. To me as an Evangelical they are decisive. This does not mean to say they are all to be taken literally. Literalism is extremely foolish to apply, say, to apocalyptic, and there is no lack of apocalyptic in the Gospels. Thus, when Matthew, for instance, records that at the Crucifixion, the rocks were rent, the tombs opened and the bodies of the saints were raised, and emerging from their tombs, they went into the holy city after Christ's Resurrection and appeared to many, I am not shut up to one possible interpretation. Is he being literal? Then what were those raised bodies doing between his Crucifixion and their going to Jerusalem after his Resurrection? Is he using apocalyptic imagery, to show the cosmic significance of the death of Christ? That death opens the door of eternal life to all the people of God, past and present, but their newness of life is 'after his resurrection' and causally linked to it. On this view 'the holy city' might be heaven rather than Jerusalem, and Matthew might be making a profound theological interpretation of the meaning of Jesus' death. Other possibilities are also open. My point is simply that literalism is no part of Evangelical faith, and that the task of the Biblical exegete is to attempt to discover what category of literature he is dealing with and apply the criteria appropriate to it. The man who attempts to work out with wooden literalness the carat-rating of the golden streets of the heavenly Jerusalem, or listens with a metronome for the sound of the last trump is not honouring the God of the Bible. He is showing that he has no sense of discrimination in the categories of the Biblical material under discussion.

But there is one area where Evangelical hackles do rise over the question of authorship. They do not rise over the attribution of the Gospels; they do not rise when Hebrews is dubbed non-Pauline, or when the Apocalypse is assigned to a different author from that of the Fourth Gospel. There is no question of falsifying New Testament claims in any of these cases. But the matter is different when 1 and 2 Peter are deemed non-Petrine; or Colossians, Ephesians and the Pastorals, non-Pauline. Here the question of truth seems to be involved. Most Evangelicals will want a lot of convincing that these documents do not derive from their putative source. They will critically evaluate the arguments which are held to prove them pseudepigraphical. And rightly. For it does not seem to us likely that God should have used false claims in these documents as vehicles for his truth. We are right to give them the benefit of the doubt unless the case against them is presented a great deal more cogently than it has been hitherto. But should it be conclusively demonstrated that, say, 2 Peter is not from the hand of the Apostle (even granting a good deal of freedom to an amanuensis) then we should have to rethink. We should either have to conclude that the Church was wrong in reckoning this document among the New Testament, and exclude it from our operational canon, or else conclude that, odd though it might seem to us, God used the practice of pseudepigraphy, which was after all common enough in the ancient world, and deigned to reveal something of Himself through it. I would gladly adopt that second position if the arguments against 2 Peter were better deployed. They do not seem to me conclusive. I have argued this in print. And the majority of scholarly opinion fails to meet the arguments adduced but continues to regard 2 Peter as pseudepigraphical! Is obscurantism, I am sometimes tempted to wonder, confined to Evangelicals?

It is not only textual and source criticism to which we are committed as Evangelical scholars, but *form criticism*. To be sure, this is regarded with deep suspicion in some parts of the Evangelical camp. But this is because of the presuppositions of some of its leading practitioners, not because of anything inherently wrong with the methodology employed. The whole purpose of this discipline is to analyse and classify the forms in which the Christian material circulated before it came to be written down in the New Testament. This undertaking is admittedly speculative, but it is highly useful. It enables us to penetrate that thirty-year gap between the events and the writing of the Gospels. It enables us to see how these early missionaries shaped and used the stories. It poses perhaps the most interesting question one could possibly ask of a Gospel story: 'Why was that remembered? What use did it have in the life of the early Church? Why this and not other stories?' Now once you have found the life-setting of the story in the early Church, you may, if you are a sceptical German scholar, conclude that the early Church made it up and that it had no setting in the life of Jesus. But that is a gratuitous assumption.

There is a gross logical mistake in making an analysis of form and then jumping from it to a judgement on content. Eyewitnesses remained. There is, moreover, a methodological mistake in supposing that because there are parallels to some event recorded of Jesus in Hellenistic literature, therefore the Christians must have made up their story. They may have; they may not. It has to be evaluated on grounds other than form. There is often a contextual mistake in the more destructive work of some form critics. They use as comparison Homeric or Norse legends which took centuries to take shape, and neglect the factor of the survival of eyewitnesses in the New Testament situation. There were plenty of people around in the sixties who knew Jesus well, and, if the Christians had in fact been dreaming up words to put in his mouth, and actions to attribute to him, it is not likely that the whole body of these eyewitnesses would have remained silent. Indeed, many of the most sceptical form-critics pin their faith on parallels from the Hellenistic world and forget the essentially Jewish character of the early Church, where accurate memorization played the major part in educational method. Form-critics sometimes make a presuppositional mistake, too; they assume that the early Church could not have been interested in anything simply because it was about Jesus, unless it had a specific use in the catechesis or apologetic or worship of the Church. I find that naïve in the extreme. Are we the first generation to be interested in history? And, finally, there is the psychological mistake of supposing that arresting material is capable of being created by that shadowy entity, the early Church. On the whole, communities and committees do not create memorable stuff. That is done by commanding individuals. Read the reports of Church Commissions if you do not believe me!

So there is a powerful critique that can be mounted against the sceptical use of form-criticism. But what a valuable tool when freed from existentialist, anti-supernaturalist, and anti-historical presuppositions! It gives us a better understanding of the nature of the Gospels once we understand the problems which pre-occupied the early Christians. We realize how much the needs of the community shaped the form in which the tradition has come down to us. We get a fresh understanding of the individuality of each evangelist as one of the early preachers. And we see the good news in each of the short *pericopae* into which the form-critics analyse the material. 'The light of the sun is glitteringly reflected in every drop in the dewy meadow. Similarly the complete personality of our Lord confronts us in every brief story', wrote Martin Kähler. Faith in Jesus Christ did not come later than the tradition. It is in the light of faith alone that the tradition can be understood.

Most recently, form-criticism has developed into a further stage, redaction-criticism. This concentrates attention not so much on the beads of early tradition which the evangelist has strung together on his necklace of a Gospel, but on the way each evangelist has polished his stones, arranged them, and what sort of string he has used. Here again the Evangelical can rejoice and enter wholeheartedly into the quest for the distinctive emphases and theology of the particular evangelist. Dr Howard Marshall has given an excellent and highly constructive use of this redaction-critical method recently in his *Luke, Historian and Theologian*. Instead of being asked to see the evangelists as mere scissors-and-paste men, as they were under the source-critical hypothesis; or as mere beachcombers, looking for other men's pearls to put on their string, as they were in the hey-day of form-criticism, they are now given a chance to appear in their rightful guise as theologians and evangelists within the surging life of the early Church which they helped to shape. Men with a message, men with a distinctive point of view about Jesus. This does not mean that the Evangelical will go along with redaction-critics like Conzelmann in seeing in St Luke a profound theological break from his predecessors, or subtle geographical factors determining his theology. The evidence on which Conzelmann builds his theories is flimsy, and sometimes is perversely handled. What it does mean is that the Evangelical is not at all opposed to the methodology employed. He welcomes it.

This leads naturally into another area of critical study to which the Evangelical is committed, that of unity and diversity within the New Testament witness. We have been over-simplistic here for a long time. We have too easily allowed ourselves to claim 'The New Testament says', when what we mean is that one small strand of the material says that. Each New Testament writer has his own viewpoint. St Paul and nobody else in the New Testament talks about the Christian experience of grace as justification; and even he does so only in polemical contexts where 'works' are being suggested as the ground for our standing before God. St Paul does not, however, unlike St John and St Peter, talk about the new birth. They do not talk about adoption. Each writer has a distinctiveness in his testimony to Jesus. It is not all the same. It does not all proceed from the same viewpoint. It is directed towards different constituencies and its form of expression is influenced by different external pressures. It is our job as Evangelicals to study the differentia of the sacred writers and put them together to gain a wider appreciation of the many-splendoured person of Christ. But to pretend that they are all saying the same thing is not to be Evangelical but to be insensitive.

This diversity does not apply only to forms of expression but to Christological understanding and to eschatology. The teaching on the last things is profoundly different in St John, for instance, from Paul in 1 Thessalonians, Chapter 4. The teaching on the Christian attitude to the state is very different in Revelation 13 from Romans 13. But there is a harmony and a complementariness in the New Testament witness taken together which is the more impressive the more you study it. The unity is none the less real for being diverse.

Ah, it is said, but it is when you come to try and apply New

Testament teaching to modern church life that the rub comes. Our world is so different from theirs; our problems so dissimilar. Their witness is so unsystematic, so partial, so fragmentary, so historically conditioned by the situation which evoked those pastoral letters which largely comprise the New Testament.

I do not think we need see this as a problem, rather as a challenge. What, in point of fact, are those New Testament writers doing as they write to persecuted Christians in the Apocalypse, doctrinally mistaken Christians in Colossians, enthusiastic Christians at Corinth? They are seeking to apply Christ to that situation. No more, no less. To believe that they were inspired in so doing does not relieve us of the responsibility of thought and study and initiative. It rather demands these qualities. We have to understand the principles they laid down and apply them imaginatively, lovingly and above all, Christocentrically, to the present situation. We shall often get it wrong. But at least we know where to return for direction and inspiration—to the New Testament itself. Sometimes we shall be at a loss to know whether a specific teaching of the New Testament was conditioned by the circumstances of the day or not. St Paul's teaching about women wearing hats in church is now seen, rightly or wrongly, by most Christians to have been historically conditioned by what was seemly at the time. But the principle for which Paul contended applies just as strongly as ever. A Christian woman in twentieth-century England should avoid any suggestion of impropriety just as carefully as her Corinthian sister was told to.

It may be that St Paul's teaching about women's ministry was also conditioned by the fact that at the time women did not occupy any position of leadership in mixed society among pagans or Jews, and therefore he did not want to bring discredit on the Christian cause by women teaching in public. It may be that his embargo is to be seen as divine truth for all time. This is something that must be hammered out by patient discussion and diligent study of all the available evidence. There is no one Evangelical party line on the matter which delivers us from the obligation of using our God-given reason and experience alongside the God-given Scriptures, themselves inspired by the God-given Spirit who indwells us. To have a conservative view of Scripture does not mean an easy life, as if one had only to go to the book and read off all the answers. It involves the difficult procedure of seeking to apply the teaching of the book to daily life, utterly different as it is from the circumstances of those days when it was written. That is why the internal illumination of the Lord the Spirit along with the hermeneutical tradition of the people of God down the ages are so important in interpreting the Scriptures in our situation. The Holy Spirit's illumination is indispensable: he inspired it in the first place, and he can interpret it. Similarly, the history of interpretation by God's people down the ages is a helpful safeguard against my misinterpreting my bright ideas for the leading of the Spirit of God.

Perhaps, after all, 'problems' is the wrong heading for the second part of this chapter. For the most distinctive thing about the Evangelical in his approach to the Scriptures is that he does not simply go there for the problems that so engross most of his New Testament colleagues, problems which absorb attention to such an extent that whole areas of the New Testament are entirely neglected. He comes not for problems (though he will not shirk them when he finds them) but for food. It is here that he encounters Christ. It is here that he seeks the illumination of Christ upon matters of contemporary belief and behaviour. It is here that he tests his understanding of the good news and the Christian way by the touchstone of the original documents. It is thus that the Evangelical seeks to be *non solum reformatus sed semper reformandus*. And perhaps that is not so reprehensible an attitude for a Christian to take up.

4

THE OLD TESTAMENT

Alec Motyer

Nothing is easier than for defence to become defensiveness. If an extensive ideological perimeter is under attack, and the defenders (maybe not over-equipped for the task) are under necessity to rush hither and thither as one point after another is stormed, the temptation soon arises simply to ignore that any breach has been made, to substitute denial for reply, and presently to allow not only dialogue but also thought to cease.

Is this too exaggerated a picture of the Evangelical reaction to the onset and presently the triumphalism of the so-called 'higher criticism'? To recall from earlier days the encyclopedic minds and largely unanswered counterattacks of men like B. B. Warfield and James Orr is to see how our broad generalization has distorted the facts; but on the other hand to recall the large-scale retreat of Evangelicals from the field of intellectual combat into the more sheltered and in some ways more profitable paths of personal piety and monochrome fellowship, is to become aware that even such a broad generalization contains its quota of the truth. We need to acknowledge this without surprise and certainly without condemnation. Views of the Bible, especially of the Old Testament, for which there had never been any call to formulate a defence, were suddenly under assault. A whole world of learning came rapidly to espouse a view of Scripture radically different from the traditional orthodoxy of the Christian Church, and as the attack proliferated on point after point until nothing seemed sacred, defence deteriorated into defensiveness. For, after all, however one might be ready to admit that the headings in the Authorized Version were no part of sacred Scripture, yet they did enshrine what the Church had ever believed and which few devout minds had ever questioned. What sort of defence is required by that which has never before needed defending?

Nearly a century later we are invited to 'take stock'. The task is no easy one, for two main reasons. First of all, from within, Evangelicals are by no means monochrome! From outside, those who try to adopt and work out the traditional orthodox Christian view of Scripture can be lumped together—'Some people believe that every word of the Bible is true. Other people think that parts of it are told in parables', wrote J. Kamm, in *A New look at the Old Testament* (p. 11), but such a foolish generalization only shows that the present-day so-called liberal makes as little attempt to understand his Evangelical contemporary as happened in reverse at the end of the nineteenth century. Evangelicals are a diverse bunch when it comes to their understanding of the Bible. The doctrine of Baptism is the best illustration of this: folk who hold high and identical views on inspiration, and have an identical determination to discover and obey what 'God's Word' teaches, nevertheless reach so far irreconcilable conclusions. And if we remain strictly within our appointed brief of the Old Testament, the same is true. Some will find room for evolution within the early chapters of Genesis—others would die in the defence of the opposite view; some are persuaded by the evidence for multiple authorship of Isaiah—others would describe this as an arrant nonsense; some feast their souls on typology in the Tabernacle or in the Song of Songs, but to others the former is a bygone portable shrine and the latter a delightful collection of songs in praise of human love as God intended it. The list could be prolonged considerably.

A second reason complicates our task. The points at which Evangelicals (in the sense of those who adopt what is commonly called a 'conservative' approach to the Bible) oppose alternative views are not so clearly demarcated as was the case when the tides of criticism first rolled in. It is interesting, of course, to observe that there is now a 'critical orthodoxy' and a good deal of evidence of a defensive and closed mentality among those who espouse the so-called liberal approach to the Bible. The prize for today's most pointless exercise could well go to the man who asks for the question of the authorship of Isaiah to be re-opened, or, failing that, to the simpleton who suggests that the (virtually credal) belief that *bethulah* is the Hebrew technical term for *virgo intacta* and that the *almah* of Isaiah 7: 14 must mean a 'young married woman' can be overthrown with no stronger a weaponry than Young's *Analytical Concordance*, or to the person who inclines to scepticism about the faceless four, J, E, D and P. Yet, true though this is, Old Testament study is in a fascinating flux impossible to foresee in the hey-day of Oesterley and Robinson. In many ways the possibility of delineating the Evangelical by contrast with others is as difficult a way forward for us as to define him by common factors within his own grouping. Yet, on each side, there are common features of immense significance.

Basic to the Evangelical view of the Bible as a whole, and of the Old Testament within it, is the principle that the Bible is to be taken at its own testimony, and that this alone is sound methodology. Essentially, this view of the Old Testament arises through taking the highest view of the Incarnation. The Old Testament does not appear to be concerned to face its reader with the concept of the Inspired Book. As it stands, it invites the reader to share in a story about God and the world which He created. The story, as it develops, is well integrated and reaches forward by discernible steps of promise and fulfilment: the Lord's vow to Eve (Gen. 3: 15) is known to Noah (Gen. 5: 29); reiterated to Abraham (Gen. 12: 1f; 22: 18) and, as it transpires, finally established in the family of David (2 Sam. 7; etc.). The promise to Abraham of land for his descendants (Gen. 15: 18ff) was fulfilled in Joshua; the threat to Moses (e.g. Deut. 28: 36; etc.) was fulfilled in the Captivity; equally, the unfinished purpose of God, revealed to Moses (Deut. 30: 1ff) and to Jeremiah (29: 10ff), was continued in the Return from Babylon (Ezra 1: 1ff). Yet, in spite of so much fulfilment, the Old Testament ends with its major dreams unrealized: the new covenant has not come (Jer. 31: 31), the Servant of the Lord (Isa. 42: 1ff, etc.) has not come, the prophet like Moses (Deut. 18: 15ff) has not come, the promised David (Ezek. 34: 23) has not come, the Lord himself, scheduled to come to his temple (Mal. 3: 1ff), has not come. The silent centuries roll troublously by until Mary's baby is born, and first as an eight-day-old infant, then as a boy of twelve, next as a grown man with a whip in his hand and finally as the Lamb of God whose rent flesh rends the veil, the Lord comes to his temple. Jesus fulfils the Old Testament expectation of the divine

Messiah. Furthermore he amplifies his claim to be heard by the spotless perfection of his human life, and ultimately God sets the seal of authority upon everything which Jesus claimed, taught, said and did, by raising him from the dead on the third day — the final, heaven-sent proof that this is indeed the Son of God and God the Son.

It is the Christian's highest duty and his richest privilege to model not only his conduct but much more his mind upon the mind of Jesus, and in particular to do this in respect of the known attitude of Jesus to the Bible.[1] The controversy of Jesus with the Pharisees on the question of Sabbath-keeping, highlights the intensity of his insistence that the total testimony of the Old Testament be accepted as the Word of God, whether it is given as example (Matt. 12 : 3, 4), precept (Matt. 12 : 5), or principle (Matt. 12 : 7).

The attitude of the majority of Evangelicals on the question of Moses and the Pentateuch springs not out of a traditionalist mentality, nor may it be shrugged off as something which has become a King Charles' Head, but arises through reverence for the normative attitude towards Scripture of the incarnate Son of God and a determination to follow through the rigour of taking the Bible at its own total testimony. Within the Pentateuch, of course, Genesis is a case apart. It clearly implies in its recurrent formula 'These are the generations' that it rests on original sources,[2] and leaves us to imagine an editorial hand (unnamed) piecing this magnificent book into its present subtle unity. The Mosaic authorship of Genesis can never be more than inferen-

---

[1] To say, as many do, 'Jesus, and not a book, is my final authority' has a greater appearance of piety than it has reality of usefulness. For the essential question is this: how does the Jesus whom all Christians acknowledge to possess all authority make his supreme authority felt by the individual and the church? How does he express his will? Once the only objectively known Jesus, the Jesus of the Gospels, is in the least degree set aside (e.g. when his own recorded testimony to his personal, visible return in glory is rejected as being unacceptable to twentieth-century scientific man) final authority comes to repose not any longer in Jesus but in human opinion or even in idiosyncratic whim. On such questions, see J. W. Wenham, *Our Lord's View of the Old Testament*, London, 1953; J. R. W. Stott, *Christ the Controversialist*, London, 1970.

[2] The translation of this key phrase unfortunately varies from place to place in RSV, and in this, as in so much else, one needs the steady help of RV. But cf. in particular Gen. 5 : 1.

tial.[1] But it is very different with the remaining four books. They are dominated by Moses to the extent that apart from him only a mere handful of named characters take part in the action. At least one hundred and twenty-three passages between Exodus and Deuteronomy are similar to Exodus 3, 4 in that they must either stem directly from Moses (by authorship, dictation, or narrative tradition) or else be classed as fictional, with no basis outside human imagination. Most of the content of the post-patriarchal Pentateuch in fact specifically claims to depend directly on Mosaic mediation, and indeed the claim is made most strongly (i.e. in Leviticus and Deuteronomy) where it is most confidently denied by the majority of Old Testament specialists.

Two related matters must be taken into our survey at this point. First, if we are determined to take the Old Testament, and not least the Pentateuch, at its own testimony, then we must treat the concept of editing with the utmost seriousness. The Pentateuch contains some post-Mosaic (e.g. Gen. 36: 31) and some non-Mosaic (e.g. Deut. 34) material. The Book of Deuteronomy as a whole bears clear editorial marks.[2] In the light of this we cannot subsume the total Pentateuch under some such bland phrase as 'Mosaic authorship'. Yet at the same time it is little short of ludicrous to note the mileage of paper covered in pursuit of the provenance of, say, Deuteronomy, without the tiniest reference to Moses and the land of Moab.[3]

[1] The strength of the inference, however, is very considerable. Cf. K. A. Kitchen, *Pentateuchal Criticism and Interpretation* (1965), available from The Theological Students' Fellowship, 39 Bedford Square, London, W.C.1.

[2] Cf. G. C. Aalders, *A Short Introduction to the Pentateuch*, (London, 1949); K. A. Kitchen, *op. cit. supra.*; G. T. Manley, *The Book of the Law* (London, 1957). The differences of opinion between Aalders, whose book is now sadly out of print, and Kitchen should be observed as showing the vitality of the debate among conservatives on these points.

[3] A passing reference to the 'Deuteronomic History' or the 'Deuteronomic Editor' of Joshua-Kings is in order here. This notion has unfortunately become intimately associated with the supposition of a late date for the production of Deuteronomy itself, but this connection is not inevitable. A book such as Deuteronomy is clearly the Old Testament's primary statement of its view of history and would necessarily be the formative influence (especially if its Mosaic claim is accepted as genuine) on any serious attempt to write up the history of the people of God. The books of Kings are confessedly compilations based on some principle of selection. That Deuteronomy provided that principle should come as no surprise.

This brings us to the second matter, the theory of pseudonymity, namely, that in books like Leviticus and Deuteronomy the
Mosaic ascription was a literary convention designed to denote
nothing more than the reverence in which this material (from
whatever source it arose) was held. Without a doubt this supposition is open to grave moral questioning. A fraud remains a
fraud even when perpetrated from pious motives; a lie is still a
lie even when told in order to commend the truth. The opinion
of E. K. Simpson is all the more memorable for the cultivated
preciousness of its expression: 'Such sanctimonious knaveries are
the antipole of the code of veracity taught by Christ and his
Apostles, with its drastic disavowal of all disingenuous artifices.'[1]
But unfortunately archaeology has delivered us from having to
settle this matter on grounds of moral principle (or scruple).
The Pentateuchal literature can no longer be held to be ana-
chronistic. Both in its large-scale features (e.g. extensive law-
codes, and in its minutiae (e.g. the alternation of singular and
plural forms of address); both in its social depictions (e.g. the
patriarchal customs) and in its religious externals (e.g. the
Tabernacle); and in its literary formulations (e.g. the Covenant
form), to mention but a few features, the Pentateuch belongs in
the Mosaic and pre-Mosaic period which it testifies to present
to the reader. The arbitrament of objective archaeological
evidence cannot but in the long run press Old Testament special-
ism into a more realistic acceptance of what this ancient literature claims to be.[2]

But does not all this savour a little of healing wounds too
superficially? This charge might well be levelled against some
Evangelical counters to the reigning Old Testament hypotheses,
and we do well to heed it. There is, after all, a very impressive
array of arguments against the possibility of the Pentateuch
arising substantially from one authorship-source. Aage Bentzen[3]

[1] E. K. Simpson, *The Pastoral Epistles* (London, 1953), p. 6. The whole
section should certainly be studied as a classic statement on this point.
[2] Cf. K. A. Kitchen, *op. cit. supra.*; also *Ancient Orient and Old Testament*
(London, 1966); R. K. Harrison, *Archaeology of the Old Testament*, London, 1963,
and *Introduction to the Old Testament* (London, 1970).
[3] A. Bentzen, *Introduction to the Old Testament* (Copenhagen, 1948), Vol. 2,
p. 11 f. For a more recent statement following the same line, cf. A. Weiser,
Introduction to the Old Testament (London, 1961), pp. 71 ff. For a conservative
appraisal, cf. R. K. Harrison, *Introduction, ut supra.*

appraised the evidence as indicating that 'it cannot be proved that Moses must be the author of the Pentateuch' but 'on the contrary, it can be proved that Moses cannot be the author of the Pentateuch.' And he went on to set out the evidence requiring multiple authorship, the use of the divine name, duplicate narratives, discrepancies and the rest.

Conservatives genuinely try to be open to such evidence as is offered along these lines, and they cannot refuse to acknowledge that there is a hard core of genuine problems, amongst which the problem of the divine Name takes pride of place, but others, such as the relationship of the first two chapters of Genesis or the apparent differences between items of legislation in Deuteronomy and the enactments on the same subject elsewhere in the Pentateuch, run it a close second.

The fact that these problems must be tackled one by one inevitably gives the conservative reply to the documentary theory a piecemeal appearance which can easily obscure the single and fundamental principle underlying the reply. If the first principle of our approach to the Old Testament is the determination to take it at its own testimony, then the second is this, the primacy of exegesis over every other task.[1]

In the case of the Pentateuch, for example, Exodus 6 : 2, 3 offers an obvious problem, and the documentary solution appears to offer at least the broad lines of a solution, but to the conservative it is a solution which leaves the mind ill-at-ease, for he approaches the problem from his readiness to accept the Pentateuch in the light of its preponderant Mosaic claim. To allow this solidly-established claim to Mosaic unity to sunder because of one apparent difficulty has, to him, the suggestion that the nut has managed to crack the sledge-hammer! Therefore he will labour rather at the task of exegesis, seeking a solution to the individual difficulty which accords with the requirements of the overall claim.[2]

---

[1] For a superb statement and exemplification of this principle see, e.g. the commentaries of U. Cassuto, *From Adam to Noah, From Noah to Abraham*, and *A Commentary on the Book of Exodus* (Jerusalem, 1961, 1964 and 1967, respectively).

[2] Cf. W. J. Martin, *Stylistic Criteria and the Analysis of the Pentateuch* (London, 1955); J. A. Motyer, *The Revelation of the Divine Name* (London, 1959); J. S. Wright, *How Moses Compiled Genesis* (London, 1946).

It is not surprising, then, to find the Evangelical unwilling to acquiesce lightly in most of the arguments put forward in favour of the reigning pentateuchal hypothesis. The so-called duplicate narratives are exposed by exegetical examination to contain more difference than similarities; discrepant narratives are revealed as dealing either with different situations or with different aspects of the same situation;[1] the varying styles and titles of Deity arise (apart from those which reflect the natural desire of the writer for variety) from the theological colouring which each imparts to its own narrative;[2] and through it all the student enjoys the genuine thrill of living exegesis of the text.

The same exegetical determination governs the conservative in many other areas of Biblical enquiry. He is less ready than his liberal contemporary to allow interpolations in the books of the prophets, for example, or dislocations in the order of verses or in the placing of sections. The reason for this is that he believes that an interpretation which harmonizes is weightier than an unprovable assertion of irrelevance or of dislocation, that unity is the natural basis on which interpretation must rest until the contrary has been proved, and that where unity cannot be demonstrated (particularly in harmonizing facts in the historical books) it is usually best to let the matter lie, awaiting further knowledge or greater exegetical skill, rather than to make hasty accusations of insertion or of error or misunderstanding.[3] The Evangelical is frankly not convinced that the founding fathers of the liberal school were either zealous or skilful or discerning enough in their exegesis. Too often they seem to have said: 'There is no connection between section A and section B', where

[1] Thus, for example (in the opinion of the present writer), the allegation that Genesis 1 and 2 are discrepant accounts of Creation arises out of failure to understand the formula 'These are the generations' in Gen. 2: 4. The documentary hypothesis makes this the *concluding* sentence of the 'P' account—though everywhere else P is alleged to have *prefixed* the formula! But if the formula is taken as introductory to Gen. 2: 4–25 it offers the following heading: 'This is the continuing story'—i.e. Genesis 1 (however it is to be understood) is a great theocentric rhapsody upon the Creator's work. Gen. 2: 4 begins to open out the story of man upon earth. In other words, it is not intended to be an 'account of Creation' at all.

[2] See U. Cassuto, *The Documentary Hypothesis* (Jerusalem, 1961).

[3] *The New Bible Commentary Revised* (London, 1970) affords many illustrations of this principle in practice. The articles on Job, Isaiah and Amos should be consulted.

they ought rather to have said: 'I can find no connection'. Whether to call this exegetical disregard or exegetical ineptitude is a question which need not be pursued, but its result has been extremely damaging to sound Biblical understanding. Surely the time has come for a cessation of this insupportable appeal to some anonymous 'editor' or 'glossator' or whatever. For what, after all, is solved if section B is declared to be the work of a 'second/later hand'. Was he such a stupid person as to import an irrelevance into the passage? Or did he perhaps see a connection hidden from the modern eye? And if there is such a connection, why, then there is no need to find the work of a glossator![1]

Before leaving this brief consideration of the principle of the primacy of exegesis, we must say a word about its dangers and its excitements. The ever-present danger is that some principle of interpretation will be imported which is alien to the Old Testament. This can be illustrated first by recalling the large part played by the concept of the evolution of religion in the development and maintenance of the Graf-Wellhausen hypotheses, where the dating of the 'documents' was possible only on the assumption that everything had its due place on a line reaching from the early/primitive to the late/developed. Or, in another area of enquiry, Amos 4: 13; 5: 8, 9; and 9: 5, 6 were often denied to Amos because they reflected a doctrine of God the Creator proper only to the time of Deutero-Isaiah.[2] Such an interpretative procedure is anathema to the Evangelical, not because an emotive word like evolution makes his senses swim, but because it is wholly and utterly contrary to the evidence of the Bible itself to make what it insists is a story of God's progressive revelation of Himself into a story of man's gradual rising to the heights. Archaeology has, of course, blown the evolutionary pre-supposition sky-high and the antiquity of higher culture is now the known and established fact.[3]

A second illustration of the danger from importing alien principles of interpretation is afforded in connection with the

[1] For a penetrating examination of methods and criteria in exegesis, cf. S. Erlandsson, *The Burden of Babylon*, pp. 54 ff. (Lund, 1970).
[2] Thus even such a discerning writer as H. W. Robinson, *Inspiration and Revelation in the Old Testament*, p. 22 (Oxford, 1946).
[3] Cf. G. E. Wright, *The Old Testament against its Environment* (London, 1950); W. F. Albright, *From Stone Age to Christianity* (New York, 1957).

study of Old Testament prophecy. Without a doubt the moving cause for the dislocation of Isaiah into three parts was a rationalistic disavowal of the possibility of prediction. And, indeed, Old Testament study has not entirely shaken itself free from the effects of this nineteenth century prejudice.[1]

But what in fact is the position? Old Testament prophecy is a subject on which the Old Testament is a source document, not a take-it-or-leave-it tradition. Its clear testimony is that certain men were endowed by God with a predictive gift. Certainly their predictions arose from current situations and were relevant to those situations, but they were not locked into or restricted by those situations. It is to be hoped that Isaiah-study in particular may yet be freed from this rationalistic embarrassment,[2] but once the foreign element has been introduced it not only prolongs its own presence but gathers other irrelevances to its aid. Thus, for example, it is commonplace for proponents of the division of Isaiah to ask whatever use could be served by Isaiah of Jerusalem predicting an event still 150 years ahead. They do not stop to notice that Isaiah says nothing about 150 years, and that there is no need to assume that he even knew that this time factor was involved. The evidence as it rests in Isaiah 39 is simply this: that in a given historical context Isaiah made a directly relevant prediction of Babylonian captivity, a captivity politically possible within the foreseeable future.[3] Nothing in the so-called modern view of prophecy should discount such a prediction.[4] Isaiah would have been a man with a peculiar, even questionable cast of mind if, having pronounced doom and thus contradicted his entire foregoing theology, he did not then seek from God some light on what might or might not lie beyond the captivity.

Turning now briefly to the excitements of exegesis, few if

[1] Cf. O. T. Allis, *The Unity of Isaiah, A Study in Prophecy*, London, 1951, ch. 1; N.B. the drastically qualifying phrase 'even if detailed prediction were theoretically possible' in E. W. Heaton, *The Old Testament Prophets*, London, 1961, p. 126.

[2] Not all Evangelicals, of course, share the author's conviction concerning the unity of Isaiah, nor indeed his enthusiasm for its acceptance! Were it not that the topic fitted here in the development of our theme it could well have joined other illustrations below of the excitement of unfettered exegesis.

[3] Cf. Erlandsson, *op. cit. supra*.

[4] Cf. J. Mauchline, *Isaiah*, London, 1962, *ad loc*.

any outside the Evangelical camp can appreciate what an open book the Bible is to the conservative. Because, in general, our determination to accept the Bible at its own testimony and our practice of putting exegesis first tend to mean that there is broad Evangelical agreement on certain controversial matters, the appearance is given (or assumed) of a party-line or of the premature closure of really debatable questions. This is very unfair and very inexact, certainly at this present time. Let it be said loud and clear that the doctrine of inspiration settles no questions of interpretation. We are admittedly ready to use expressions like 'verbal inspiration' and so forth, but while this may for some (even many?) of us describe our attitude towards the Bible text, and offer a reason why we think it worth taking pains over, it does not begin to tell us what the text means nor to solve its conundrums. The enormous question of literary *genre*, for example, is still wide open, even when one holds that the words used in a particular passage are God's words. It would be simply impossible today to establish any unity amongst conservative Evangelicals as to the book of Jonah. Maybe we would tend towards its historicity,[1] but we would prefer to recognize it as a book about which much has yet to be established. For could it not be the case that, along with, say, Genesis 3, it represents a category of literature where the historical and the figurative are interwoven? Thus, one could accept the historicity of Adam (indeed, does the narrative as such, and the Bible as a whole leave us any option? Surely not!) and yet find ground in Genesis

---

[1] The 'we' in this sentence refers to Evangelicals as a group. For myself, I accept the historicity of Jonah and of the events recorded in the Book of Jonah. I can find no ground in Scripture for denying that God the Creator both could and would deal with His servant in this way if He so chose. Likewise I can find no ground for refusing to accord historicity to the record in Gen. 2, 3. Possibly the narrative of the creation of woman is one about which agnosticism is the best position; or maybe one should treat it as an intentional parable of the God-intended relation of the man and his wife. But, again, the event was unique, and who is to say it was not exactly as the Hebrew text reports? As to the talking serpent, since sin had as yet no internal lodgment in man, the tempting voice must come from without, the inscrutable divine sovereignty which decreed the temptation and the divine mercy which would go to the limit in alerting man to the real situation are well brought together in the absurdity of a brute creature which not only usurps the human faculty of speech but the divine prerogative of direction. Cf. E. J. Young, *The Theology of the Old Testament Today* (London, 1960).

3: 15 for the interweaving of factual and parabolic understandings of the fall and its consequences.

The excitement of exegesis could be illustrated in relation to Ecclesiastes, that profound (not sceptical) Old Testament apologist for Yahwism, or in tracing the diversity of approach to the Song of Songs,[1] or in dwelling on the entrancing vistas of interpretation opened up by modern Psalm-study, with its arms branching out towards the cult, containing the possibility of festivals and rituals hitherto unknown, and then reaching forward to a more realistic Messianism, rooted in the contemporary actuality of the Davidic king.[2] But space is running out and discussion of detail must give place to the description of aspects of contemporary Evangelical appraisal of the Old Testament.

We have so far been occupied in discussing two principles dear to Evangelicals in their approach to the Old Testament, the normative function of the Old Testament's testimony to itself, and the primacy of the exegetical task. But behind these (and, as we saw but did not elaborate, especially behind the former) lies the principle that the Old Testament is to be held within the unity of the Bible.[3] This at once raises the question of inspiration and authority.

The Old Testament is a very diverse body of literature. Prose and poetry, history and parable, theology and sociology, good men and bad men, great devotion and great betrayal, high-mindedness and sensuality, sublime truths and human errors—it is all there. In what sense then can the one word 'inspiration' cover such a diversity? The New Testament teaches us to think of the Old Testament as 'sacred writings' 'breathed out by God'

---

[1] Contrast, for example, the approach to the Song in J. H. Taylor, *Union and Communion*, London, 1962; and in the New Bible Commentary Revised *ut. supra*.

[2] See the article on *Messiah* in the New Bible Dictionary, London, 1962, and the introduction to Psalms in the New Bible Commentary Revised.

[3] Cf. J. Bright, *The Authority of the Old Testament*, London, 1967, where the relation between the testaments is described as Act 1 and Act 2 of a single drama. Thus the individuality of each testament considered by itself is held in tension with the incompleteness of each testament without the other. This is exactly correct, and removes the suspicion that in speaking of the necessity to hold the Old Testament within the unity of the Bible one is trying to short-circuit the discussion of Old Testament problems by providing ready made New Testament solutions.

(as we might amplify 2 Tim. 3: 16),[1] and the Old Testament testifies from time to time to its own sense of inspiration. Can these testimonies be sustained in the face of some confessedly erroneous material and some that is downright uninspiring? For example, in what sense are the errors of Job's friends inspired by God, and in what sense is the record of David's adultery or his nauseating human sacrifice of Saul's descendants (2 Sam: 21) part of inspired Scripture? The same might be asked of the imprecatory psalms. John Bright (*op. cit. supra*) warns of the way in which every man can so easily become his own Marcion in relation to the Old Testament, picking and choosing what he is pleased to accept as inspired and what he rejects as worthless. We are in fact in no position to arbitrate concerning inspiration, because it is a miracle of which we have no experience and do not possess canons and criteria by which to assess it. It will not do to speak of some parts of the Bible as 'more inspired' than others, for when this thought is analysed it means no more than that some parts of the Bible are at that present moment, and to that individual observer, more inspiring than others. The objective fact of inspiration must not be confused in this way with the subjective experience of enjoyment, benefit, or uplift.

Possibly it is more exact to speak of the diverse aims of the inspiring God. Some things are inspired as to their fact and essence (e.g. the messages of the prophets, subsumed under the heading 'Thus saith the Lord', and intending precisely that: that the words spoken were God's words, cf. Ezek. 3: 7), and some things are inspired only as to their record (e.g. inspiration guaranteed the exact recording of the sentiments of Job's friends because it was only in dialogue with error or half-truth that the truth could in the end shine forth). But as soon as we press this distinction we face again the rigorous task of exegesis. It is clear, for example, that Elihu considered himself inspired by God, yet we would have to account him mistaken. Did Joshua then equally mistake the will of God when he understood him to command the slaughter of the Canaanites? Can we accept the Bible's testimony that the Spirit of God moved Samson against the Philistines? The answer to these questions is that the Bible is not at every point fully self-explanatory but is always in the

[1] Cf. B. B. Warfield, *The Inspiration and Authority of the Bible*, London, 1951, especially ch. 3.

long run self-correcting. In the case of Elihu, his claim to inspiration is found to be bogus within the book of Job itself: the
testimony of the whole corrects the claim of the part. In the case
of Joshua, his sense of God's will accords with the view of history
sketched in Gen. 15: 16, elaborated into a total view in Deut. 28,
29, and undenied right through to the end of the New Testament.
As to Samson, while the mere reading of his story might trap the
unwary into thinking that the Lord was implicated in his mis-
deeds, the later elucidation of the career of Sennacherib (Isa.
10: 5–15; 37: 26–29) reveals the nature of the activity of the
Spirit of the Lord as one of executive superintendency over the
wicked, self-willed acts of sinners: the boisterous, headstrong
movement is native to the horse; the direction is decided by the
one who holds the bridle.[1]

In a very real sense the essence of the Evangelical understanding of the Old Testament is summed up by the honoured words,
progressive revelation. The thrust of this concept is best felt by
contrasting it with the idea of religious evolution. In the case of
evolution, the upward path is littered with that which must be
discarded because it is unworthy, erroneous, a mere stepping-
stone on the way up. But there are no stepping-stones in progressive revelation; only stones great and small steadily built
into, and each occupying for ever its place as part of the whole
edifice of truth. In progressive revelation there are no false
starts, no untruths to be discarded, but the unfolding of truth, an

[1] The same approach must be made to the so-called moral problems of the
Old Testament. The total evidence shows that Old Testament history is very
selective (but not on that account by any means either falsified or tendentious).
It does not record all of which it could approve nor approve of all which it
records. The folly of David's seeking to propitiate God by human sacrifice in
2 Sam. 21 is revealed not in the story itself but in the total Old Testament
context. Sometimes, of course, as well as making certain that we have grasped
the requirements of the total context, we need to be sure that the translation is
not needlessly biassed. For example, 'small boys' in 2 Kings 2: 23 is quite
needless, and creates a totally wrong conception—that the prophet snarled
vindictively at the thoughtless cheek of some Bethelite 'play-school' which he
happened to pass, rather than (as was surely the case) that he was set upon by
a rabble of young layabouts. Regarding the imprecatory psalms, the straight
question whether there is such a thing as righteous anger and whether prayer
(for all the imprecations are prayers) ought to be couched in terms of the
reality for which it is asking go a long way to clear the air. See, however,
J. R. W. Stott, *The Canticles and Selected Psalms*, London, 1966, pp. 11, 12;
J. A. Motyer, *Psalms*, in the New Bible Commentary Revised.

onward march from truth to more truth, an accumulating truth. The Evangelical, when he comes to the most seemingly anti-quated, remote, way-out Old Testament fact or feature, gives no place to the patronizing spirit which takes note of man's by-gone quaintnesses and then passes on. Rather, he asks what is the truth here, what is the testimony here about God.

In brief illustration, let us allude to a feature of Old Testament religion which more than any other makes it seem remote and out of touch with modern man—and a feature incidentally on which the Evangelical is generally found occupying a minority position in relation to specialist opinion—the insistence of the Old Testament on sacrifice and blood-ritual. If modern specialist opinion is correct, then here is something without a message for us. Who today could possibly believe that by obtaining the blood as it flowed from the animal, one gained possession of its precious life and that by giving this life to God one 'somehow' achieved new acceptance before him and a new vitality of relationship with him? Even if we are speaking not of animal blood but of the blood of Jesus, this 'somehow' is ludicrous and inadequate. But a 'person for person' relationship whereby the one takes the blame for the other, and if necessary, bears the penalty and dis-charges the obligation before the law, is a timeless reality. It happens almost every day between the parent and his growing family; it is recognized by the law of the land even if only in the matter of permitting one person to accept and discharge the fine laid on another; it harmonizes with the accepted concept of human solidarity. It has ever been a characteristic Evangelical insistence that in the Bible 'blood' stands for death, and that, in connection with the sacrifices, this death speaks of God's judicial penalty falling on the innocent in the place of the guilty.[1] In that most remote of all the Old Testament books, Leviticus, we come face to face with Jesus. How lengthily and satisfyingly this precious truth could occupy our thoughts! This alone can be said: no better place could be found to round out a review of the Old Testament which started with the Incarnation than that it should now focus upon the Cross, asserting an identity of inter-pretation reaching from the passover lamb in Egypt to the Lamb of Calvary, and the progressive revelation of the one God who,

[1] Cf. L. Morris, *The Apostolic Preaching of the Cross*, London, 1955; A. M. Stibbs, *The Meaning of the Word 'Blood' in Scripture*, London, 1947.

from before the foundation of the world, had it in mind to place the sins of those whom he would save to the account and upon the head of his own Son. Yet, to end just like that would be an insufficient appraisal of the Old Testament. We must encourage our imaginations to allow us to walk in company with the risen Jesus as far as Emmaus, and then to hasten back in time to be with him in the upper room in Jerusalem: for, by doing this, we become certain that he, demarcated as the Son of God in power by the Resurrection from the dead, took the Bible he knew and loved and set it first between us and himself (Luke 24: 27) as his authorized means whereby we would understand and know him, and then set it between us and the world (Luke 24: 44–48) as definitive of the good news of him which we are to declare to others.

5

LITURGY

Colin Buchanan

'Taking stock' makes little sense unless one does it regularly, and compares the situation at one stock-take with that of the previous one. In this way gains and losses can be assessed, and trends established. The problem in liturgy is: when was the last stock-take against which to measure this present one?

For my purposes here the best time for the last stock-take was just ten years ago from the time of writing (January, 1972). It provides a good occasion both as the last time events could be measured before the real changes came, and also, to put it in personal terms, as a point to which I can refer back in my own memory and experience in a way which I could not if the point of reference were twenty years ago. However, it is my suspicion that to go back twenty years would not produce a picture very different from that which will follow. Before 1962 the trends in liturgy for Evangelicals were nil—everything was static. By a curious coincidence, if I were a Roman Catholic I might almost take the same date—early 1962—and in the same way assert that little or nothing changed in the decades before that, and very much has changed in the one decade since. No one would allege that Evangelicals or Roman Catholics have been consciously imitating each other. The best guess therefore is that similar forces have been at work upon both of them.

'Liturgy' as a title conveys nothing. But clearly the subject is Church worship in its widest interpretation. For convenience, it will be helpful to classify Evangelical changes under three heads: liturgical texts; patterns of Sunday worship; ethos, atmosphere, and mood. The chosen period of ten years inevitably means that the best way of illustrating the changes will often be from personal experience, and it is my hope that writing in the first person singular will help both to illustrate the trends I discern, and also to warn the reader that it may be only my idiosyncratic view he is seeing, and not an objective liturgical history of the decade.

Texts

Let us go back ten years. The normal Evangelical approach to the Prayer Book was to cling to it as (second only to the Articles) the bastion of Protestant orthodoxy. In my own theological college days (1959–61) I was taught the Prayer Book service by service, with each difficult point expounded historically and Biblically so that it could only be understood in a Protestant sense, with the strong inference that the other people in the Church of England were cheating. The stance of the Church of England could be proved to be Protestant by this appeal to the Prayer Book; there was no further appeal, and if the Catholic were an honest man he would obviously leave the Church of England (so it showed he was not very honest that he stayed). The Church Society sold reprints of Bishop Ryle and Dyson Hague on the Prayer Book. In 1962 they reprinted *The Tutorial Prayer Book* in its original 1911 text, with a supplement by the aged Sydney Carter, himself a veteran of 1928 controversies. The Hodder *Prayer Book Commentaries* by Evangelicals were first issued between 1961 and 1964. In 1964 I inherited, coming on to the staff of the London College of Divinity, a worship course of two years. The first of these ran historically from the apostles' times down to and including the 1552 Prayer Book. The second year worked solidly through the 1662 Prayer Book. I took up the task where I had myself finished in my student days. If anything, I made the thrust of the course slightly more Protestant.

Nor were parish practices different. Morning and Evening Prayer varied little on Sundays from the Prayer Book. Holy Communion followed it even more closely. The Ten Commandments were read Sunday after Sunday at 8 a.m. (even if to only a handful of worshippers). The prayer for the monarch was never omitted. 'North side' reigned supreme (the last publication deploring Westward position was published in 1963 by the Church Pastoral-Aid Society—and then it was only deploring something *before* it happened to Evangelicals—the practice was almost unknown, save perhaps at St John's, Harborne, Birmingham, in

Evangelical parishes at the time). Evangelical clergy never wore
stoles—and knew exactly why the Ornaments rubric excluded
them! Some were already posturing threatening secession if the
Vesture of Ministers Measure went through (which it did in
Summer 1964). The text of the Prayer Book controlled everything.

This is not to say that the business was harsh and legalistic.
On the contrary, Evangelicals really believed in what they were
doing. They felt this to be not only a good defence in the Church
of England of their position, but also pastorally the best possible
provision for men's souls. Others might use the 1662 Communion
service with farcing and grudging compliance—not so the
Evangelicals. They pitched themselves into it with wholehearted
belief. They *knew* what was best for themselves, their congregations and the whole Church of England.

These were years of grave suspicion therefore in respect of any
proposed changes. Evangelicals felt that a policy of '1662 or bust'
had served them well in the 1928 crisis, the glories of which
still echoed in their corporate memories. All changes actually
proposed were almost certainly going to be worse than the Prayer
Book, so Evangelicals were opposed even to the principle of
change. Various rationalizations were issued to cover this defensiveness: 'These are times of doctrinal confusion—a bad time for
revision'—'Cranmer's handiwork is incomparable—we have no
skill like his.' And, in particular, Evangelicals found themselves
both addicted to uniformity (once they could bring those awful
Anglo-Catholics back on to the Prayer Book), and unwilling to
allow experiment (which might get out of hand). They were
therefore not well able to contemplate either the content or the
authority which any new services might have.

Around 1963 first signs of updating in language for youth
services and other non-sacramental occasions were found at parish
level. These normally followed the Prayer Book closely in thought
and structure, but rewrote the actual words: 'Christian friends,
the Bible repeatedly urges us to acknowledge and confess...'
If anything, this was a concession to the non-Christian elements
who might be present, and resulted from the tactics of the
times. These involved getting the unbelievers and half-believers
to a service and then preaching to them. Such 'modern language'
services tended to be for special occasions only, and rarely if

anywhere were found as the staple Sunday diet of worshipping Christians.

Sacramental services were almost equivalent to the Ark of the Covenant (though for the century since Gorham's day Evangelicals had been restive over 'Seeing this child is regenerate'). It was a major new departure when the Latimer House Liturgy Group embarked on writing new services (theoretically for not much more than internal consumption, and for advising Evangelicals in Chile and elsewhere) in 1961–62. At first we worked on Confirmation, for reasons which could be explained, but need not delay us now. In 1963 we moved on to Baptism, and for these purposes joined with another group from the 'Eclectics' (younger progressive Evangelical clergy) who had had the same thought. The upshot of this finally saw the light of day in 1967 (*Baptism and Confirmation*, edited by R. T. Beckwith, C. O. Buchanan, K. F. W. Prior, Marcham Manor Press), and in the meantime had been overtaken by the official work of the Liturgical Commission. The difference in mood between 1961 and 1967 should already be appearing. That which was daring originally had little such glamour by the time it came out. The reason for delay lay in the assumption we all shared, that we must produce something representative of Evangelicals as a whole, something around which all could rally, something semi-definitive as to our desires in liturgical revision. That assumption is itself open now to questioning. Certainly it delayed our work.

With eucharistic liturgy (one sign of changing times is that I can now write 'eucharistic' and not feel a traitor) the timetable of Evangelical stirrings was roughly similar. In 1962 the staffs of four Evangelical Colleges asked one of their number, the Rev. Leo Stephens-Hodge, to draw up an 'Evangelical Eucharist' for comment and revision by them. In the event it remained a one-man piece of work, but being modelled on a different structure from Cranmer's, and including reference to the Resurrection and Ascension, it marked a bold departure from the adherence to 1662 ways which had betokened Evangelicals up to that point. It appeared in duplicated form for specific occasions in 1963 and 1964, but through lack of publicity, presentation and marketing remained a private enterprise.

It was, therefore, upon an Evangelical world which neither expected nor wanted it that Series Two burst in its draft order in 1965, its revisions in 1966, and its final form in 1967. I had myself been brought on to the Liturgical Commission in September, 1964, when the work on this service was under way; and when I objected to parts of the text I was told 'But Evangelicals will never use it anyway, so you are just being dog-in-the-manger'. The evidence was that they would not, at least at first sight, and this view was understandable. Nevertheless, the stirrings I encountered made me take the opposite view, and I insisted that Evangelicals would be heavily involved in using revised services, so long as they were doctrinally usable by them. This in time proved to be the case, and Series Two both focused and created new approaches to liturgical texts amongst Evangelicals. Many put in a cautious toe and found that despite serious losses doctrinally, there were also gains, some doctrinal, some more practical and pastoral. The service came at just the right time in terms of Evangelicals' confidence about their future in the Church of England. It was authorized three months after the Keele Congress, and it fitted well into the more 'open' and questing mood which Evangelicals found in themselves as they faced the new agenda in the life of the Church.

Since then times have moved very fast. Series Two Morning and Evening Prayer have come in in some places; Series Two Infant Baptism in many more. Informal family services (as e.g. the one published by CPAS and contained in the back of Michael Botting's *Reaching the Families* (CPAS 1969), have been added. The upshot is that many Evangelical parishes now only use their 1662 Prayer Books for collects and psalms. As '1662 or bust' has gone, so it has been possible for 1662 to go without many people busting.

Evangelicals have gone further than this with texts, and, perhaps most significantly, with eucharistic texts. The Latimer House Liturgy Group started work on eucharistic liturgy around 1965. After some agonies (again arising from the desire all to say the same thing in a definitive way) two members of the Group were permitted to publish over their own names a service which the Group as a whole would not underwrite, on the grounds it was too *avant-garde* and kite-flying. This was *Eucharist for the Seventies*, edited by C. H. B. Byworth and B. T. Lloyd, and published originally with an introductory essay by Northwood Christian Book Centre in 1968. The service itself has been off-printed twice since (now available from Grove Books Bramcote at 5p) and has clearly passed into a large amount of unofficial use. The Seventies have caught up with it, so that it has a much shorter lead now over the official texts, but in spring, 1968, it was most daring, and it anticipated all other revisions which later called God 'You'.

On reflection, it was probably most significant in that Evangelicals at last were interested in 'kite-flying' and in 'unofficial use'. Such would have been almost unthinkable only six years before. Meanwhile the whole Liturgy Group soldiered on at a more definitive work, and this was completed in 1971 and published as *Holy Communion*, edited by R. T. Beckwith and J. E. Tiller, published by Marcham Manor again. This includes a more scholarly review of trends in eucharistic revision, and detailed criticism of Series Two and Series Three.

At the time of writing, Series Three is not yet finally amended and authorized. However, it represents a turning of the tide away from the trends feared by Evangelicals. Sin ranks as more sinful and more demanding of repentance than in Series Two. The cross is the better emphasized and underlined as the point of our Lord's sacrifice and atonement than in Series Two. The Biblical material and provision is richer and fuller. Here at St John's, once it was used, there was little or no desire on anyone's part to return to either Cranmer or Series Two.

So too with hymnody. The *Anglican Hymn Book*, the last of the Victorian-type of hymn books, was published by the Church Book Room Press in 1965. A fine job of work it was too. Doctrinally, typographically, and musically, nothing that Evangelicals were already using could beat it. It was a resounding success. It was indeed definitive. But no one seemed to know then that the day of the definitive was passing. In seven years since then we have moved on to needing a more modern language (to fit the wording and idiom of modern prayers) and a less lasting format. Hymns do not have to be Kleenex-like, but they do better on sheets like the famous carol sheets than in weighty and expensive productions aimed to last for a century or more.

All this has put a great strain upon those brought up, as I was myself as a student in the late Fifties, to expect the Church of England to be unchangeable, and the Evangelical 'party' to be a powerful reinforcement of that unchangeability. In ten short years it has all turned full circle. Now, Evangelicals not only want their texts changed, they themselves want to pioneer the writing of such texts, they want the door to further change to be ever open, and they have ideas about what they hope to bring in through that door. The agenda for lecturing in liturgy and worship has altered almost beyond recognition in the seven years since I took up my present job.

Patterns of Sunday Worship

In 1962 the mainstream of Evangelical Sunday practice was an 8 a.m. Holy Communion, 10.45 or 11 a.m. Morning Prayer and Sermon, and 6.30 p.m. Evening Prayer and Sermon. The pattern might be completed by afternoon Sunday schools and Bible classes, and by 4 or 4.15 p.m. Baptisms. Thus it had been since the turn of the century or before, thus it still remained. The services were valued for the preaching at them (it was still thought that evangelism was conducted by preaching, and up to a point it was). Evening services catered for young people, because informal activities could follow the service. Whereas others who had moved to a parish Communion had started to run their evening services down towards vanishing-point, Evangelicals could still show large evening congregations. The enthusiastic nucleus of congregations attended services twice each Sunday. Outwardly all seemed well and stable.

What then of Holy Communion? The Evangelical clergyman would be at Communion weekly (or more often) when in training; daily when on ordination retreats and suchlike occasions; and probably twice weekly when he became a minister. The services existed—they were on offer. But the laity were not regular communicants. Some effort to provide for them (apart from the famous eight o'clock) was made with the 'staying-behind' services. Once a month in the morning, or once a month in the evening, or both, the devout could stay behind and receive communion. Sometimes this was charmingly introduced by 'Mangled Matins' —which ensured that the worshippers got two penitential sections, four readings from Scripture, and possibly no intercessions at all. But whether it was mangled matins or a new beginning at 'Ye that do truly and earnestly . . .' the impact was the same. Those who valued communion could receive; the others were almost encouraged to leave. What this pattern never did was to *foster* a valuing of Communion amongst the laity.

The next move was just starting round the country in 1962. Now, very daringly, parishes substituted Holy Communion for Morning or Evening Prayer on one Sunday of the month. This was meant not only to give opportunity to the devout, but also to nudge the regular morning and evening congregations into an awareness of Holy Communion. Sometimes there was a sense that this service was meant to be a gathering-point for the local church, and it was entitled 'parish' or 'family' Communion. It is a pattern that perseveres today, and is possibly the 'mainstream' practice of Evangelical parishes.

It is, however, in strictly objective terms unsatisfactory. It is meant not to disturb the non-communicating, but regular, worshipper who attends morning or evening services. He still has his own service most Sundays of the month, and he has fair warning as to when he will not like the diet. He then stays away, and the Communion service, far from gathering the people of God, actually often has the lowest attendance of the month. Others simply take the service as it comes—'Oh, it's Communion this week, I can never remember'—but that does not sound as though there were any convictions or determination about Communion. Others, with the best intentions in the world, are away for a weekend here, unwell for a weekend there, and by chance are still not in Communion services more than eight to ten times a year. What alternative sort of programme can the Evangelical clergyman offer them or an evangelical parish devise?

Here, of course, the question of weekly Communion comes straight on to the agenda. Could there be good reason for having Communion as the central service every Sunday? After all, the Anglo-Catholics do—and the Brethren Assemblies do. The evidence on this point suggests that Evangelical heads are now convinced, but their wills are not screwed up sufficiently. The Keele Congress (mentioned above) stated the determination of its 1,000 members to move towards a weekly celebration of Holy Communion as the central corporate service of local churches. This was a controversial subject at Keele and a large minority (which some thought might even have been a majority) wanted to say only 'towards a regular, some would say a weekly, celebration . . .' Nevertheless, the subject was becoming a live one on the Evangelical agenda, and it may be helpful to trace out some of the objections which get set out in letters to the Church press and elsewhere. Their weightiness or otherwise can be assessed by examination.

(1) *We do not need Holy Communion. Having Christ we have all things and to put so much weight upon the sacramental means of grace as to fall into a catholic trap and belittle the authentic approach to God by faith alone.* There is a sense in which this is the classic form of Evangelical anti-sacramentalism. It may value Holy Communion as an occasional *experience*, but abjures it as a basic rhythm of Christian living. From a Biblical standpoint it ignores our Lord's *command*. 'Do this'—but we do not do it. Surely the *prima facie* case is that Christians ought to meet weekly for Holy Communion, and the onus is on those who would show otherwise. If some are false sacramentalists, that should not make us false anti-sacramentalists. If Holy Communion is a sacramental means of grace, it is surely not to be opposed to direct access to God by the priestly people of God? Is not the one the occasion and the setting for the other? Is not the sacrament of Communion a sacrament of the continued application of the free grace of the Gospel to the people of God? The disjunction should not be made.

(2) *Weekly communion would drive into the sacrament the unconverted and uncommitted in our congregations, and thus profane the sacrament, and harden them in unbelief.* This sort of objection reveals the traditional Evangelical presupposition in thinking about a worshipping congregation. All present might sing Christian hymns, and say Christian prayers, but in every congregation the sheep and the goats existed alongside each other, and the careful pastor, preacher, and leader of liturgy had to take account of the fact. Preaching was either to believers or to unbelievers (and often the preacher would make clear which). But the sacrament was only for believers, and no unbeliever must be admitted. To lay the service on, as it were promiscuously, was to frustrate it of its effects, and to verge on blasphemy.

There is a core of truth here. No one wants to drive unbelievers into Holy Communion in a wanton way. But there is also a faulty presupposition. In a parish of 10,000, where one hundred go to Sunday services, are these one hundred not entitled to some tentative assumption that they actually mean what they are doing? If in the past people went to church out of habit or a desire for respectability, that is hardly so today. Are not those who worship as much to be treated as Christians to the point of our putting the bread and wine of the Lord in their mouths as they are when we quite happily invite them to sing Christian hymns? As Church and society drive ever further apart (and this is strongly in trend compared with ten years ago) then we have ever better warrant for treating worshippers as Christians.

One fears the traditional Evangelical will still be on the look-out for hypocrites. To this there are two answers. The first is that in the last resort the responsibility is upon the man himself. The second is that the Holy Communion is a challenge to him. The problem with many churchgoers today is that they are never brought to a sticking-point. Preaching services are drift-in, drift-out performances in essence. There are no sanctions to them. If individuals think that they can get just as good sermons on TV (or at least on wet Sundays) then who can quarrel with them? The only point of commitment to the worshipping con-gregation is, in the providence of God, at Holy Communion. It is only the 'do this' which makes men stand up and be counted. One suspects that many many congregations do indeed have the half-converted and the half-believing attending preaching ser-vices in a half-hearted way, and they are curiously confirmed in their halfway position by the very pattern of services they attend. Were the Holy Communion to be put before them as the *sine qua non* of discipleship to our Lord, then no doubt some would fade away—but others would be brought to commitment. It is a challenge which many congregations need.

Of course services still gather all sorts of casual attenders, and probably will do so right up until such time as we are driven back to the catacombs. Casual attenders are, however, no more of a problem when Communion comes each Sunday than they are on the 'one Sunday in the month' pattern. In each case they are simply there on a specific occasion. They may have come because their banns are being read (how much longer will *this* last?), or because someone has died, or because they are at a loose end, or because they are searching. We can cope with these people. They must be made to feel at home, to be unembarrassed, and dis-tinctly *not* to be forced to communicate, nor to be evicted halfway through. Admittedly, non-communicating attendance was op-posed by the Reformers, but it was opposed as improper for

Christian people, leading to an improper celebration. Today, the presence of a fringe of doubters or unbelievers or enquirers who choose not to communicate, but to watch Christians at their most distinctive activity, should be welcomed, rather than opposed.

(3) *Weekly Communion is to invite worshippers to take it for granted, to drop into slipshod ways, and to come without preparation.* It may be true that Anglican celebrations of Communion can and will never rival the great heights of the old-fashioned Scottish practice where the sacrament was held four times yearly, and was preceded by services of preparation and followed by further services of thanksgiving. No Anglican pattern can give us that. The point of the Presbyterian pattern is that the service is *corporate*. One could have sympathy with a programme which had the sacrament but rarely, and really gathered the congregation for it. But the Evangelical patterns of the 1960s leave the sacrament still occurring each week, but simply on offer to those who happen to care for that sort of thing. Some communicants are simply in Communion by surprise—it was not the service they were expecting. Others take it for granted as the particular feature of that week of the month. But there is little or no evidence that Evangelicals prepare themselves by vigorous self-examination for Communion nowadays at all. It would not be cheapening the service to make it central every week—it is cheap already. What it would do would be to make the sacrament self-evidently the proper activity for Christians, rather than an infrequent and slightly unregulated one. It is an open question whether this would really bring the worshippers more or less prepared to the service.

From such a balancing out of reasoning some Evangelical parishes have moved on in the last five years from 'once a month' to a genuinely parish Communion situation. They have been helped in so doing by Series Two. They should have been helped also by the new situation in which any number of laymen may assist in the administration of both elements (though Evangelical parishes can be as clericalist as anyone on this point). If the length of time of the administration can be kept down, then more opportunity for teaching can be gained.

Finally, Evangelicals are now grappling with other questions in the Sunday pattern. The questions are posed the more strongly because few Christians, it seems, attend services twice on a

Sunday now. Ten years have seen a great falling off here. But family services have grown in place of traditional Sunday schools, or at least made some inroads into them. Baptismal questions, which have pressed ever more urgently in recent years, have led at least to more baptisms in the main services of the day, and the existing pattern of Evening Prayer and Sermon is itself under review in many places.

Yet with all this, are not certain vital matters overlooked? Two spring at once to mind. The first relates to the quality of Christian fellowship, and will come under review in the section following this. The other is directly related to what we do on Sundays when we meet. It is simply this—the clergy and other preachers and officiants are not teaching the people God's truth. It is as simple as that. No doubt about it—they are going through the motions most conscientiously. But they are not teaching them. The sheer undiluted, unmitigated theological ignorance of virtually every worshipper in our congregations is breath taking. Could so much didactic energy go to so little result? It could, and it does, and it is frightening. If patterns of the use of Sunday are to be restructured, then along with the well-known problem of the place of Communion must come the less recognized problem of the null effect of existing teaching and preaching.

Ethos, Atmosphere and Mood

The core of Evangelicals are used to close Christian fellowship. They have always experienced it in extempore prayer meetings, on camps and house-parties and in Bible study groups. It has been their glory, but it has happened in severe separation from the liturgy of the Church. This has meant that fellowship has been mentally defined in subjective ways ('people with whom I have a deep sense of warmth and oneness') and not in the more objective New Testament way ('those who are in Christ with me'). The recovery of the doctrine of the Church which has characterized the Liturgical Movement in other parts of Christendom is now finding some echo amongst Evangelicals. It may have been promoted by the ecumenical pressures which have made Evangelicals ask 'What is the Church?' Or it may spring from the more full-orbed Biblical theology which, growing from the Calvinist renascence of the fifties and early sixties, has caused the 'party' to ask itself questions about its own place in the larger life of the Church of England. Or it may spring from pastoral need—the minister at least cannot narrow his awareness of the local body down to simply those with whom he 'clicks'. For whatever reason, Anglicans who are Evangelicals are now much more Church-conscious than a decade ago. And their Church-consciousness is grappling with how the Church can really unite its members into harmony. What does the Church do when it meets? And what has this to do with uniting it in depth and enabling it to be and to act as a supernatural fellowship?

The answer seems to be that traditional formal worship is not building up the fellowship, or not sufficiently, and traditional informal Evangelical activities tend to cut across the goal of fellowship which we are seeking. The need that cries out is that Christian people should *meet* each other, and meet each other in depth. Worship, in the New Testament, was an informal activity 'from house to house with joy'. The disciples loved one another and shared with one another. Food and money and teaching and praying and joy (and even fun?) all figured in their meetings. Set prayers there may well have been—the New Testament is littered with liturgical allusions. But community was the setting. Nowadays formal worship has become the enemy of community and has set apart two things which in the New Testament belong together.

Evangelicals, both college students and more progressive parishes, are still at early stages of analysing their needs here. But informalizing the formal is beginning to happen. There are great obstacles. The sheer weight of traditional ways is one. The size of worship-buildings and of congregations is another. The fixed pews are a third. The protective shells we are accustomed to use to prevent others really knowing us is a fourth. The shyness of speech of those who know themselves to be ignorant in the Scriptures, and the brashness of speech of those who fancy themselves to be knowledgeable constitute a sixth. But slowly and painfully, through house-groups and house communions, through *agapes* and informal family worship, through dialogue forms of teaching and congregational participation, a frozen situation is unfreezing. Some Evangelicals would see the natural next step as the incorporating into Sunday gatherings of the various gifts of the Spirit. Tongues and kindred gifts have reappeared in Evangelical Anglican circles (and elsewhere of course) almost exactly in the last decade. Other gifts (yours truly, for lack of others, offers administration—1 Cor. 12: 28) are recognized and used in harmony also. We are still at the beginning of assimilating such 'every-member' ministry into corporate worship. But in some few parishes it is already a regular Sunday occurrence.

How absurd then is our liturgical freeze-up? If Communion comes during a meal, how can it always have its super-seriousness? If children take their place as well—and Keele foresightedly looked forward at least as far as the 1971 Initiation Report on this—then how can we all be sober-sided? Our meetings for worship must be authentic and contemporary and human. Otherwise the liturgy, however true in objective terms, remains a masked pretence which will not bring us near God or each other. And, curiously, if only we actually *met*, that might be the context within which effective teaching could be recreated too. In 1972 it is hard to think of a greater priority for Christians. The first steps have been taken? Where are the second?

6

SECULAR SOCIETY, MORALITY, AND THE LAW

Norman Anderson

It is impossible to make any dogmatic statement about the attitude adopted by Evangelicals in general regarding their responsibilities towards secular society. This attitude has in fact varied widely down the years, and from one group, or even individual, to another. At the time of the Reformation, and again at the time of the Evangelical Revival, these responsibilities certainly received widespread recognition. But it would, I think, be true to say that in the last two or three generations the dominant trend has been somewhat pietistic. The Biblical verses which depict the 'world' as evil, estranged from God, and even under what may be termed enemy occupation, have received much more emphasis than those which declare God's love for, delight in and continued sovereignty over the world he has made. The injunction to Christians to 'come out and be separate' has been stressed much more strongly and persistently than the affirmation that 'You are the salt of the earth'; and the duty to call individuals out of a corrupt society, 'snatching them as it were out of the fire', has been taken far more seriously than the obligation to proclaim God's will and purpose for society as such.

But with the present generation of Evangelicals the pendulum has begun to swing the other way. It is increasingly realized that no clear-cut line can be drawn between the secular and religious, the material and spiritual, the temporal and eternal, for God is vitally concerned with *every* aspect of human life. There is, of course, a very real sense in which this has never been completely forgotten, for there has almost always been a healthy emphasis in Evangelical circles on personal charity—partly, no doubt, as an effective aid to evangelism, but partly also out of a genuine care for those in any sort of need. The major change has been in the renewed interest and involvement of contemporary Evangelicals in what we may term preventive rather than remedial measures. Instead of concentrating almost exclusively on the salvage of individual casualties on the Jericho road (to adopt the metaphor taken from the Parable of the Good Samaritan which was used of Martin Luther King), Evangelicals have become vitally concerned with the need to rid the road itself of the robbers who cause the casualties. In other words, it is not only individuals who must be succoured, but society which must be changed.

Some, no doubt, would attribute this new emphasis to the fact that Evangelicals of the last two or three generations usually had a much more vital expectation of the Second Coming than is commonly found today. In the comparatively recent past, as in the primitive Church, there was a widespread feeling that the Advent was so imminent that nothing really mattered except individual evangelism and personal holiness. Our true citizenship was in heaven, not on earth; we were to look for the almost immediate 'consummation of all things', so no time could be spared for political action in a world which was doomed to destruction; the predominant emphasis must always be on redemption, not reform.

In so far as this represents a true diagnosis we must acknowledge a loss as well as a gain. It may be unbalanced, and even untrue, to insist that the Advent must be imminent, but we should suffer spiritual impoverishment if we were to cease, in Paul's phrase, to 'love his appearing' or no longer to live our lives in the light of the Advent hope. Today there is, we must confess, a considerable danger of this. But the Bible is surely explicit in its teaching that we cannot know for certain when the Advent is to be, that we are to 'occupy till he comes', and that the hope of that coming is to inspire us to do his will, and obey all his injunctions, in our day and generation. And these injunctions are not confined to evangelism or to the nurture of our own spiritual lives, but include the passionate denunciations of social injustice, and the imperative call to moral reformation, which are so characteristic of the Old Testament prophets.

This dual responsibility—the negative duty to take our stand against evil and injustice, and the positive obligation to promote the health and well-being of society—was summed up by Jesus himself when he said that his Disciples were to be both the salt of the earth and the light of the world. The metaphor of salt emphasizes the fact that it was their presence and witness which would keep society from the decay and even putrefaction which always threatens it, while the metaphor of light clearly implies that they should not only expose, but pierce and illumine, the darkness around them.

Now it is perfectly true that, in the New Testament, Christians are primarily exhorted to fulfil this double duty in terms of personal witness rather than political action. John the Baptist certainly rebuked the moral evils of society and called whole classes of men to repentance; but it is the example of Jesus himself and his apostles which is usually cited as normative for the Christian in this context. It must always be remembered, however, that Jesus had a wholly unique mission to fulfil. He came primarily to redeem men from sin and reconcile them to God—and this inevitably involved his willing acceptance of vicarious suffering and an atoning death. He was concerned, moreover, to change men's hearts rather than the political system under which they lived; to transform their whole attitude to life rather than their circumstances; to treat the sickness of their hearts rather than the problems of their environment. To have become politically involved with Rome, or to have fought for the radical change of the society to which he came, would have fatally detracted from, or even frustrated, his primary mission. And while his disciples could have no share in his redemptive work, they had the all-important charge and responsibility to make that redemption known. They represented, moreover, an infinitesimal and insignificant minority in a vast autocracy; and any attempt to crusade for the abolition of slavery or for democratic rights, for example, would have been, at best, completely counter-productive.

But there is nothing in the New Testament to suggest that the burning proclamation by the Old Testament prophets of the divine demands for social justice, and their equally pungent pronouncements of God's judgement on injustice, cruelty and social wrong, had in any way been abrogated. On the contrary, there are many indications that the moral standards of the New

Testament are even more exacting than those of the Old. But it was only within the narrow sphere of personal life and witness, and the somewhat wider sphere of the corporate life of the local church, that these standards could, in New Testament days, be given immediate and practical expression. Hence the injunctions to obey the civil power, to pay taxes, to render to every man his due, and (above all) to love one's neighbour as oneself—rather than to campaign for a better government, to protest against the methods of tax collection and the purposes to which the money so collected was put, or the reform of the social system as such. But it is significant that the doom on 'plutocrats' with their 'wicked hoarding', their denial of wages to their employees, their 'swindling' and the ruin of innocent men which their self-aggrandisement involved, is pronounced, in the Epistle of James, in the immediate context of the expectation of the Second Coming.[1]

The Epistle to Philemon provides an admirable example of the point I am trying to make. The early Church has been repeatedly criticized for acquiescing in the system of slavery rather than denouncing it as inherently evil, and for exhorting Christian slaves to give meticulous and loyal service even to harsh and inconsiderate masters. It must be remembered, however, that the ideal of the immediate abolition of slavery was not only something which the little band of early Christians could never have hoped to achieve but which, in the circumstances of the contemporary world, would have produced utter chaos. Instead, Paul makes the most moving (indeed, virtually irresistible) appeal to Philemon to receive his runaway slave as Paul's own son, a part of his very self, and as a 'brother beloved'—and asks him to put anything Philemon had stolen down to Paul's own account. Nor should the exhortation to Christian slaves to serve their masters conscientiously, and to regard their work as service to Christ himself, cause any surprise; for it is of the essence of the Christian message to hearten and empower men who find themselves in seemingly intolerable circumstances from which there is no way of escape, and to encourage them to commend their faith by manifesting a supernatural quality of life in those very conditions. These exhortations were, moreover, matched by similar injunctions as to how masters should treat their slaves, together with explicit advice that a slave who had the oppor-

[1] Cf. James 5: 1–7, Phillips' version.

tunity to obtain his freedom should avail himself of it. But it is equally true to say that the very institution of slavery is wholly incompatible with New Testament teaching when properly understood; and it is part of the abiding shame of Christians that it took them so long to realize this, to act on it themselves, and—when this was possible—to mount a political campaign to persuade society as a whole to give it practical expression.

It is precisely at this point that the position is so radically different today from the situation in which the apostles and their immediate followers found themselves. The only way of influencing secular society open to them then was the standard of personal example set by the infant Church and the extension of that Church by the winning of individual converts. Both of these methods are, of course, equally open to, and incumbent on, the present generation of Christians; and there can be no more effective way of starting a transformation in a man's whole attitude of mind towards his social responsibilities than to lead him to that radical change of heart inherent in true conversion. But there are other methods, too, by which those who live in a democracy can influence secular society—particularly when they represent what is, at least, a not inconsiderable minority; for it is open to them to make an effective protest against injustice and moral evil, and to do all in their power to induce a change not only in public opinion but in the law. Today, this is, in my view, an inescapable ingredient in loving one's neighbour as oneself.

It is obvious, of course, that the limits within which Christians can give legislative effect to what they believe to be God's purpose for society are considerably more restricted now than was the case throughout long periods in preceding centuries. It was possible then to make a wide appeal to Christian dogma and Christian ethics as the common coinage of the West—acknowledged in theory, if not put into circulation in practice, by the vast majority of the community. This situation has substantially changed, and today we live in an essentially plural—or pluralistic —society. The general heritage of Christian morality no doubt subsists; but much of this is sharply challenged by humanists, materialists, and followers of other religions and cults. We stand half-way, as it were, between the precarious position of the early Church and the entrenched position of the dominant Church of the intervening centuries. We have far more liberty for political as well as personal witness than was true in apostolic and sub-apostolic times; and we have the numbers and influence to ensure that our witness, if unequivocally given, will carry considerable weight. But we are today up against a powerful and articulate challenge to all our doctrinal beliefs and many of our ethical convictions.

How, then, can Christians presume to legislate for a pluralistic society, many of whose members are indifferent to, and some of whose members positively repudiate, Christian presuppositions? The answer is, of course, that in a democracy they cannot, in the very nature of things, impose their views on a resistant community; and that, even were they in fact in the majority, they should always accord to others that liberty of conscience which they would in other circumstances have claimed for themselves. But surely Christians have an incontestable right to do all in their power to persuade their fellow-countrymen to accept those laws and principles for the regulation of community life which they believe to have been revealed, not as the special rules of a Christian or theistic club, but as what they regard as the 'Maker's directions' for mankind as a whole—directions without which it is impossible for men and women to fulfil the purpose, and enjoy the quality of life, for which he made them.

A simple illustration of the point I am trying to make can be found in the Christian's attitude to Sunday observance. Clearly he cannot impose on the community at large any obligation to attend a place of worship, to take a day of rest or to regard Sunday as in any way different from the remainder of the week. Equally, however, he is perfectly free to tell his fellow citizens that he is convinced that their very constitution is such that they would live happier, healthier, and more effective lives if they made a practice of taking one day's rest in seven[1]—and also that they have souls as well as bodies, and will be following these 'Maker's directions' in a wholly inadequate way if they ignore the spiritual dimension to human life. On both these counts—physical and mental recreation, on the one hand, and spiritual enlightenment and enrichment, on the other—he can try, moreover, to persuade them that it is to the advantage of the community as a whole that as many people as possible should observe the same

[1] Incidentally, the Russian experiment of one day in ten was soon abandoned as a failure.

day of rest, rather than stagger individual days-off throughout the week; for only so could the community in general, and families in particular, be in a position to rest—and to worship—in the way they should. And he can also do his best to convince the legislature that reasonable regulations should be enacted with the purpose of protecting those who want to avail themselves of this opportunity from being unnecessarily prevented from so doing.

But this, in its turn, leads us to the much wider subject of how far—if at all—the criminal law may rightly be called in aid to support moral standards.[1] It was the strenuous contention of John Stuart Mill that 'the sole end for which mankind are warranted, individually or collectively, in interfering with the liberty of action of any of their number, is self-protection', and that 'the only purpose for which power can be rightfully exercised over any member of a civilized community, against his will, is to prevent harm to others. His own good, either physical or moral, is not a sufficient warrant. He cannot rightfully be compelled to do or forbear because it will be better for him to do so, because it will make him happier, because, in the opinion of others, to do so would be wise, or even right.'[2] It is this fundamental thesis which was accepted as a presupposition in the Report of the Committee on Homosexual Offences and Prostitution (commonly known as the Wolfenden Report), where it is categorically stated that the function of the criminal law 'is to preserve public order and decency, to protect the citizen from what is offensive or injurious, and to provide sufficient safeguards against exploitation and corruption of others, particularly those who are specially vulnerable because they are young, weak in body or mind, inexperienced, or in a state of special physical, official or economic dependence.' *Per contra,* the Report continues, it is *not* the function of the criminal law 'to intervene in the private lives of citizens, or to seek to enforce any particular pattern of behaviour, further than is necessary to carry out the purposes we have outlined.'[3] It was this basic thesis which was challenged by

[1] I have discussed this subject in much more detail in my recent book *Morality, Law and Grace*, Tyndale Press, 1972.

[2] J. S. Mill, *On Liberty*, London, 1859. Reprinted in *Utilitarianism, Liberty and Representative Government*, J. M. Dent, London, 1910, Everyman's Library No. 482, pp. 72 f.

[3] Report, paragraph 13.

Lord Devlin in his Maccabean Lecture in 1958 on 'The Enforcement of Morals', where he contended that the community had as
much right, in suitable circumstances, to make use of the criminal
law to protect the integrity of its common ideology as to employ
the law of treason to protect that of its accepted political structure.

This contention was almost immediately challenged by
Professor H. L. A. Hart, who gave general support to the views of
John Stuart Mill—but with a very significant exception. For
although he is as emphatic as Mill that the criminal law should
never be employed to enforce standards of personal morality, he
fully accepts the fact that the State may at times adopt a paternalistic attitude and try to prevent even a responsible adult
from doing what is manifestly bad for him, however much he may
himself want to do this.

The simplest illustration of this concession—which would have
been anathema to Mill—is legislation designed to prevent even
responsible adults from obtaining free access to hard drugs, on
the grounds that such drugs constitute a demonstrable danger to
health and all too easily lead to addiction. But Hart would also
explain the fact that our law does not recognize as a defence to
a charge of murder, or of inflicting grievous bodily harm, the
fact that the victim had consented to (or even requested) this
action, as another example of paternalism in the law, rather than
an application of the moral principle of the sanctity of life and
limb. But where, on the other hand, the criminal law includes
provisions which can be explained only in terms of what he would
regard as an attempt to enforce morality as such (e.g. 'bestiality,
incest, living on the earnings of prostitution, keeping a house for
prostitution')—these should, in his view, be totally expunged.[1]

The weakness in this position seems to me obvious. If it is
permissible for the State to be influenced by paternalistic considerations in framing its criminal law, then where, precisely,
must the line be drawn? May a man be protected in this way
only from physical harm, or may not the concept of paternalism
be extended to protecting him from moral harm too? The
answer to this question which Hart would give, if I am not mistaken, is that the damaging effects of hard drugs on the body and
mind are demonstrable and undeniable; whereas the moral
harm which incest or living on the proceeds of prostitution does

[1] *Law Liberty and Morality*, O.U.P., 1963, p. 25.

to the individuals concerned, or to the community as a whole, is much more questionable. But is it? It may be conceded that it is far simpler to demonstrate and quantify the one than the other; but if the basic assumption is that the harm done by drugs to physical health is undeniable, whereas what is commonly regarded as moral evil amounts to no more than a harmless deviation from accepted norms (which are themselves essentially relative and dubious), this is distinctly open to challenge.

It can, in fact, be challenged from a number of different angles. First, why does it seem to be a matter of common agreement that safeguards should be provided against the exploitation of the young, the weak, the dependent, the inexperienced, and also, according to Mill, members of backward races? In the Wolfenden Report reference to 'exploitation' in this context is immediately followed by 'corruption', which certainly implies that the exploitation in view is not confined merely to persuading them to do something which older and more experienced persons might refuse to do, but that there *is* such a thing as moral corruption and that certain acts or behaviour are liable to promote it. To persuade a minor to agree to homosexual relations, for example, is unlikely to cause him any purely physical harm. So the question arises as to whether the argument is that acts or behaviour which tend to corrupt the young, the weak and members of backward societies, have no such effect on normal adults from civilized societies; or whether the contention is, rather, that the latter must be allowed to submit themselves to such corruption— or potential corruption—if they so wish. If this is the argument, then the contention about accepted norms which are purely relative, and of dubious validity, is scarcely in place.

Secondly, it seems obvious that to live on the proceeds of prostitution must often involve the actual exploitation of one who is 'specially vulnerable', at least by reason of some kind of dependence. It is deeply significant, moreover, that Hart himself, when explaining why it is difficult today to go all the way with Mill in excluding any form of paternalism in regard to a responsible, civilized adult, justly comments on an 'increased awareness of a great range of factors which diminish the significance to be attached to an apparently free choice'. Choices, he says, 'may be made or consent given without adequate reflection or appreciation of the consequences; or in pursuit of merely transitory desires; or in various predicaments when the judgement is likely to be clouded; or under inner psychological compulsion; or under pressure by others of a kind too subtle to be susceptible of proof in a law court. Underlying Mill's extreme fear of paternalism there is perhaps a conception of what a normal human being is like which now seems not to correspond to the facts.'[1] Precisely.

Thirdly, it is noteworthy that even Mill himself found it impossible to decide whether an adult member of a civilized society should be allowed to be a pimp or to keep a gaming house. This would certainly seem a natural deduction from his basic principles; for his attitude towards both prostitution and gambling was that they were essentially undesirable activities, but did not lie within the category of what should be proscribed by the criminal law. Yet in regard to pimps and keepers of gambling dens he saw much force in the argument that 'if society believes conduct to be bad, it must be at least a disputable question whether it is good or bad: that being so, society is entitled to exclude the influence of solicitations which are not disinterested.' But this seems to me to undermine the logical consistency of his whole thesis.

Fourthly, this last statement of Mill's underlines the fact that we cannot concern ourselves exclusively with the protection of individual citizens, but must extend our care to the protection of society as a whole, and of its basic institutions. Among the most fundamental of these, in our community, is that of the family; so this means that the criminal law may be invoked, within reasonable limits, to uphold the integrity of monogamous marriage, for it is on this that the structure of the family, in our society, is based. But what, it may be asked, should be regarded as 'reasonable limits' in this regard? This question raises the whole problem of those criteria which must determine, in any given context, whether criminal sanctions are, or are not, the appropriate remedy; and to this problem we must presently revert. Suffice it to say that there seem to be sufficient reasons why bigamy should be prohibited and punished, why divorce should, in suitable cases, be permitted, but why adultery as such should not be made liable to criminal sanctions.

This leads us to three fundamental questions. First, what is

[1] *Ibid*, p. 32f.

the basis of those moral imperatives which should govern the lives of individuals and of society as a whole? Secondly, do these imperatives constitute moral 'laws' of abiding validity, or are they no more than 'guidelines'—and what is to be done when two of them appear to clash? Thirdly, to what extent, and in what circumstances, should these imperatives be given statutory authority in a plural society, whether by means of the civil or criminal law (provided always, of course, that the community can be persuaded to enact the necessary legislation)?

First, then, the basis of moral imperatives as such. Here the Christian must inevitably part company with many of those whose code of moral behaviour may, in practice, be almost identical with his own. He cannot, of course, be in any way indifferent to the Utilitarian's plea for the greatest good of the greatest number, or his condemnation of actions which add in any way to the sum total of human suffering. Up to a point, moreover, he can equally agree with the Intuitivist, for he will take seriously Paul's assertion that all men in some measure 'show that what the law requires is written on their hearts'.[1] But he will of necessity reject the teaching of those writers on moral philosophy who subscribe to the 'Emotive Theory,'[2] however much he may admit that individual attitudes to moral questions are all too often based on prejudice and emotion rather than any more valid or reasonable criteria.

Fundamentally, the Christian will always align himself with those who base their system of ethics on metaphysical considerations; and his distinctive contribution will be his insistence that it is in the teaching of Christ, and of the Bible as a whole, that an uniquely authoritative answer can be found to the problems of right and wrong. And here the particular emphasis of the Evangelical will be his wholehearted acceptance of the moral injunctions of the Gospels as a faithful record of what Jesus in fact taught; of the apostolic elaboration of that teaching as divinely inspired; and of the moral law of the Old Testament as reinforced by the authority of Christ himself.

Secondly, do these moral imperatives constitute 'laws' or principles of abiding validity, or are they to be regarded (as the

[1] Romans 2: 14 (R.S.V.)

[2] I.e., those who say that the statement 'that is good' means no more than that the speaker approves of the action concerned.

disciples of Situation Ethics so constantly and vehemently insist) as no more than 'guidelines'—as mere indications, that is, of how the only absolute command, that of love, can best, in normal circumstances, be obeyed? At first sight this doctrine sounds singularly persuasive, for did not Jesus himself sum up the Decalogue—in terms derived from the Old Testament—as loving God with all one's heart and one's neighbour as oneself; and did not Paul reiterate this when he said 'love is the fulfilling of the law'? Closer examination of Situation Ethics, however, reveals what appear to me to constitute certain fundamental defects in its reasoning. How can fallen man possibly discern, in all the complexities of social, national, and international problems, and in all the stresses and tensions of his own turbulent emotions, where the path of absolute love really lies? It is simply not good enough to say, with Dr John A. T. Robinson, that 'Love alone, because, as it were, it has a built-in moral compass, enabling it to "home" intuitively upon the deepest need of the other, can allow itself to be directed completely by the situation . . . It is able to embrace an ethic of radical responsiveness, meeting every situation on its own merits with no prescriptive laws.'[1] It is, of course, only fair to note that Dr Robinson does not intend in this passage to promote moral laxity, for he adds that 'love's gate is strict and narrow' and its requirements are 'infinitely deeper and more penetrating' than many may think; but the fact remains, as I see it, that his statement reveals an inadequate view of the essential sinfulness of the human heart: a belief, indeed, in 'man come of age' which is much closer to wishful thinking than the realities of contemporary life. It is much more consonant with human nature to agree with B. H. Streeter when he writes that 'When passion is the arbiter, my own case is always recognized to be exceptional . . . When Aphrodite whispers in my ear, a principle which admits of no exception may nerve me to resist, but if any exception is admitted, my case is certain to be one.'[2]

But is it realistic to speak of principles which admit of no exception, or moral laws which are really 'absolute'? Is it not a fact that, in this very imperfect world, two moral 'laws' or

[1] *Honest to God*, p. 115.
[2] *Adventure, the Faith of Science and the Science of Faith*, Macmillan, London, 1937, p. 125.

principles may conflict with each other? Many different examples of this could be cited; but those which come most readily to mind are situations in which the law of truthfulness, or the prohibition of lying, has to give way to some other moral law which, in the circumstances of the case, must of necessity be given priority. So the question may be asked whether this does not, in fact, imply a capitulation to the central thesis of Situation Ethics? Not really, as I see it; for in such a case the disciple of Situation Ethics would say that the lie which the situation required was, *per se*, absolutely right—that the law of truthfulness is not, in fact, an abiding moral principle but only a guide-line as to how the law of love will usually find expression. But this seems to me remote from the teaching of the Bible; and the Evangelical, as I understand it, will feel compelled to affirm that truthfulness is an abiding moral law or principle which one can never transgress without a sense that this is something which is, intrinsically, morally wrong—however much one may recognize that, in this particular case, it represents the lesser of two evils, and must therefore necessarily be regarded as the 'right' choice in all the attendant circumstances.

Finally, then, what are some of the criteria which must be taken into account before any moral principle, however valid, can properly be supported by a criminal sanction? First, it is almost always a mistake to allow the criminal law to get seriously out of step with public opinion, even if the legislature itself is prepared to enact, or to maintain, such legislation. There are certainly some occasions when the legislature can, and in my view should, give a lead to public opinion; but unless the law is— or comes to be—substantially supported by the common conscience of the community it cannot be effectively administered. Similarly, it is normally wrong to enact or maintain legal prohibitions which the police cannot enforce effectively or fairly; for a legal requirement which is openly and continually flouted, or which is put into operation in a manifestly unjust way brings the law itself, and its enforcement agencies, into disrepute and contempt. Yet again, there is little to commend a law which carries with it such undesirable side-effects (such, for example, as widespread blackmail) as to counterbalance the good it is designed to effect.

Many different examples could be given of problems under

current debate in our society, on which Evangelicals are themselves often divided, to which one or another of the principles outlined in this chapter must necessarily be applied. Elsewhere I have discussed in this context such matters as abortion, euthanasia and divorce. In abortion, for example, almost all Evangelicals, I should think, would oppose 'abortion on demand', because the basic principle of the sanctity of life must surely mean that an unwanted baby cannot be equated with a troublesome tooth. Equally, however, I cannot go all the way with the prohibitionists; for where a choice must necessarily be made between the life—or basic physical or mental health—of the mother, as a *developed* human personality, and the life of the embryo, as a *potential* human being, then I would have no hesitation in giving priority to the mother. All the same, acute difficulties arise when an attempt is made to draft the necessary legislation—legislation, that is, which will give adequate liberty to the conscientious doctor, on the one hand, and will be sufficiently tight to restrain those who are determined, whether for financial gain or from a wholly different mental approach, to exploit any loophole they can find.

Divorce, on the other hand, represents a very different problem, for here it is the civil rather than the criminal law which is involved. The basic question for the Christian is how far he believes that he should co-operate in securing as satisfactory a law on this subject for a pluralistic society as the facts of contemporary life would seem to demand—a law, that is, which gives relief where this appears to be necessary while yet upholding, so far as is possible, the sanctity of marriage and the stability of family life. Evangelicals will believe that what the Bible reveals as the Creator's intention for his creatures—lifelong fidelity in monogamous marriage—must be taken seriously, and openly proclaimed; but many Evangelicals will also be impressed with the fact that Jesus did not in any way suggest that Moses mistook the divine voice when he sanctioned suitable provisions to meet the 'hardness' of men's hearts.

A final example can be found in the vexed problem of pornography and the widespread dissemination today of the blatantly obscene in literature, pictures, films, and plays. An artist must always be free, it is constantly reiterated, to depict life precisely as he sees it, without any inhibition; and it is intolerable that those who are squeamish in such matters should try to restrict the freedom of those who are not. But even the most 'liberal' opinion will usually agree that the young stand in need of protection from what might deeply upset them, retard their healthy emotional development and thereby endanger their ability to enjoy a mature and satisfying sex life; and most would also agree that those who are offended by such material have a perfect right to object to having it imposed upon them against their will—whether by unsolicited distribution or public display. The law, it is true, should seek to protect rather than restrict; but it cannot protect those who need protection without some restrictions on the liberty of those who menace them.

But two further questions necessarily arise: whether pornographic magazines and 'blue' films should be available for those adults who want them, or allegedly 'need' them, provided they are not foisted upon others; and whether it is in fact possible to give any satisfactory definition of the sort of material which should be covered, in one way or another, by the relevant legislation. Here my own opinion is that the law should not seek to invade the privacy of a home or prohibit the private possession of even the most indecent material, but that there is very good reason to draft legislation which will restrict the activities of those who purvey such material for commercial gain. To suggest that pornography 'does no one any harm' seems to me absurd. Of course it is exceedingly difficult, if not impossible, to prove that one book or one film has had the direct effect of depraving or corrupting any of those who read or saw it. But the analogy of the pollution of air or water is singularly cogent; for while it is unlikely that a little pollution of these elements will seriously upset a healthy body, it is obvious that a sufficient concentration of pollution will adversely affect almost anyone, and that even a minor degree of pollution may upset a child or one whose health is already precarious. So, too, with pollution of the mind.

These examples—none of which can, of course, be adequately discussed or developed in the scope of a single chapter—may serve to illustrate the attitude adopted to the secular world by a great many Evangelicals today. They have resolved to come out of the ghetto of pietistic indifference to secular life in which they have (in popular opinion, at least) been recently incarcerated. They find in their wholehearted acceptance of the authority of the

Bible a firm foundation not only for morality, but for a 'theology of the secular'; and while their starting-point for this theology goes back, in many respects, to the doctrine of creation rather than redemption, their whole attitude to the world is centred on the incarnation, the atonement, and the advent hope. But they are also conscious that they cannot impose their convictions about moral standards and legislative enactments on a pluralistic community, but can only commend these convictions to the judgement and consciences of their fellow citizens. I would myself gladly adopt, in this context, the words of T. A. Lacey:

> It is the duty of a Christian to support the authority of the State.[1] It may be his duty also to labour for the reformation of the laws of the State. In doing this he has no right to put aside what he has learnt as a Christian, and in the quality of citizenship to act as a mere natural man. Such a division of personality is intolerable. But neither is he bound to insist that the laws of the State, in regard to marriage or in regard to anything else, shall conform exactly to Christian teaching. Not all the subjects of the State are Christian, and the State must legislate for all. He is bound, however, to use his Christian illumination for ascertaining what is naturally just, and he is no less bound to ensue peace by endeavouring to bring the law into such a frame that it will not actually conflict with his obligations to the Church.[2]

[1] I have discussed the special problem posed by a tyrannical Government and utterly unjust regime in *Morality, Law, and Grace*, chapter 4.

[2] Lacey, T. A., *Marriage in Church and State*, SPCK, 1912 (revised 1947) page 224.

7

EVANGELICALS AND CULTURE

Rob Pearman

This essay is an attempt to approach the question of culture, and specifically the relationship between evangelicalism and certain of the Arts. Certain basic assumptions underlie what will be written: that the nature of our particular culture is at present undergoing significant change; that those arts upon which this writer feels competent to comment (namely theatre, cinema, and television drama) are more an expression of, than creators of, this change; that this change has an effect on the form rather than on the content of Evangelical expression of faith; that there is an obligation upon Evangelicals to come to some coherent position in this area; and that the important cultural changes through which we are passing need to be carefully examined in order to prevent the existing wide *spectrum* of viewpoint within evangelicalism from becoming a radical and irreversible *division* among those who share our faith.

The 'significant change' affecting our culture could be expressed in any one of several ways: it could be approached as an expression of the changing nature of the class system as, for instance, the 'working class' experience enters fully into national education, entertainment, and communication media. Or it could be seen in terms of the growing international awareness of the possibility of total destruction by nuclear or ecological disaster.

My approach will be along another path: that which concerns the means of expression and communication.

Along this path, we must begin with the arch-prophet of cultural change, Marshall McLuhan. His argument that we have moved out of a period of 'written culture' and into what he calls the 'ear-culture' is an essential definition that needs to be examined before we can proceed.

We are quite unconsciously accustomed to living in a world of print and the alphabet. And it is hard for us to imagine what life was like before men first began to depend on the written and printed word. To put it simply, they must just have talked, listened and drawn pictures.

McLuhan is saying that it is precisely this sort of culture into which we are again moving. The increasing importance in our lives of pictures, colours, the television screen and music, are evidence of this.

Perhaps we need to look back at something of what was felt at the time about the change from an earlier ear-culture to the present 'word-culture' in order to proceed to face the fact of the current reversal.

From ear to word

McLuhan uses a short quotation from Socrates to illustrate the conflict between the two cultures:

> 'the discovery of the alphabet will create forgetfulness in the learners' souls, because they will not use their memories; they will trust to the external written characters and not remember of themselves . . . You give your disciples not truth, but only the semblance of truth; they will be heroes of many things, and will have learned nothing; they will appear to be omniscient and will generally know nothing.'[1]

What Socrates is here arguing for is the retention of the poetic and dramatic culture which had been the traditional way of passing on guidance in the spiritual, ethical and social life of man.

What he was regretting and reacting against was the demand for a more precise means of communicating and classifying, a greater stress on facts, reasoning, precision, conduct, and human nature. What he wanted was the safeguarding of metaphor, music, rhythm, and song. Socrates lost—inevitably.

And we are products of the 'precise' culture of the written word. Our society as a whole is one that is based upon a technocratic system of exact definitions and categories. Technocracy,

---

[1] *The Medium is the Massage*, Marshall McLuhan and Quentin Fiore, p. 113. (Penguin Paperback 2816).

in fact, is the logical end of a word-culture. Whether it is also to
be the ultimate end of humanity depends largely on how we act
now and in the near future.

It is very difficult for contemporary Christianity (and particularly for contemporary evangelicalism) to come to terms with
the current swing back to a new ear culture. The rôle of print,
the written word, 'the written word of God', is clear in the history
of evangelicalism, which is literate, based on precise definitions
and generally alien to the use of metaphor or symbol. And yet,
unless it comes to terms with the fact that the old culture is
dying, evangelicalism could well move slowly towards its own
extinction.

This threatened extinction will be avoided, I believe, just
because, consciously and unconsciously, evangelicalism *is*
adapting; it *is* coming to terms with the new culture. There are,
and will be, small pockets of resistance to any such adaptation.
But these will die slowly, and with some possible bitterness,
because it is inconceivable to imagine that young people will
emerge in sufficient numbers to sustain their ranks.

No future generation will be, *can be*, uninfluenced by the visual
and aural culture that we are entering: no child can escape the
influence, not simply of the content of television, but more
importantly of the *form* or *medium* itself. He will therefore be
unable to maintain or be maintained in a purely written word
culture. However well protected he may be in his own home, he
will not be able to evade the influences beyond the front door.

And even if small pockets were to survive and to retain their
old culture in the midst of an alien one, for what would they be
retaining it? Was Christianity originally a word-culture faith?
It can hardly have been so, since the truly universal word-
culture did not emerge till much later.

The failure of words

If we go back to McLuhan's quotation from Socrates, we can
look more closely at what he said, and see how his strictures on
the use of written, precise words to communicate spiritual,
ethical and social faith apply to us and to the Evangelical tradition.

What Socrates said is important, because it is, in a sense,
exactly what is being said by the new ear-culture to our old

word-culture. And the accusation that dependence on words, terminology and definitions is to the detriment of the content and meaning behind those words is addressed precisely to evangelicalism.

There can be few life-styles which are so full of categories and classifications as is evangelicalism. One can, with some justification, point to a similarity, in the concern for precise theology and clearly defined modes of conduct, between evangelicalism and ideological Marxism.

The comparison is inevitable, of course, because both the latter political faith and the former religious faith are determinedly 'aggressive'—in that they both have a firm basis of conviction, assurance and awareness of possessing *the* answer to all of life's problems.

In saying that, I am not attempting to parody, but simply to illustrate what I mean by the historical dependence of evangelicalism on the more precise method of communication.

My aim is straightforward: to suggest how far evangelicalism has become dependent on a form of communication and on a particular culture which is being radically attacked, undermined or developed (whichever term one prefers).

Has the Evangelical use of precise, written words, of exact, defined classifications, in both theology and conduct, led into the trap or pitfall which Socrates describes? Has the absolute dependence on the written word in the Evangelical tradition caused 'forgetfulness in the learners' souls'? In other words, has it taught us the correct terminology whilst allowing us to forget the true meaning?

Socrates feared that the precise word-culture would provide its disciples with the semblance of the truth. We would then know all the correct theological and ethical words, and we would know what they all meant, and yet we would have absorbed so much at a technical level as to block our experiencing of the *content* that the words are attempting to describe.

Have we come to trust to the external written characters and failed to remember the experiences they aimed to depict? Words are shorthand attempts to give us a concrete presentation of that which cannot be contained within such a concrete embrace. Have we allowed the words to become the experience, the end—instead of the useful reference points?

If we have (as I believe that the absence of imagination from so much of evangelicalism proves), then there is a quite definite cause for concern, and an important decision to be taken.

If we have, then Evangelical preachers and laymen should not be surprised if they experience a failure to communicate in depth. Evangelical communication, having the support of little mystery, symbolic ritual or theatrical wrappings, has been almost totally in 'written word' form. This form does not only, of course, refer to the printed word itself, but also to those means of communication which are derivative of it: in particular that form of preaching and counselling which is no more than the printed word in disguise. The word-culture is a whole way of thinking.

A new language

Evangelicals in general, in common with the word-culture of which they are part, are probably unaware of the situation of language in recent times, and in particular of the suspicion with which many people approach the use of words.

Why is it, for instance, that a representative of the counter-culture, alternative society, underground—call it what you will—why is it that such a person will often seem to be rambling incoherently around and around apparently searching for words? Is it simply youthfulness, lack of education or social grace? In part it may be all these, but it is also a conscious, or more likely unconscious, fear or rejection of precise language, a determination to avoid the quick label or term which we all know he could use, and which we are tempted to shout out to him. There is the sense in which he is being asked to express himself in the language and form of a culture (the word-culture) which is alien to him. If he could communicate his meaning to us in picture form, or in music or colours, or better still by being with us for a greater length of time, by sharing in action or work—then he could 'tell' us clearly what he means.

Let me quote again from McLuhan—not because I am blind to any other source, but because he has found a way of expressing, in printed words, this new post-print culture.

> Listening to the simultaneous messages of Dublin, James Joyce released the greatest flood of oral linguistic music that was ever manipulated into art:

The prouts who will invent a writing there ultimately is the poets, still more learned, who discovered the raiding there originally. That's the point of eschatology our book of kills reaches for now in soandso many counterpoint words. What can't be coded can be decoded if an ear aye seize what no eye ere grieved for. Now the doctrine obtains, we have occasioning cause causing effects and affects occasionally recausing altereffects.

Joyce is, in the *Wake* (*Finnegan's Wake*), making his own Altamura cave drawings of the entire history of the human mind, in terms of its basic gestures and postures during all the phases of human culture and technology. As his title indicates, he saw that the wake of human progress can disappear again into the night of sacral or auditory man. The Finn cycle of tribal institutions can return in the electric age, but if again, then let's make it a wake or awake or both. Joyce could see no advantage in our remaining locked up in each cultural cycle as in a trance or dream. He discovered the means of living simultaneously in all cultural modes while quite conscious.[1]

Now some may well find this incomprehensible if not complete rubbish. Yet I hope they will not leave it there, but will go back to read it again in order to get some sense of what is meant by ear-culture. Through reading this section from Joyce with an Irish accent, I have discovered that the more I hear it, the more I see that it contains all that I have tried to say so far about the cultural change now in process.

It is unnecessary to go at length into what Joyce was trying to do in *Finnegan's Wake*—to do so would be to take a further step off-course. It is sufficient to use him as an example to prove that the current situation of language is not just a post-war phenomenon, but is simply reaching fruition now. And it is sufficient to hear his words in order to experience something of what is meant by 'auditory man', and to note the symbolic nature of the alphabet.

The crucial point is this: our time is not just a time of great social upheaval, not just a period of experimentation and re-examination of fundamentals. It is a period of radical cultural change, and however long or short that period may be—whether

[1] *The Medium is the Massage*, Marshall McLuhan and Quentin Fiore, p. 120 (Penguin Paperback 2816).

it is a sudden moment of transition or a gradual process—until we look it firmly in the face, we have not yet begun to find an answer.

One out of four

Let me repeat again, at this stage, that this great cultural change affects us not primarily at the point of content of our faith, but at the level of communication and expression of it. This leaves, I believe, four possible paths to take in the current situation.

1. *Refusal* It is possible to refuse steadfastly to acknowledge the significance of culture and cultural change. This is a short-term view, presupposing, it seems to me, an imminent end to terrestrial life. I fail to see how one can ignore one's cultural environment and yet still anticipate any effective communication beyond the life-span of the ever-dwindling number of people who remain unaffected (apparently) by the cultural change. This 'refusal to look' viewpoint seems to have the examples of Christ and Paul to contend with: both were, in terms of communication, children of their age—using the language and imagery of their day.

2. *Fight* It is also possible to acknowledge the cultural situation and to fight against it, to reject it. There is a built-in inevitability of failure in this position—and that inevitability lies in the fact that television (that great purveyor of the ear-culture) is unlikely to hold itself back in the future.

To fight the ear-culture is also to see it as a necessarily 'bad thing' and to identify evangelicalism with one particular (technological) cultural epoch. To fight it in this way is also to attempt to limit God to one's own era and experience, and seems not significantly different from that other disastrous attempt to identify Christianity with one particular social *class*. And if it is now recognized that the Christian faith should not have been confined to the middle-classes, then it should also now be recognized that outright rejection of the ear-culture may be a similar mistake.

3. *Surrender* Another possible course of action is to surrender to the spirit of the age, to drift into subservience to the current culture. 'Be not conformed . . .' has generally been taken to refer to morality and behaviour. To fail to apply it to the area of culture (as we have been using that term) is clearly wrong. It is

7

wrong in that it is to succumb to subjectivism and relativism, to lose all theology and definitions, and to forget, for instance, that Christ ever spoke distinctly on any issue. This is when faith surrenders to the notion that words and the alphabet are *mere* symbols of a greater truth, that the individual's subjective experience is the *only* arbiter and interpreter. This is when the individual exists in complete isolation from the influence of shared ideas.

And it is also when the crowd chants, the ranks sway, and feelings and emotions are put at too high a premium. It is ironic that this could ever happen within evangelicalism—but I believe that relativism always waits at the end of the road for those who put too high a stake on emotionalism.

4. *A better way* This is where we face up to the new cultural situation, acknowledge the unavoidable fact that we are part of it, thereby attempting to avoid cultural schizophrenia, and at the same time try to master the culture rather than let it master us. This means rejecting the purely word-culture approach to communication, rejecting the sterility of subservience to the precise, factual, classified culture of what Socrates called 'the external written characters'. It means the rejection of fragmented living in favour of making connections. That is to say, seeing all things as inextricably inter-related; refusing to accept such precise areas as 'the ethical', 'the political', 'the theological', 'the social'. It means seeing that each of these shorthand classifications is in fact no more than just that: a handy label to be used as such, and not an absolutely definable area.

(That sentence about the rejection of fragmented living in favour of making connections is a useful example of the sort of spectrum of understanding involved in the cultural situation. To some people the sentence is instantly clear; whilst to others it will sound like esoteric jargon. It is important to note this division of reaction, and further to note that any attempt to explain or expand it necessarily deforms it by adding more precise definitions. The best understanding of it is in 'listening' to it imaginatively—something that the word-culture has taught us to forget to do.)

But in addition to rejecting the dominance of the word-culture, it also entails rejection of absolute control by the new ear-culture.

Whilst it will by now be fairly clear why I reject the old culture's stranglehold, it will not be so obvious why I refuse to slip over to subservience to the new one. And yet the reasoning is the same in both cases: there is nothing absolute in either culture; neither 'word' nor 'ear' is good or bad in itself, but either will go bad if left to control us, the participants.

In the case of word-culture, the path leads inevitably towards the sterility of cold dogma, unfelt words, imposed theories. At the farthest end of that path stands, perhaps, the notion of 'rapid reading courses'—those arch-disciples of a purely technocratic approach to life!

In the case of ear-culture, subservience leads to another sterility namely, that of total subjectivism, of surrender to the idea of absolute insecurity of language. Just as it was bad to lean too heavily on a whole battery of word-definitions, so it will be bad now to reject the use of common language altogether.

What we have to do is to accept that (as far as language is concerned) we have reached a point of breakdown in standards of value and significance, and having done so to begin to re-create a common language.

Some may not agree that we have now reached such a serious breakdown (or rather are acknowledging a breakdown that was there before). Let me illustrate by referring to a discussion on BBC 2 in December, 1971. 'Man Alive' put a group of established, literate journalists of the old word-culture tradition alongside another group of young, volatile producers of alternative or underground newspapers.

On the one side, articulate, practised users of the printed word, accustomed to the careful structuring of sentence and paragraph, and the division of news into separate, clearly defined topics (politics, home and international, sport, women's page, court cases).

On the other side, apparently incoherent but equally committed users of colours and shapes to present attractive, entertaining, visual papers, rejecting such division of the news; making sport into politics, mixing legal with metaphysical matters—and not just making these 'connections' as a deliberate rejection of 'society's norm', but doing so out of pure, natural inclination. Such connections are an inevitable and often unconscious part of the ear-culture.

The conflict between the two sides was not simply one of generation, but of culture.

And if the future lies with the ear-culture (as the inevitable continual growth of television promises) then it is up to the old 'word men' to look out.

The challenge

And if, as I have tried to maintain, evangelicalism has become dependent on the word-culture, then it too must look out. But it need not do so with fear and foreboding, for it has a very striking precedent.

In his book *The Making of the Counter Culture*, Theodore Roszak illustrates this precedent to advance his own particular argument:

> The Christian example is one that many of the hip young are quick to invoke, perhaps with more appropriateness than many of their critics may recognize. Hopelessly estranged by ethos and social class from the official culture, the primitive Christian culture awkwardly fashioned of Judaism and the mystery cults a minority culture that could not but seem an absurdity to Greco-Roman orthodoxy. But the absurdity, far from being felt as a disgrace, became a banner of the community.

> 'For it is written (St Paul boasted), I will destroy the wisdom of the wise, and will bring to nothing the understanding of the prudent ... For the Jews require a sign, and the Greeks seek after wisdom ... But God hath chosen the weak things of the world to confound the things which are mighty.' 1 Cor. 1: 19, 22, 27.

> It is a familiar passage from what is now an oppressively respectable source. So familiar and so respectable that we easily lose sight of how aggressively perverse a declaration it is ... how loaded with unabashed contempt for a long-established culture rich with achievement. And whose contempt was this? That of absolute nobodies, the very scum of the earth, whose own counter culture was, at this early stage, little more than a scattering of suggestive ideas, a few crude symbols and a desperate longing. It was the longing that counted most, for not all the grandeur of the Greco-

Roman civilization could fill the desolation of spirit Christianity bred upon.[1]

If we decide then that the present technocratic word-culture is one that evangelicalism should look upon and face up to as 'alien', then we have a more than helpful precedent.

Roszak not only uses stirring words to describe this essential precedent; he also refers to the Bible as 'an oppressively respectable source'. I believe that he is wrong in his phrasing: the Bible has only become oppressively respectable in so far as the means used to communicate its content have become so.

And this is because evangelicalism has identified itself with the word-culture, and is therefore identified with the established technocratic culture. It has become the unwitting dependent of a culture pattern which should be seen to be fundamentally alien to its very nature.

It is surely the job of this generation of Evangelicals to re-create the dramatic and poetic means of passing on guidance in the spiritual, ethical and social life of man.

But how is this to be done?

Rebuilding a language

Not being competent to deal with music, poetry, or such arts as painting and sculpture, I must necessarily restrict myself to suggesting one possible way to create a new language: through the art of drama.

Drama is a good example of one area in which Evangelicals can imaginatively attempt to rebuild a language in which to express the timeless truths of their faith.

Drama, after all, has a long and honourable history as a survivor from the earlier ear-culture.

Perhaps many Evangelicals react against the very word 'drama'. The Evangelical tradition, after all, has tended to put theatre, cinema and such arts into a general category labelled 'highly suspicious'. Now, whilst to many of us this seems strange, it is important to acknowledge the fact and to attempt to mellow the reaction.

[1] *The Making of a Counter Culture*, Theodore Roszak, pp. 43–44 (Faber & Faber, 1970).

A brief history of the relationship between drama and religion would show that theatre was born out of early religions, and developed to a very high standard by the Greeks, for whom it was a significant means of expressing religious truth. When the theatre was crushed by the early Roman Christian powers, this was because it had become a cheap form of sensationalist, spectacular entertainment, not unconnected with prostitution and real or simulated violence.

Time passed, and in England the theatre was reborn out of Medieval Church liturgy and incidents from the Old Testament. It was quite natural that it should be thus reborn—drama after all is one of the greatest means of communication in a pre-literate ear-culture. Unfortunately, the theatre was soon deemed to have again become sensationalist and a centre (and even cause) of vice, and was put down by the Puritans. Its consequent rebirth under the restored King Charles II and the continued existence of Puritanism as an expression of fundamental Christian faith meant that there was an inevitable alienation between this faith and drama: far from being born out of religion for a third time, the theatre was now a friend of the hedonistic, anti-Puritan Royal Court.

This is clearly a very simplified history; but I believe that it set the scene for a long time. Evangelicals since have generally stood alienated from the theatre and other expressions of the art of drama and this has produced an inevitable ignorance about the art itself. It has also allowed 'rumours' of the immorality of theatre life to become 'facts', and has, of course, left the theatre without much influence from those who attempt to live and express fundamental Christian faith.

But the sort of cultural change to which I have referred (whether caused by the advent of television, and hence the intrusion of drama into the home, or by the effects of a commonly shared, national education, or by confusion of the old class-structures) has created a division within evangelicalism today.

Many Evangelicals, particularly those who have come in 'from outside', not only have no particular hesitations themselves about participating fully in the practice or viewing of drama, but also find it difficult to understand the traditional suspicions about drama. Other Evangelicals have gone back to the Scriptural source and have discovered that, as far as they can see, the traditional objections were far less Scriptural and far more 'cultural' than they had supposed. Other Evangelicals continue in deep-seated reserve towards this and other arts.

It is essential, in view of the cultural changes as I have tried to express them, to acknowledge these differences and to create some useful dialogue between the viewpoints, and I shall use the remaining space to comment briefly on the nature, possibilities and limitations of drama.

Drama is first of all entertainment. In a competitive, technocratic society like ours, we must understand the problems of theatre managers, cinema distributors and television programme planners. Short of sufficient state subsidies, they have to put financial survival as a very high priority. Drama is very expensive to produce, and theatre managers, for instance, know only too well that nothing succeeds in the West End so well as the good old romantic, light-hearted (not to say trivial) situation comedy with a touch of adultery or suggested infidelity. Most of those concerned with drama would like to put out the *best* material all the time. But if this leads to bankruptcy, then there is little future in it.

Having said that, and having acknowledged that entertainment is a valid part of drama, it is important to be able to distinguish between the run-of-the-mill material which is what most Evangelicals probably think of when they refer to drama, and other drama which is of more lasting significance.

True drama is more than mere, trivial entertainment. Apart from being a means of creating a community of people sharing together certain emotions and experiences (an important role for any art to play), it has also been concerned with the basic themes of human existence.

To put it simply, drama can explore the realm of man's search for meaning and purpose in life, and it can explore human relationships. This is to ignore, for lack of space, many recent attempts to present political drama, whether in theatres or in street-shows. (It is a development which should not be ignored, particularly as it is one of the only ways in which radically alternative political or social viewpoints can be expressed in a society where most means of communication are firmly controlled by 'the establishment'.)

There are countless examples of drama which explore man's

search for meaning, from the Greeks to Shakespeare, from Ibsen and Strindberg to Pinter and Storey. In Samuel Beckett's 'Waiting for Godot', for instance, there can be found just about all the questions man has ever asked in a world where the ultimate meaning is 'invisible'. What is it all about? Why am I here? Am I the same person as I was yesterday? Do I find ultimate meaning through my relationship with another person?

And then there are the many other plays which present and explore human relationships—usually under stress, of course, for there can be no true drama without conflict in some form. A play like Edward Albee's 'Who's Afraid of Virginia Woolf?' is one that forces the viewer to examine his own motives and behaviour within his relationships.

These are stage examples to illustrate my simplified description, but the same sort of material can be found in television and cinema drama.

And if this is what drama is about, then it is clearly of importance to those whose faith is seen in terms of both ultimate meaning and human relationships. If that is as patently obvious as it sounds, then it hardly seems necessary to argue for a serious and determined approach to drama by Evangelicals. And, of course, for the many Evangelicals who have been actively engaged, privately and publicly, in appreciating drama, it is not at all necessary.

However, my concern is to point towards a means to rediscovering a language in which Evangelicals can express their faith in an age of ear-culture—recreating, in effect, a dramatic and poetic, imaginative tradition by which to pass on this faith. This will entail not only study and appreciation of drama which already exists, but active encouragement to those with the talent to create new material. This in turn will demand a far greater awareness of the place of metaphor, parable, and allegory than the Evangelical tradition has perhaps allowed.

The old word-culture way of telling a truth is to tell it straight. My contention has been both that this is becoming an alien culture form, and that it has drifted into that sterility or loss of the deeper, experienced content against which McLuhan uses Socrates' words to warn us.

We shall also need to make some study of the possibilities of creative drama and an awareness of its limitations.

Drama

To put it very briefly, I see the usefulness of drama as being threefold: firstly, it is a group activity, and as such it can help to create community or fellowship among the active participants and between participants and audience.

Secondly, it can take the form of inspirational or meditative material—attempting to create a deeper, personal awareness of the content of faith, perhaps through metaphorical or symbolic presentations. When this sort of drama is created, the participants must avoid killing the effect by adding word-culture definitions at the end. Let the drama do its own work.

Thirdly, it can be seen as a means 'to create discussion. It is no mere accident that medical students at one American college have been taken away from their old patterns of instruction. Their psychology teachers have set up a situation where professional actors perform selected parts of modern plays in order to reveal to the students some examples of human behaviour which they will be encountering in their later work.

One teacher quoted Freud: 'Imaginative writers are valuable colleagues; in the knowledge of the human heart, they are far ahead of us common folk.' (*Time* Magazine, November 29, 1971).

One of the things that these psychology teachers are saying is that the practisers of the ear-culture (actors and playwrights) can better communicate the nature and expressions of the human soul than can the old word-culture methods of lecture and textbook. They would then add, of course, that these ear-culture exponents are not the end of the process of learning, but rather the beginning, the means to experiencing from which discussion and study can move forward towards better understanding. Those teachers were presumably themselves educated and instructed according to the word-culture pattern, but they have been able to perceive the changes around them and have acted accordingly.

Discussion which follows drama which has succeeded in communicating to the inner self of the audience can be at a level which involves the experience and feelings of all concerned. In other words, a language is being created as a consequence of the medium of drama. When the questions have been raised in a way that the audience can 'hear' (using that term in its full ear-culture sense), then the participants should be able to work towards the answers in a more involved way than if they had simply been subjected to a sermon or lecture.

Only practice will prove how much and which aspects of faith can be communicated through drama and through discussion based on a judicious use of contemporary cinema, theatre and television material.

But, if we take the notion of a changing culture seriously, if we note the growing, universal effects of an ear-culture, then we must be prepared to see such arts as drama back in their original place as communication media of vital importance—and not just as a 'secular activity' or simply as 'something to keep the young people happy'.

8

EVANGELICALS AND EDUCATION

PETER COUSINS

All religious or political groups which are strongly committed to a particular—and especially to a minority—viewpoint are bound to ascribe great importance to education, in some sense of the word. It is, after all, not only the Jesuits who attach significance to the first five years of life. It is quite natural therefore that Evangelicals, along with other Christians, should be concerned about education. Natural too that this concern should often have taken a form not easily distinguishable from indoctrination. For if the rôle of education has been to induct the child into the customs, beliefs, and values of a community, then it is quite understandable that this should include the inculcation of religious and ideological dogmas and presuppositions.

It is not surprising then, that the Church has been until quite recently the chief educational agency in western culture. Yet there has been another less overtly ideological reason for this concern. Education is generally regarded as a good thing, so that establishing and running schools has been seen by Christians not just as a convenient means of indoctrination, nor even as a vehicle for transmitting the Faith, but also as an act of charity or love.

Alongside the hospitals founded in the name of Christ and his saints to care for men's bodies, schools have been established to benefit their minds. It is no accident that mission hospitals and schools still supply the bulk of medical or educational provision in many countries, especially of the Third World.

So the Evangelical concern for education is closely connected with an interest in evangelism, and all over the world hospitals and schools are a tangible witness to the good news proclaimed in and alongside them by the large number of missionaries who have not abandoned or traded in the New Testament gospel.

There are further especial reasons why Evangelicals, more perhaps than some others, are concerned about education. At first sight, for example, it may seem odd that a body so conservative in its theology as the Wycliffe Bible Translators should devote immense effort to recording the languages of remote tribes and undertaking literary work. For most of the peoples concerned can already understand one of the better-known languages, even if they cannot read, and those who know only their own tongue could surely be helped by simply listening to the missionary.

The principle at stake goes back to the Reformation and beyond that, even to (for example) Ulficas and the Goths. Evangelicals, more than most Christians, take seriously the basic Biblical affirmation that God has spoken to men, not just generally but 'through the prophets' in particular. Since the Bible is God's word written, it is overwhelmingly important that men should be able to read and respond to it for themselves.

The need for an individual response is little less significant than the existence of the written word. Whatever truth may be found in the view that the sixteenth-century emphasis on the importance of the individual was linked with social and economic changes, it remains no less true that the Reformed emphasis on individual response to God, the duty (not merely the right) of private judgement, and the priesthood of all believers is grounded in Scripture.

As a result, it has been the policy of Protestant churches, both in their homelands and on the mission field, to make it possible for men to read and understand the Scriptures for themselves.

A Biblical View of Culture

Although this policy has been largely responsible for a great deal of evangelical work in education, yet evangelicalism is not committed to a narrow or exclusive concern with 'religious education' in any restrictive sense. The Reformed view of the full effects of the Fall is especially relevant here. All Christians would have agreed (until comparatively recently) on the necessity of special revelation for salvation; but outside the Reformed churches there has been a tendency (to say the least) to assume that for all other matters the light of reason would be adequate. The Reformed churches, by contrast, have maintained that the effects of the

Fall extend so far as to distort man's understanding both of himself and the world he lives in.

Evangelicalism has to a great extent accepted this position, and as a result sees God's self-revelation as relevant to the whole of human culture, so that the Evangelical concern for education is not limited to ensuring the provision of orthodox religious education. Because of the noetic effects of the Fall, all education must be subject to God's revelation of himself in the Scriptures as well as in his creation.

This does not mean that Evangelicals are called upon to deny that men who reject God's authority may discover or respond to truth. In spite of the Fall, all men remain in the image of God, however sadly defaced this may appear, and the Bible itself shows clearly that unbelievers can be aware of religious, moral, historical, and scientific truth. But their refusal to acknowledge God's authority is bound to lead them (as they turn every way possible to avoid encounter with him) into inconsistencies and error. Thus, the Evangelical and Biblical idea of education involves the sovereignty of God in every area of knowledge.

It must be admitted that this concern has sometimes led Evangelicals into obscurantism and anti-intellectualism. They have joined with other Christians in defending a particular interpretation of Scripture in the teeth of well-based scientific opinion (e.g. in the Galilean controversy and the chronology of creation). They have sometimes been biassed in their interpretation; Paul's injunction to think on goodness and beauty does not, for example, imply an adverse verdict on all art that deals with what is evil or repulsive.

Paradoxically, this danger has been accompanied by another threat to genuine education. Evangelicals have been particularly liable to echo Tertullian's question: What has Athens to do with Jerusalem? They have often shared with him a negative attitude to human culture, and have seemed, on occasion, to believe that Satan's power over the world is so great that education is at best a necessary evil. On this view, children should learn the Scriptures in order to be saved from this present evil age, and beyond this be taught only what will be necessary to equip them to gain a reputable living. Such a view still characterizes sects such as Jehovah's Witnesses, and may be encountered here and there in all denominations, even today.

This fear of human culture plainly owes something to the Bible and to the observable condition of western civilization. The Bible speaks of the world as being in Satan's power. The New Testament makes it clear that far from human wisdom facilitating salvation it is—like all forms of riches—more hindrance than help. And nothing can mitigate the truth that it was the cultural worlds of religion, learning, and government, which crucified the Lord of Glory. No wonder Paul warns Christians in Rome against letting the world squeeze them into its mould!

So one finds Evangelicals who despise—and, rather worse, who profess to despise—every activity that is not directly linked with redemption from sin. They approve of the successful salesman who claims that: 'My business is saving souls; I sell cars to cover my expenses.' In point of fact, this attitude rarely leads Evangelicals to discourage their children from passing examinations, for reasons we shall discuss later, but it does go along with a tendency to mistrust intelligence, academic excellence or artistic achievement. It is not very long ago that some university Christian unions would look askance at any member who got a first, fearing that this implied a low state of spiritual health.

Yet although there is Biblical ground for setting a supreme value on salvation and for mistrusting the 'wisdom of this world' the Bible also contains some far more positive teaching about human culture. The divine command to exercise authority over the earth is carried out wherever men build, farm, create, and govern. The privilege of work and the institution of marriage are not rescinded by the Fall, and are God's plan for every man— not the redeemed alone. In Romans 13 Paul makes it clear that even a pagan Emperor is God's agent to restrain evil and encourage good. So it is wrong to assume that God is concerned only with redeeming the world He has created. Preserving it is also part of His purpose.

Education is thus of value, even if it does not lead to a man's conversion, provided that it leads him to live in a way more conformable to God's will. Society benefits if (even) unbelieving and rebellious men and women try to live their lives in accordance with God's purpose for mankind.

This means that the Evangelical teacher—whether or not he works in a school with a Christian foundation—will see his teaching in the context not only for God's saving grace, but of His common grace given to all men. He can serve God, not only by witnessing to his pupils or by teaching religious education with an evangelistic purpose, but also by instructing pupils in any discipline, since every one of these represents some aspect of man's 'dominion'.

Realizing this has given many Evangelical teachers fresh confidence. For too long, many of them could see Biblical significance in their work only in terms of its evangelistic impact, immediate or (hopefully) delayed. The R.E. specialist was felt to be more spiritually significant than any other kind of teacher; for others, the spiritual focus of their work lay in the school Christian society. Several influences brought about this change. One is the work of the Christian Education Fellowship, now absorbed in the Association of Christian Teachers, catering for the needs of Christian teachers in general, not solely for religious education specialists. Another is the widespread influence of Calvinism, with its emphasis on the sovereignty of God extending to all aspects of human life.

A steady flow of books and articles witnesses to this revived Evangelical concern for education as a whole. (See, for example, *Spectrum*, the journal of the A.C.T., published at 47, Marylebone Lane, London W.1.; also *Preparing for Teaching*, edited by Philip May and Colin Holloway, published by I.V.P.)[1]

All the same, this attitude has apparently not been fully accepted. In spite of the large number of Evangelicals in education, comparatively few seem to become head teachers or to gain similar status. This is probably not because they deliberately choose to remain 'in the ranks'. One may hazard a guess that many of them feel it is rather 'unspiritual' to devote 'too much' time and effort to their careers.

Quite plainly, family responsibilities and local church activities (which most Evangelicals take very seriously), make important claims upon time and energy. In addition, there is still some prejudice against Evangelicals from educationists of more 'liberal' (!) religious views or of none. The result is that Evangelicals exercise far less influence in education than their numbers might lead one to expect.

Evangelicals and Religious Education

There is also room for concern about the future of religious

[1] And Philip May, *Which Way to School?*, Lion Press, 1972.

education. Although a large proportion of R.E. specialists are Evangelical in their sympathies, there seems to be a falling-off in the numbers training for this work. At the same time, changes are being suggested in the type of religious education given in maintained schools which may make committed Christians generally far less enthusiastic about teaching the subject.

It is worth while giving some attention to the question of religious education, since this is a matter on which Evangelicals have strong but mixed feelings. Their general approval has depended on the fact that until recently religious education has been based on the Bible. So parents, while often unhappy about the quality of teaching provided, have hoped that the overall result would be beneficial. Although they have disliked—not always without reason—the 'liberal' approach adopted by some teachers, and have been even more disturbed by the cynical way in which too many head teachers have allowed the subject to be taught by teachers equally irreligious and ignorant, they have nevertheless tended to feel that exposure to the Scriptures would benefit their children.

For similar reasons, many Evangelical teachers have been especially concerned to give religious education. This has not been because they intended to use the classroom for evangelism; indeed they have been quite content to see their task in terms of giving children an insight into religion—that is, in this country into the Christian religion—so that pupils might accept or reject it from a position of knowledge, not ignorance. (There has been less agreement about the unique position of R.E. as the only subject which is voluntary for pupils and teachers, though obligatory for schools, and about the desirability of the daily act of worship.) But there are strong pressures at present to change the pattern of religious education. Even the most enlightened classroom teaching of Christianity is condemned as neo-confessionalism. (Schools Council Working Paper 36, published by Evans/Methuen in 1971.)

The choice seems to lie between attempting to help pupils look at every experience from a point of view of 'ultimate concern', or teaching them about religion as a human phenomenon. In either event, Christianity would appear, it seems, only as an option among many. Many Evangelical teachers who have felt they were doing something worth while by introducing children to the person and teaching of Jesus, or by helping them to enjoy the Bible, will now want to re-examine their position. So may parents who have hitherto tolerated school religion. The problem is not just that teachers of religion may be expected to adopt a neutral stance which is rare indeed in our schools. What is involved is the whole question of the Biblical attitude to religion.

It is true that one can see religion as a significant and fascinating creation of the human spirit; inducting children into this approach to reality may be regarded as comparable with teaching them the arts and sciences. Evangelicals teach these without scruple, and see them as manifestations of God's grace freely given to all men.

The case of religion looks rather different. First of all, the Biblical attitude is less than enthusiastic; indeed the main thrust of the Scripture condemns religion as one of the ways in which man persistently avoids facing God. Paul even suggests in 1 Cor. 10 : 20 that religions are manipulated by demonic forces in order (presumably) to keep man in slavery. Secondly, what is at stake, according to the Bible, in a man's approach to religion is not the amount of cultural furniture he may acquire, but his eternal happiness.

Evangelicals may, of course, decide that in addition to offering fascinating possibilities as an academic study, religion also raises such important questions that they can with a clear conscience teach in the manner outlined above. And it is, in any case, by no means certain that Christianity will be so decisively dethroned. But one cannot assume that the enthusiasm for religious education shown by Evangelical parents and teachers will survive changes such as we have described.

Evangelical Parents—Expectations and Fears

It would be unreasonable, however, to imply that the educational concern of most Evangelical parents is principally directed towards either of the areas mentioned. Evangelical parents, like other mainstream Christians, are overwhelmingly middle-class, and value education for the usual middle-class reasons. Naturally they would like to see their children turn to Christ, but this is not (as they see it) the school's responsibility. The Calvinistic 'cultural mandate' means nothing to them. They want their children indoctrinated with traditional middle-class morality,

8

and equipped with as many examination passes as possible so that they can 'do well' in life, by traditional middle-class standards. On the whole, the children oblige, and achieve their potential in examination successes.

This concern has gone a long (but not the whole) way towards accounting for the large number of Evangelical independent schools, too many of which provide what is basically a dull and traditional formal education, with an increased ration of evangelically flavoured Scripture lessons and acts of worship.

Not, of course, that middle-class standards are necessarily undesirable; indeed there is a great deal of good about the values that sociologists have detected in the middle-class. But there has certainly been a tendency for Evangelicals (like other Christians) to be more concerned with middle-class than with Biblical standards and to accept with little questioning the attitudes of an apostate age. They have over-emphasized the intellect, been too ready to make worldly success their chief effective criterion, encouraged individual self-assertion as against co-operation, and confused social conformity with goodness. They have been snobbish and philistine.

All this has meant that many Evangelical parents have had their children educated outside the maintained system for reasons which are Biblically and educationally suspect.

Besides the independent schools, there are also church schools, controlled or voluntary aided. These have been regarded as a mixed blessing by Evangelicals, as by other members of the Church of England. Of course the teachers vary greatly both in competence and in Christian commitment; by no means all would call themselves Christians. When such schools are staffed by teachers whose 'Christianity' amounts to little more than theistically-tinged humanitarianism, Evangelicals and others who believe in supernatural Christianity are understandably angry.

It must be admitted, on the other hand, that there is very little to be said for narrow restrictive teaching, whether given by devout Evangelicals or by Anglo-Catholics. In the last resort, the quality of a church depends on the school head-teacher and staff. Even more influential than what they teach is what they are, and in a good church school the 'atmosphere' and quality of community life will reinforce and exemplify the overt religious teaching.

The Durham Report concluded that the chief justification for spending so much of the Church of England's income on education is that the Church cannot credibly claim to have an interest in education unless it has schools to practise what it preaches. This view raises an important question: has Christianity any distinctive contribution to make in education? Is there such a thing as 'Christian' education? Professor Paul Hirst, who is not the least eminent of Christian educationists, believes not. There is no such thing, he argues, as Christian agriculture or history. These are autonomous activities, to be judged by the criteria appropriate to them. The same holds for education; an activity either is or is not rightly categorized as education—Christianity has nothing to do with the matter. (*Faith and Thought* (Journal of the Victoria Institute), Vol. 99, No. 2).

This viewpoint has not gone unchallenged. It appears to be based on assumptions about the nature of man that are often taken for granted in western culture, but which depend ultimately on Biblical theism. It seems to entail the conclusion that a 'good' school staffed by Christians would be indistinguishable from a 'good' school staffed by Buddhists or Maoists. On the face of it, this seems unlikely.

The importance of the Biblical revelation to a philosophy of education begins with what the Bible says about God and the created order and man in God's image. As in any other area, so in education, man cannot 'get started' on any other rational basis. He can certainly postulate the existence of reality external to himself; himself as a rational being free to choose and act; a cosmos in which effect follows cause with observable regularity; moral values which he has not invented—but he is hard put to it to demonstrate the validity of all these.

Yet education can scarcely proceed without them, and since he bears the divine image man may take some or all of them as axiomatic. But in doing so he is being inconsistent and arbitrary if he denies the basic Biblical revelation which alone makes sense of them.

The importance for education of God's self-revelation goes beyond this. The Christian does not see these truths as a springboard from which he can leap into autonomous activity. Basic to his own experience and development are guilt and forgiveness, and these must inevitably—if he is consistent—colour his attitude to his pupils. It is important to be clear that 'guilt' here does not mean guilt-feelings. The Christian should be less burdened than his colleagues by these, for he has no need to deny or suppress them; he has received forgiveness through the cross of Christ. 'Guilt' here means culpability. He cannot pretend that he is virtuous and his pupils are morally inferior.

Yet neither is he prepared to gloss over moral faults as if they were of no account, mere subjective value judgements or procedure rules of no ultimate importance. In this respect he and his pupils are on the same footing, for all are sinners, all from time to time do wrong, all stand in need not only of divine but also of human forgiveness. This attitude does not mean (in spite of the incompetence of some devout and squeamish teachers) that he will never condemn an action or punish an offender. What it does mean is that he will not reprove or punish aggressively or self-righteously. He knows that he stands condemned by the same moral law that puts his pupil in the wrong, and that he has it in him to behave worse than the delinquent he is dealing with.

It would be a great comfort to many Christian parents if they could believe that schools are no worse for being staffed by teachers who reject the authority not only of God, but also of the moral law, a state of affairs which is inevitable today since schools are bound to reflect the state of society. It is hopefully suggested that there is sufficient agreement about moral values even in the 1970s for the schools to reach some sort of consensus about what they are going to inculcate. Evangelical parents are not so sure, and they are by no means alone in their uncertainty.

The 'middle class' package has disintegrated. The media have familiarized people with the idea that 'anything goes' so far as personal morality is concerned. There is general feeling that moral judgements are essentially subjective and irrational, so that nobody has the right to tell anybody else what is right or wrong. The effect of this on Christian parents must ultimately be to send them back to the Bible in order to construct a moral order on surer foundations than middle-class consensus.

The effect on schools is traumatic. Teachers are confronted by children from homes where parents have lost their moral nerve. Too often teachers are in the same position, unwilling and indeed unable to give a clear moral lead because of their lack of clear moral conviction. They cannot even offer adolescents a coherent personal viewpoint to dissent from, since they themselves possess no defined set of principles. Their abdication is already proving disastrous in some schools where 'soft' secularist head-teachers and housemasters are trying to build a community on a foundation of relativistic blancmange.

No wonder Evangelical parents feel they have good reason for disquiet. Of course tension between home and school is nothing new. Over and above their not infrequent class prejudice ('look at the type of child he'll have to mix with!') they have in the past been concerned about a number of issues. There have been the R.E. teachers who seemed (even when they were qualified) more concerned to destroy their pupils' faith than help it to mature; teachers of science and history who used their position in order to oppose Biblical Christianity. Never far away has been the Evangelical bogey of 'the world' especially present (according to prejudice) in school dances, theatre and cinema visits, involvement in school plays, Sunday rehearsals and non-Christian friends.

It is not just a question today of the standards of other pupils from godless homes; the use of drugs (other than socially acceptable alcohol, nicotine and barbiturates); the stealing; talk of sexual experimentation; the hostility to all authority. More serious are the attitudes inculcated by the schools themselves, intentionally or by default. The tension is even more acute. 'The world' is encountered in more significant ways. There is sex education which ignores marriage, or values, implying that pre-marital restraint is an irrational phobia; set-books which would not have been on sale to adults in the not so distant past; teaching which affirms that moral choices are irrational, and that life is futile and absurd; communities where the so-called authorities do not seem to know what values they stand for, and are either disinclined or incompetent to prevent disturbed or rebellious children from disrupting community life.

Christian Schools?

Of course there are many schools still comparatively (but only comparatively) free from these tendencies. Yet, the poison is sufficiently widespread for many parents, and especially Christian ones, to fear for their children. Evangelicals in particular may wish to consider very seriously the possibility of using Christian day-schools where they exist.

We have already seen why they would not necessarily be enthusiastic about sending their children to church schools. Irrespective of parents' wishes, there are in any case comparatively few church secondary schools, and most of them are Roman Catholic. The sort of school that might appeal quite strongly would be on the lines of Christian schools in the U.S.A., staffed by believers and explicitly founded on the principle of the authority of the Bible.

The most obvious difficulty is financial. Whereas in America charitable gifts to such schools would be exempt from tax, this relief would extend in Britain only to covenanted gifts. In any case, most potential donors would have no personal interest in such schools, owing to the prestige attaching, in England at any rate, to boarding-schools, committed though they are to keeping asunder that which God has joined together.

Some Evangelicals look enviously towards Holland. There every encouragement is given to the foundation of private schools.[1] For example, under the Act of 1920 the following criteria govern the establishment of private schools. There must be: (a) a corporate association or institution; (b) an application to the municipal council with a declaration (usually by parents) that a sufficient number of children will attend the school; (c) a statement of the anticipated number of pupils and classrooms; (d) a declaration of willingness to provide security of ten per cent of the costs of foundation. The sufficient number of pupils varies with the size of the community served, from 50 to 125.

Once these data have been supplied, the school is automatically founded, and owned by the governing body, with the state paying the teachers' salaries and operating costs similar to those applicable in maintained schools.

Teachers are appointed and dismissed by governing bodies, but committees of appeal also operate, each covering at least twelve subsidized schools, and having equal numbers of members elected by the governing bodies and by the teaching staffs. These schools are widely used—accounting for between sixty per cent and eighty per cent of school places.

It would certainly be interesting to see what would happen in the unlikely event of the British law being changed to facilitate the founding of such schools. Quite certainly some Evangelicals

[1] *World Year Book of Education, 1966*, Evans, pp. 78–91.

would want to take advantage of the possibility. But however generous the support given, and however great the pressure to remove children from a corrupt maintained school system, many Evangelical parents would hesitate to use such Christian schools, which might prove less attractive than a first glance would suggest.

First of all, would they not tend to weaken the children educated in their 'hot-house' atmosphere? Some Christian schools, aware of this danger, currently try to avoid it by welcoming children from deprived backgrounds, who are sent by local authorities. Another problem is that while it would no doubt be possible for teachers to encourage pupils to face questions of contemporary relevance, some parents or governors might well disapprove. The question remains whether such a protected environment is a sound preparation for life in a secular society.

There is another serious difficulty. A school such as is being considered would presumably impose doctrinal tests on its teachers, and would be controlled by a governing body of strong Evangelical faith. It would indeed be very easy for narrow restrictions to be imposed also on the conduct of teachers; some colleges in the U.S.A. demand that lecturers abjure the use of tobacco and alcohol. Nor would these pressures always originate with the governors.

There are, after all, obscurantist parents, some of whom would send their children to Christian schools. It is not at all alarmist to foresee such parents protesting vigorously about a good deal that might be educationally sound, while others less bigoted, fearful or concerned keep quiet. This sort of pressure, if it was not resisted by a strong board of governors, might severely inhibit teaching in such areas as art, literature, science, and philosophy.

The establishment of Christian schools might also contribute to a 'ghetto' mentality, totally opposed to the 'salt' and 'light' metaphors used by Jesus. Many people think that the substantial absence from the U.S.A. public school system of children and young people from committed Christian backgrounds has harmed the community. At the time when anarchism and the New Left were making the greatest impact there were clearly powerful arguments for segregating Christian young people; yet a positive Christian witness was never more needed than at that moment. And if young people from Christian homes do not learn at school or college to relate to unbelievers among their peers, then this seems very unlikely to happen in later life.

Perhaps it could be one part of God's judgement on our society if direct Christian influence disappeared to a great extent from our education system, but this would mean Christians turning their back on society in a way difficult to reconcile with the New Testament, except on the assumption that society has become so corrupt that the risks could no longer be accepted of sending children to maintained schools.

A significant recent development has been the interest shown by the radical left in founding so-called 'free schools', based on the principles of self-government, education as self-fulfilment, lack of coercion, and the ultimate goal of creating a new society. An article on 'Free Schools and the Law' which appeared in the magazine *Children's Rights* (No. 2) discusses the law to achieve registered independent status, and suggests that Section 36 of the 1944 Act may offer an alternative possibility of having part-time, preferably unpaid tutors educating children at home. Evangelicals should be keenly interested in the experience of other groups of parents who find themselves disagreeing with the educational aims and practice of our society.

Future Trends

Changes of the kind we have been discussing seem unlikely to happen in the near future. Evangelical influence in education will, however, continue to be felt in other ways. We have already mentioned the considerable number of schools in the independent sector which are run on Evangelical lines. Unless they are made illegal by doctrinaire politicians (a possibility that should be actively fought by everybody who values individual freedom) their influence seems likely to increase, as the greater mobility of professional and business men, together with higher divorce rates, make boarding-schools more necessary.

So long as religious education is given in schools, many Evangelical teachers will be involved. If the subject develops in a way that displaces Jesus Christ from a position of central importance, then the number of Evangelicals—as of other committed Christians—doing this work will decline. Our children might then be taught religion chiefly by teachers having some sort of interest in religions generally, although unwilling to commit themselves to any one in particular. How many teachers are able and willing to do this is completely unknown; very few, one suspects.

Quite apart from religious education, there are always likely to be large numbers of Evangelicals teaching in both the maintained and 'independent' sectors. Like medicine, teaching is bound to make an appeal to people who want to help others. This motivation operates across the whole range of subject-matter, age, and ability. Just as there are Christian ward orderlies and Christian consultants, so a Christian commitment may inspire both infant teachers and university professors.

We may conclude this brief forecast of future Evangelical involvement in education by pointing to an area where the Evangelical contribution seems likely to grow. Evangelicals are beginning to realize that 'the basis of Christian action in the field of education must be in genuinely Christian thinking about education' (*Preparing for Teaching*, p. 9). Just as the last twenty-five years have seen the emergence of a recognizable body of conservative Evangelical Biblical scholarship, so in the future we may anticipate greatly increased activity among Evangelical educationists concerned, both to derive from the Scriptures guidelines for education and to relate these guidelines to significant developments in educational thought and practice.

Evangelicals are at last beginning to realize that children must be educated, not for life in pre-Christian Judah, nor yet in first-century Greece, but for the kaleidoscopic culture of the nineteen-seventies and -eighties. And they have acquired a new confidence that God's self-revelation is relevant to the cultural needs of the twentieth century.

9

THE URBAN SCENE

BRYAN ELLIS

'I have laboured in vain,
I have spent my strength for nothing and vanity.'
(Isa. 49: 4)

'You are my witnesses', says the Lord
(Isa. 43: 10)

'What is your parish strategy?' he said.

'We haven't got one. We go where the Spirit leads', I replied.

He went elsewhere for his curacy. I don't blame him; but I had told him the truth.

I had come to work in this inner city area in Leeds in 1962. In those days it was a solid working-class area. But it had deteriorated and a lot of the housing was in poor condition and designated for slum clearance. No one knew when it was going to happen. When it did come in 1963, the area around the church emptied in three months. Three thousand people moved away and our small congregation was halved in this short time. Vandalism in the area increased. The church and the old church hall both suffered. We had to close the hall and, as the vicarage was a mile and a half outside the parish, there was no centre to work from or meet at. I had no previous experience of this sort of situation. I had learnt nothing about it at college and no one else seemed to know what to do. How could I have a strategy for a disappearing parish?

This was just one of the traumas that hit me over the years. The first happened on the first Sunday I took services in the church. At the evening service I read myself in (as all Anglican vicars are supposed to do) by reading out the Thirty-nine Articles.

I sensed that I might just as well have been reading Chinese for all the understanding that the listeners had of what was being said.[1] I discovered that most of the elder members had left school at twelve or thirteen. The Tudor language was beyond them. Some were very intelligent but lacked formal training. I had been trained to think in the abstract. They thought in concrete terms and pictures. I found subsequently that almost all Christian literature was quite unsuitable for this area. The assumption behind it was that all were capable of grammar school thinking. Only recently has some literature appeared which is suitable,[2] and then it has to be used in a certain way. It is difficult for educated people to realize how big a problem communication is and remains in a working-class area.

Like many grey and underprivileged areas in cities, the educational standard was low. Teachers came and went very quickly. Little was expected of the children and little was achieved. Now and then I found a child with an unusual talent, but, because of depressing surroundings and the pressure to conform, the gift was not developed.[3] It was not surprising but heartbreaking, for the schools of the area were old, with poor heating, overcrowding, inadequate facilities inside and outside. This carried over into the church's life. There was only one teenager when I arrived. Others came along. But we never succeeded in integrating them into the church. We were too late in understanding their world.

Another trauma was the condition in which people lived. All homes were terraced. Some were 'through', some were 'back to back'. Some had hot water, some did not. Most toilets were outside or down the street. It took me some time to realize why a group of young people visiting the vicarage were so interested in the bathroom. Some cooking still took place on the old Yorkshire ranges which baked delicious bread, but, together with the open fires from 2,000 stacks and the industrial chimneys, blackened buildings and lungs. The smoke and smuts also blackened the washing which hung across the streets from house

[1] See *The Gagging of God*, p. 22, by Gavin Reid. This book is particularly relevant to our area where the break-up of community means no communication.

[2] E.g. the 4 booklets by the Bishop of Woolwich, 'Today' notes, S.U.

[3] See chapter 10, Section A, 'Scholarship boy', p. 241, *The Uses of Literacy*, R. Hoggart.

to house. There were no gardens; here and there the square yard of grass or flowers. The children played on the cobbles perilously near the busy main road, which claimed its victims. It had been a very respectable working-class area but for thirty years the threat of clearance had existed. So landlords refused to do repairs, and roofs leaked and wood rotted. When the wind blew strongly it was dangerous to walk along the streets.

The insecurity of the buildings was matched by the insecurity of the people. 'We may not be here next month, Vicar', was a sufficient excuse to put off doing anything in forward planning in the church. Yet who could blame people for feeling this? So the ambitious and energetic people moved away. The old people remained. Many had lived in the same street or the one nearby for seventy years. They suffered most. There were many extended families in the area; but mobility of population and the threat of clearance left them on their own. If they survived uprooting, and some did not, they found themselves scattered from their relatives and friends and placed on unknown estates. Life, with its poverty and lack of opportunity, had not prepared them for such an experience.

The noisy teenagers who had grouped near the church wall went, unless they belonged to the very poor families who could not afford to move. Into the area came young marrieds wanting cheap accommodation on their way to something better, or the problem family or those who hoped to get rehoused by the Corporation.

Though the church now stood as an enclave in 100 acres of rubble and rat-infested refuse, there were other areas in the parish. There was the new housing estate at the bottom end, but this was some way from us. It had a new Baptist church in the middle of it with two Anglican churches and a Roman Catholic church in close proximity. So we had few contacts there. But there were still the older areas. One was near the church. We also had two other areas whose usefulness as parish areas was compromised by the recent building of another Anglican church too near to us. However, there seemed to be opportunity enough, and I was confident that the Gospel would soon have its effect and that a strong church would be built up.

It was not the decaying area or the creaming of its leadership that defeated my hopes, though they added to my problems. I was to discover, as others working in similar areas have done, that there are two massive matters I had not appreciated. One is cultural difference and the other is the irrelevance of the Church and its Gospel to the working man. These were the two greatest shocks.

The cultural difference is not at first apparent. When I moved from serving in two middle class parishes, I found a church with fewer people, poorer, less leadership but with the services I was used to and a congregation who seemed to understand me and my faithful predecessors. It was a middle-class church. We were not eclectic but what had happened was simple. Those who had become members of it, had conformed to middle-class ways, whether by aspiration or pressure. Gradually I began to understand that 'C. of E.' meant middle-class to the working man and was culturally alien to him.

There are some very good descriptions of working-class culture and life available.[1] Any description of working-class life today is of course a description of yesterday. Making generalizations about class is dangerous, but there are certain features about the working-class that were true ten years ago and are still true today in spite of very rapid change.

For example, 'working-class solidarity' is a politician's myth. Yet there is sufficient truth in it to indicate a large cultural difference from the middle-class. The forbears of urban man and woman came to the cities to find work. They found it and they found also immense struggle and suffering. Early death, to which our local necropolis with its jostling, grimy headstones on the common graves bears abundant testimony; poor living conditions, factory work, poverty, exploitation, and industrial depression, produced a community of self-interest and defence. Seabrook shows the bottom limits of this solidarity. Yet it is there in a way that I have not found present among those who live in their semi-detached islands. The family supports its members. The youth gangs stand by one another. Neighbours help each other out in crises. The groups are many and various, but bound together in common need. They throw up their spokesman who expresses a common mind, and the middle-class boss does not easily understand the strength or nature of this grouping

[1] Hoggart, *The Uses of Literacy*; Rose, *The Working Class*; and Seabrook, *The Unprivileged*, and others. Seabrook's account is very readable, but grim.

in his labour relations. One hears accusations of 'Communist agitators' at work when what is really happening is the group saying what it thinks through its articulate members. If this solidarity is sometimes negative, defensive, and primitive, the phenomenon is much nearer to the Biblical pattern than the individualistic approach of the Evangelical. In contrast, when affluence comes, solidarity is diminished.

Poverty, overcrowding, underprivilege, have also dictated other social and cultural patterns. Lack of hope and security has reinforced an epicurean attitude to life. Thus the adolescent with strong sexuality and not much else to do looks for satisfaction for his need, and permissiveness is nothing new in working-class areas. The smallness of the homes means that social life takes place in the streets and at the clubs and pubs. The inability of the parent to communicate with the child often means that discipline is brutal and physical. A blow is an argument. The drabness of the surroundings and the monotony of work are relieved by Saturday night at the club. Enjoyment is sought in a social context and few have individual interests. There has been no chance to acquire them.

The culture[1] is changing. The mass media, especially television, and greater affluence mark out the young from the old. But the difference from C. of E. middle class is real enough. It was expressed to me by a churchwarden in suburbia who said about their curate that it was nice to have an educated man. I know what he meant though he was right for the wrong reason. That it is felt also the other way is shown by an experience of the late Henri Godin, a French Roman Catholic priest,[2] who came from a working-class home. On his return from the seminary for the holidays one of his friends remarked: 'You've changed. You don't belong to our class any more.' Godin in fact managed to remain working-class, but C. of E. clergy I know who come from this background have not. Their training at university and college has cut them off from their culture and they have found it impossible to return. So a middle-class clergy ministers in a working-class area, uneasily aware of a barrier and trying to overcome it by imposing middle-class norms on a working-class culture.

[1] Hoggart's book *The Uses of Literacy* gives a full description of this culture, and much of it remains true.
[2] *France Pagan? The Mission of Abbé Godin*, p. 8.

But the greatest shock of all was for me to discover what the Church thought about industrial areas and what these thought about the Church. 'Don't bury yourself there', a bishop said to me. 'Keep in touch and we will find you something in about five years.' 'It's just the sort of place for a young man with energy to go to. You can make your mistakes and it doesn't matter' was another view expressed to me. And 'You're wasting your time. They should find you something better.' These views appear to me outrageous, yet they adequately express that these areas are the cinderellas of the Church's interest.

I soon became aware that such axioms as 'A visiting parson makes a full church', and 'Prayer and hard work is all you need' were not true. The vast mass of the parish remained unmoved, unmovable. I later found out that the explanation for this was not just me. This alienation of the Church and working-class goes back a long way.[1] It started when rural poverty and industrial growth brought millions to the cities. The Established Church was unable to adapt itself to changing conditions. It had in any case become at the height of the industrial revolution a middle-class church. Other churches followed in the same path. Pew rents, paternalism and privilege, made it impossible for the poor to be reached. There were some momentary exceptions, like the beginnings of the Methodist revival, Anglo Catholic work in the East End of London and Booth's early Salvation Army.

This failure to reach the poor was recognized and lamented. Booth left the Methodists because of this. Dr Hume, Vicar of All Souls, Liverpool, in 1849, wrote of his parish of 24,000: 'They are all lost sheep of the Church of England . . . the seed of neglect having produced a harvest of home heathenism.' This lack of concern and urgency on the part of the Church at the beginning of the nineteenth century resulted in working-class culture growing up without the practice of religion.[2]

When the churches later realized what was happening, the direction of their work was paternalistic and concentrated on rescuing men and women from poverty, ignorance, and Godlessness. Though this desire was right, they failed to understand and alleviate the causes of these evils. This desire to improve meant a

[1] See especially *Church and people in an Industrial City*, E. R. Wickham.
Churches and the Working Classes in Victorian England, K. S. Inglis.
[2] See Wickham, p. 14; also *A Sociology of English Religion*, David Martin.

going up the social scale, and there has been a consequent drift of converted people out of their environment ever since. Thus there has been a complete failure to build indigenous church life within the working-class culture. There was hardly any attempt to penetrate by involvement and identification. The only sustained success has been by the Roman Catholics, and this is for ethnic reasons. So the illusion that the converted working man will make his way by 'A' levels to Ruskin College, Oxford, dies hard among the middle class. This attitude is resented. A Christian shop steward writes: 'What really gets up my nose is the way "Christians" have exalted certain kinds of work, usually the clean hand type. X, writing in the *C.E.N.* some time ago, spoke of "a couple of lads who were converted. Previously they had worked on a building site but once converted they got some 'O' levels and got a *more creative job*." . . . Adam was a farmer and that's a dirty hands job.'

But the working man who rejects this pressure to rise and leave his culture has also some other matters to concern him. He is surrounded by pre-utterance factors.[1] Culture difference says that to be a Christian you have to be middle class. Sunday best (coat, trousers, collar and tie) must be worn to worship God and an obscure language used. Christianity means privilege, for the clergy live in large houses, like the bosses; while the workers live in small garden-less back-to-backs around the two-acre vicarage grounds. Leadership is in the hands of the bourgeois, who cannot trust the working-class to lead. The large and showy bookstall near the church entrance tells him that Christianity is books. The insistence on certain standards of behaviour before he can be accepted into membership confirms his belief that Christianity is not swearing, drinking or smoking.[2] These and other factors, like the divided churches, strangle the Gospel of Grace before it can breathe into his soul. There are all sorts of variations from the setting I work in. Besides the old slum areas, there are the

---

[1] *The Gagging of God*, chapter 5. These are the factors that reinforce or destroy our response to the message: e.g., a fat man extolling frugality.

[2] *Come out the Wilderness* p. 89 (see also p. 91). 'It almost seemed as if the first concern was not to bring the sheep home but to keep the lost sheep out in case they impaired the Church's reputation for respectability.' *France Pagan*, p. 98. 'Why first convert to a culture and make acceptance of that culture a condition of acceptance of faith?'

pre 1939 council estates with their often neglected gardens;[1] the big problem areas, with drugs, prostitution, and crime; and the new industrial housing estates. They all share the alienation I have described. The problem in the cities gets worse. The parish next to mine has not one but nine major cultures represented in strength, as well as a number of sub-cultures.

It is not surprising that the minister in these areas after a sojourn of five years looks longingly at the greener fields of middle-class suburbia. Or worse, fed by the unfailing deluge of success stories in the Evangelical magazines, he accepts non-parochial work, and, just as the first green shoots of new faith are coming up, he leaves and they are trampled down. Or worse, he loses his faith. Read chapter one of *The Gagging of God* and realize that he is the victim of pressures he does not understand.

'Perhaps, first of all, there is a need for Christian leaders to have a more coherent understanding of how the modern city operates and grows, and of the forces at work in its life. Many sections of urban population are untouched because their rôle in city life is not appreciated.'[2]

The Old Testament prophets were men who were keenly aware of what was going on around them. Their knowledge covered national and international affairs. It was because of this awareness that they were able to bring a relevant word of God to the nation. My own ignorance of the urban scene before I came here and my experience since suggests that the quotation above is an understatement. This lack of awareness is disclosed by the almost total absence until recently of any serious Evangelical study of the matter. The books that have been written come from the bosses' side and are often irrelevant to the urban situation. The first book I read that helped was *Come out the Wilderness*, by Bruce Kenrick. This describes the work of the Protestant East Harlem Parish in New York. Though the circumstances that produced this huge area of underprivilege are different from our own, it does speak realistically of their attempt to establish a church among people who are trapped by their environment. Their work began with a social survey so that they could become

[1] A planner's folly. Putting a working man with no experience of gardening into a house with one is like putting a suburban man into a large country estate. He would not manage any better.

[2] *On the Other Side*, p. 36, S.U.

9

aware of what people were thinking and suffering.[1] They found a church irrelevant, where there was one at all, for most Christians had moved out of the area. Hence our first duty is to find out what has happened and is happening around us; then to bring Biblical reflection to bear; then to apply the insights of God's will.

My experiences have made me reflect, and I offer these as Presence, Witness, and Ministry.

Presence

'The Christian need not live between the gas-works and the linoleum factory if he can afford to live somewhere more salubrious.'[2] But a very large number of people have to. If the Christians move out as they do, who is to witness to those round about? I suppose that a previous vicar of this parish thought like this when he persuaded this diocese to let him move to a vicarage one-and-a-half miles from the parish and in a very salubrious area. His parishioners had to stay where they were.

Jesus, to be a witness to heavenly things, came into this world. His presence in it could alone bring about our salvation. It was a presence without privilege or safeguards. He was born into a working home. The maternity arrangements were far from ideal. He had a provincial accent.[3] His parents had little choice in where they had to live. This was not a very good start for getting on in the world. Further, the New Testament writers show their tremendous sense of Jesus as fully human. They came to accept his divinity, but it was as a man they first met him. He partook of the same nature (Heb. 2: 14). He suffered and was tempted (Heb. 2: 17). Although he was a son, he learned obedience through what he suffered (Heb. 5: 8). Jesus at every point identified himself and was involved with mankind. Love lowered all defences and led to his ignominious end. It was this complete absence of privilege that enabled his complete involvement with people, and especially the poor.

---

[1] *Come out the Wilderness*, chapter 4.

[2] *The Christian in an Industrial Society*, H. F. R. Catherwood.

[3] When *A Man born to be King* was first produced in 1943, Jesus and his mother spoke in standard English, though the notes on accent and dialect in Gollancz edition say that for complete realism all the Galilean characters ought to have a strong local dialect.

Before Paul could become all things to all men he had to abandon his privileged past. He did not deny it but he learnt that it could not provide a platform for the claims of the Gospel (Phil. 3: 4–8). He learnt to be like his Master, wholly identified with the people to whom he went. (1 Cor. 9: 19–23).

What the working man sees of the presence of the Church, if he sees it at all, is too often a decaying building, non-residential Christians; non-involvement by the Church in the problems of his area. The only time he becomes conscious of it is for baptisms, weddings and funerals; or, as in Seabrook's Green Street, when the parson comes collecting for waifs and strays or the melody of 'Greenlands Icy Mountains' wafts down the street from the mission.

So, before all else, a Christian presence is needed. At its minimum it is summed up by a German pastor who was asked why he did not quit his wretched area and replied that he remained in order that the rumours of God should not wholly die out. I must admit that, if I had not been ordained, I should have settled for suburbia. As someone said to me 'You wouldn't be living in that area, if you weren't the vicar.' But having come, I have seen how weak the church is through lack of Christian presence and know too the help that can be given when Christian people do move in.

There is nothing romantic about this involvement. It has meant sharing in all the troubles of the area. It has brought tensions to my family that have had to be resolved, for the children too have had to share in the inadequacies of the area. But only in this way have I been able to understand and sympathize with those who live here. Recently I asked a clergyman friend living in a Liverpool slum when he expected to be cleared. He replied, 'I don't know when it's due to come down,' and added, 'We now know what other people in the area feel like and it's good for us.'

There is a great need for mature missionary-minded people besides clergy to go and live in the poorer areas of our cities and towns. The transition is far from easy, and impossible for those who want to see a church life reproduced according to the pattern of their student days. But those who are prepared to try to understand and learn will find a white harvest field, though often in black surroundings.

Sometimes fear makes converted people want to move out of these areas. They are led to believe that they and their children will be contaminated. The problem is succinctly answered by St John: 'Greater is He that is in you, than He that is in the world' (1 John 4: 4). It is strange that among those who claim to believe the Bible there is often a defensive spirit. 'That virtue which requires to be ever guarded is scarce worth the sentinel.'[1] In fact I can promise a joyful opportunity of proving the truth of God's power to keep for all who live in these areas. The experiences of the *Come out the Wilderness* team are particularly helpful here.

God needs his witnesses in suburbia. However, it seems to me that they are not lacking in these places and that many who have had the privilege of growing up spiritually under a godly and able ministry should now bring their treasure to share with those who have not. John Trevor,[2] the founder of the Labour Church movement, learnt from the Salvation Army in its early days 'that God can do nothing without love and self-sacrifice, and the witnessing spirit which may lead to martyrdom; that the "Truth" taught comfortably, however reasonable it may appear, will never redeem society; indeed, that truth without self-sacrifice is not truth but a sham'.

I quote from a letter in a recent number of 'Christians in Industrial Areas'[3] '. . . the working class Christians should stay, but it is not true that *only* "working class people" can do the job. I believe that if more and more professional and other classes other than working class would move into industrial areas, this would be not only a social good, but a spiritual breakthrough.'

Marxists are not slow to come and live in our poor areas. Can God expect less from Christians? There must be a Presence and a physical one at that.

Witness

What do we do with the Christians in the city when we have them? What is the mission of the Church? Should it be involved

---

[1] Oliver Goldsmith, *The Vicar of Wakefield.*
[2] Inglis, *op. cit.*, p. 215.
[3] No. 21, R. K. Godin.

politically and socially besides the more conventional ways which some consider outmoded?

A study outline we used recently had a section on mission. It suggested that the mission of the Church was to witness, to serve, to have fellowship, to evangelize. I would not quibble with any of these points but I have long thought that there was a muddle somewhere over mission, with many different voices saying this and that about it. This muddle stems from using the word 'mission' which is a convenient word but not a Biblical word. What in the New Testament is used as a verb has been turned into a noun. So we end up doing things and trying to justify them under one of the headings above.

The Biblical umbrella word is witness. The old Israel was a witness to God to the nations (Isa. 43: 11, 12 etc.). Thus the prophets record God's anger when the nation is corrupt, immoral or unjust, for this reflects badly on the nature of God to onlookers. Jesus was the supreme and perfect witness to God (Rev. 1: 1), and he calls his Church to continue to witness to the full range of the character of God as he did. This witness is carried on in all sorts of situations and it means being sent into these situations (Matt. 28: 20; and Acts 1: 8; 13: 3). The task of the Church is plain. It is called to be a witness by word and deed to all that God is and has done, and especially by Jesus Christ. This is spelled out in the Acts. But the witness is as manifold and wide as God himself. Different needs demand an appropriate witness. Thus the need of the Greek widows in Acts 6 is met with administrative change in the Church, and the witness to the compassion of God for widows is brought out.

It is therefore the task of every church in its own situation to seek the guidance of the Holy Spirit about the content of its witness. Following norms or precedents or what other churches are doing is of limited use. What may be right for one church in one situation may be wrong for others. The East Harlem Church found that their witness to God meant their grappling with drug addiction, education, rent rackets, sanitary arrangements, as well as the ordinary accepted matters of church life.

There is a good description of the working out of this witness in chapter 7 of *From a Mersey Wall* by Roger Sainsbury, when mess and noise from a local market led the Christians to start a Community Association which now, in an enlarged form, deals with people's living conditions. Here again problems that are never met in middle-class areas demand a witness from Christians. This is not a kind of optional extra for the socially minded but a witness to the character of God. Here again fear of contamination by the world puts some Christians on the defensive. John 7: 37, 38 makes it quite clear who will influence whom, and the interests of piety and holiness are not served by a refusal to be citizens in the world. It is in fact sinful because it misrepresents God.

But if witness to the love, justice and holiness of God carries us into some strange places, it would be an unbiblical and inadequate witness that sees man's needs fulfilled by bread alone. Our respect and love for our neighbour demands that we show him by word as well as deed his need of becoming a new creature in Christ. Seabrook sums up the poverty of the life he knew. 'I cannot imagine wanting to perpetuate proletarian culture. The conditions that created it were cruel bondage which mutilated and destroyed, and those who prolong it—even in the name of some prospective and possibly beneficial revolution—would need the ruthlessness and inhumanity of a circus owner who breeds a race of dwarfs from some dishonourable motive of personal gain.'[1] His book shows a group of people wrestling with identity, justice, meaning, relationships, communication, work, and finding no answer within their shuttered experience. These are the very problems that Jesus answers so completely, and yet the Christianity they saw seemed irrelevant. The full rich life[2] of the man who is cloistered by his circumstances is very likely to escape to the working-man's club or pub where he will have a good time, and who can blame him. For unless he can see Christians who are enriched by Christ (1 Cor. 1: 5) he will know of nothing better. Words alone are not enough.

The coming urban scene will not lack opportunities for the Church to witness to new urban man with his fragmented insular impersonal and insecure life. The city has many good points but it fails most, as old urban man did, in the poverty of his personal relationships. If Christians cannot help here who can?

---

[1] *Op. cit.*, p. 120.
[2] Hoggart, *op. cit.*, chapter 5. Also the lack of purpose in his work contributes to this. 'I only work here, but if you want to know me as I really am, come to my home and meet my family'—quoted in *The Sociology of Industry*, p. 154.

If they are not prepared to be salt in the world, then there is only one destiny promised.

Ministry

Making witness a reality in urban areas comes through ministry. The theological and historical considerations have been written about elsewhere.[1] I want to see established in these areas a positive and outgoing ministry. So here I am concerned about the *structure* and the *scope* of it.

The Early Church was not given a blueprint for either of these things. It found its way prayerfully and sometimes uneasily in and through new situations as the Spirit of God led (see Acts chapter 15 especially). The principles of ministry were never in doubt but the structure and the scope were.

The principle of ministry is enshrined in Romans 15: 16. It is bringing God to men and men to God through Jesus Christ, proclaiming a living Saviour and bringing them up in Christ. But in history we observe two polarizations. One is an extreme Catholic position that has arrogated the ministry to a priestly caste, and the other is the protestant reaction expressed in the phrase 'the priesthood of all believers'. This latter tends to an extreme of denying the different functions of ministry, and the truth is better safeguarded by using the Scriptural phrase 'Royal priesthood' (1 Pet. 2: 9) which much better states the corporate nature of ministry shown by St Paul in 1 Corinthians. It is this corporate nature of ministry that must find adequate fulfilment in structure and scope today.

Roland Allen's book *Missionary methods—St Paul's or ours* was an inspiration to the East Harlem team as they struggled with ministry in their own area. I found this sixty-year-old book prophetic and it spoke to my own situation. It confirmed me in the belief that I was working in a missionary area and that somehow the structure I was in was not valid for this place. But the least satisfactory part of the book was his attempt to square the Church of England bishops, priests and deacons with the missionary situation. It is not difficult to see why. The structure that evolved and which we have inherited from the early centuries fits static Christian community or a community whose culture is strongly influenced by Christianity. This is the ideal

[1] E.g., *Called to Serve*, Michael Green.

on which the Church of England ministry is based. One is made painfully aware in the city of the inadequacy of this structure. The older generation had at least a smattering of Christian belief, though it was non-participating and Pelagian, and it did not work for them. How much less can it work for a younger genera- tion that has hardly any background at all.

This structural difficulty in industrial areas is noted in France by the Abbé Godin in *France Pagan*, and in Germany by Horst Symanowski in *The Christian witness in an Industrial Society*. What is a missionary situation cannot be met by the existing structure when the Church is equipped for maintenance but not mission. The Morley Commission stated 'that the present way in which the Church handles the care, deployment and payment of the clergy is inadequate and wasteful. It fails to meet contemporary needs . . .'[1] It is these urgent needs that demand a radical approach; tinkering with the structure will not do. Just as the sabbath was made for man, so was the ministry. I do not see how the right structure is possible in the Church of England so long as patronage and the establishment remain as they are, and time in the cities is not on our side.

In this missionary situation it will not be possible to have, or desirable to seek, a uniform structure. There are examples al- ready where the structure has been altered to attempt to cope with the problem. There are group ministries in Liverpool and *From a Mersey Wall* tells us something of the combination of youth club and parish. The Mayflower is known to many.[2] *Open House*, by John Tanburn, tells of the establishment of house churches on a council estate at St Paul's Cray. The Heworth team in York includes university to working-class and there are alterations, as at Barton Hill, Bristol, to the ministerial leadership of the Church. But still too many men are left struggling on their own in a way that no missionary society would contemplate abroad.

It is possible that God will transform an existing structure and make it usable for the future. The class meeting, which became

---

[1] *Partners in Ministry*, p. 5.

[2] In 1958 David Sheppard accepted the challenge that if the Gospel is true it must work for the working man. He and his wife, and other Christians, went as a team to Canning Town, where the No. 1 Dockland Settlement became the Mayflower Family Centre. See his book, *Parson's Pitch*, chapter 10.

the backbone of Methodism, started as a money-raising activity, and only gradually did John Wesley realize its usefulness.[1] But if he was an opportunist, he was also a thinker and organizer. The structure he initiated, tragically and of necessity outside the parochial structure of the Church of England, helped forward the greatest revival of modern times. The missionary situation, as in his day, demands missionary methods. Change is dangerous but it is better than death.

Scope

Since the industrial revolution, men and women have worked in ever-increasing groups outside the home. Today new urban man no longer lives round his place of work. His leisure is taken in a different area. So he has three distinct parts of his life. His neighbour is the man at work or in the club or association, but he may not know the family in the next flat to his in the high rise block. It is a very different setting from what we find in the New Testament and it is to these three aspects of his life that the Church must minister.

(a) *Work* Bishop Wickham argues the case for industrial mission in his book.[2] It is a very different way of looking at mission from what Evangelicals are accustomed to call mission; but it must be taken seriously. His view is that the Church has a prophetic rôle to take and must offer a serious critique from neutral ground of the aims of industry and the way it works. It is not possible here to discuss this in a short space, but one long quotation from Horst Symanowski will show the kind of problem that the Church must speak about. He writes about his time in a factory.

'Once I experience with my own body the way in which the system of production lays hold of my life with inexorable laws determining it by its own rhythm, then I understand that the worker is no longer the master of his own free time, is no longer free to shape the life of his household. His own shift work, as well as that of his wife, his older children, allows no stable period of free time; no evening of rest in the old sense, and often not even a fixed day of rest each week. It is often no longer possible to speak of Sundays and holidays in which the whole family can be together. The modern system of production does not permit a

[1] *Journal*, April 25, 1742—quoted by Wickham, *op. cit.*, p. 268.
[2] *Op. cit.*, p. 238 *et. seq*.

man to live any longer in step with the natural rhythm of day and night, six days work and sabbath rest. Its work is directed neither by Sun nor Moon, summer nor winter. It has a rhythm of its own. Which morning prayer or which evening prayer should we teach our young men and young women who will soon be getting up in the evening and going to bed in the morning according to the demands of this rhythm? . . . The rhythm of our churchly life in villages or in certain vocational groups may still show a harmony between the rhythm of nature and the rhythm of work . . . But for millions of men who are yoked to the modern system of production there exists only this other rhythm.

'It is certain that the Church will not be able to overcome the rhythm of this other world. But the Church can, out of love for those men who are yoked to this rhythm, cease making its own rhythm the precondition for the Christian and churchly life.'[1] The working man is bound by this system. It is no use telling him that conversion will solve his problem.

There are very few Evangelical contributions on this matter which are of such importance. Before there can be, there must be those who make it as serious a study as Bishop Wickham has done and are as involved as he is.

(b) *Leisure* It seems certain that the working man will have far more leisure time than in the past. 'For most people in the present industrial society, leisure is quite clearly demarcated from work. Work contributes something for which others are willing to pay (or for which others would have to be paid if one did not do it oneself) while leisure is concerned with contributing to the satisfaction of self.'[2]

Our area is dominated by the working men's clubs. There are ten of them in and just outside the parish. Some of the clubs started years ago as providential societies but have now become entertainment centres and inward-looking. Any church ministry has therefore to take into account how it is to help its people to use its leisure. The cultural pattern, as has been noted, is to take leisure in groups, so there is a very real need for a Christian social life which will bear a positive witness to Christ. An example of this is the Men's Fellowship at Holy Trinity, Platt, Manchester, where its aims are: (1) to reach out evangelistically

[1] *Op. cit.*, pp. 37, 38.
[2] *Sociology of Industry*, p. 158.

among the ordinary men in the parish; (2) to provide a thoroughly enjoyable social evening for those who come; and (3) to use it as a bridge to Christian discipleship, and then on to Church family membership.

It is not sufficient to help only the young through youth activities in this matter. This is a part of life, recognized in the Bible and therefore to be redeemed by Christ. And how is this influence to come through the mass media or the holiday camp? We ignore these at the spiritual peril of those who are affected.

(c) *Home* It is the home and family setting that is most familiar to the ordinary parish minister. It is to this that he will give most of his time. There are of course the specialized ministries so urgently needed in cities,[1] and which should be part of the missionary structure which is so badly needed. But there is the necessity to build up those who have become members of the body of Christ so that they too may take part in the corporate ministry of the Church. The aim is to produce a whole person in Christ in a wholesome relationship with others.

It means time and patience to help people who have had little opportunity in life to grow. Yet grow they must and it is the minister's duty to provide opportunities for growth.

It means giving people the responsibility of making decisions, helping them to do so, and to live with the consequences of their decisions, for ultimately the missionary help from outside must leave behind it an indigenous Church.

It means giving people jobs to do that I could do better and faster myself, knowing that they will be done badly according to my standard, but in the hope that this will help someone to learn to give.

It means accepting that the Holy Spirit working in a different culture brings what we are not expecting. A Liverpool curate told me that the Bishop confirming his slum boys complained about their lack of regular prayer and Bible-reading when he questioned them. 'But it was', he said to me, 'the first time they had told the truth.'

It means looking for and using new means of helping people to grasp Biblical truth. Erasmus longed 'that the husbandman

[1] E.g., Immigrants and different cultures, youth, Samaritans, hospitals, industry, etc.

should sing portions of them (the Gospel and Epistle) to himself as he follows the plough, and that the weaver should hum them to the time of his shuttle . . .' So do we, but we have to reckon with a non-literate ethos. The student type of Bible study will not do.

It means helping and encouraging Christians in evangelism. Visiting, personal contact, with the natural groups, use of the home (which is against the cultural pattern), are ways of doing this. For evangelism must be done by us. Evangelism from out-side in the past has had almost no effect.

It means trying to make our common life in Christ a group experience, and trying to live as members one of another. For it is in groups that we learn in life, and it is the way the disciples learnt from Jesus, and the way the early Church progressed, and there is plenty of opportunity for forgiving and forbearing in this sort of relationship.

*   *   *

We have far to go. Often we seem to take one step forward and two back. There have been so many reverses. It has taken nine years for us to get a small but established meeting for prayer. A few have turned to the Lord, a few have been blessed. This is gold to us but no-one working in these areas can rest content until the proportion of men and women committed to the Lord is as high as it is in the middle-class areas.

I am glad to know that an Evangelical urban training project is being planned. If I had known when I started here what I know now, others could have been helped far more than they have been.

Visiting evangelists to these shores talk of seeing a Christian revival in this country. It has not been very easy to see this in our urban areas. Nor am I confident that a Church which is middle-class and wedded to capitalism will take seriously the plight of these areas. But perhaps the increasing deep concern among a few is a sign, as the preaching of the Gospel to the poor was to John the Baptist. I shall feel a lot happier when I see churches being dedicated to 'Christ the Worker'.

10

EVANGELICAL CO-OPERATION

Gordon Landreth

The story of Evangelical co-operation in modern times may conveniently be taken up in 1846, when the Evangelical Alliance was founded 'to aid in manifesting as far as practicable the unity which exists among the true disciples of Christ; to promote their union by fraternal and devotional intercourse; to discourage all envyings, strifes and divisions'—to quote a resolution at the inaugural conference proposed by an Anglican, the Rev. T. R. Birks. Among the founding fathers of the Alliance were Anglicans such as the Rev. Edward Bickersteth (whose son, Bishop Bickersteth of Exeter, became a long-standing champion of the Alliance), the Rev. and Hon. Baptist Noel (a chaplain to the Queen), the Rev. T. Byrth, and the Hon. Arthur Kinnaird.

Other Anglicans who have since been active in the work of the Alliance have included such well-known Evangelicals as Bishops Knox and Taylor Smith, Dean Wace, and Prebendary Webb-Peploe. The leadership has naturally always included a good mixture of denominations. Congregationalists, Presbyterians, Independents, Wesleyans, Baptists, and a minister in the Countess of Huntingdon's Connexion, all appear among the founding fathers.

In those early days the Evangelical Alliance maintained a strong opposition to Roman Catholicism, and could be regarded in part as a response to the emergent Anglo-Catholic party in the Church of England. But the prime reason for Evangelicals getting together, then as now, was not for controversy but in order unitedly to propagate the Gospel (as the very name Evangelical implies). Opposition to others like the Catholics was necessary because the purity of the Gospel was at stake. Today the Evangelical Alliance does not place its emphasis on a militant Protestantism (though it still feels the need to say a word from time to time in defence of the purity of the Gospel), and the violently anti-Catholic group in the Church of England sees its rallying-ground rather in a body like the Protestant Reformation Society or the Protestant Truth Society.

The creative work of Evangelical co-operation, ever since the Evangelical Revival at the end of the eighteenth century, has been in evangelistic alliances for home and foreign mission work and for serving the varied ongoing work of the Church. From the British and Foreign Bible Society through the Evangelical faith missions of the last century (China Inland Mission, World-wide Evangelization Crusade, Regions Beyond Missionary Union and many others) to the Billy Graham Crusades and the very recent TEAR Fund (Evangelical Alliance Relief Fund) this missionary concern has expressed itself in societies operating alongside the institutional churches.

Similar patterns can be seen in specialist ministries like the Keswick Convention (for deepening the spiritual life), the Scripture Union (with its children's missions, Bible-reading aids, and young people's work) and the Inter-Varsity Fellowship (working both in student evangelism and in Christian publishing). The complexity of modern life is reflected in more specialized activities, like the Shaftesbury Project (for research and education in the Biblical principles that should underlie political and social action), and Radio Worldwide (producing radio programmes for missionary use overseas). There are many others.

It is a sad commentary on the lack of evangelistic thrust in the institutional churches that these many interdenominational or undenominational mission bodies and service agencies have come into being. It is also of course a fact that once Christians set up independent societies the fissiparous tendencies continue, and every strong natural leader who comes along can be tempted to start his own show. Thus a useful form of interdenominational co-operation in evangelism can become debased into a multiplicity of small societies each with a very similar rôle. The scandal of Evangelical disunity in the field of evangelistic effort has been taken to heart in recent years and the Evangelical Missionary Alliance (in particular) has worked with some success to promote closer co-operation in foreign missionary work, and actual mergers where these are indicated. Successful mergers of small societies, like the Poona and India Village Mission and the Ceylon and India General Mission, may point the way forward; while bigger societies, like the Overseas Missionary Fellowship (successor of the China Inland Mission), and the Bible and Medical Missionary Fellowship, are actively working together in a number of spheres at both the home and the field ends of their operations.

The Evangelical Alliance has regarded its rôle as that of a linking agency to ensure that co-operation and liaison is provided between different societies and churches with a common interest in a particular Christian activity. Thus, ministers of various denominations have come together in fraternals and residential conferences to consider their evangelistic and pastoral tasks. An annual residential conference for full-time evangelists has been organized. Occasional meetings of executives of both denominational and interdenominational Evangelical youth organizations have been arranged. Special commissions and study groups have worked on the updating of evangelistic methods (the report entitled *On the Other Side*) and of missionary work (the report *One World, One Task*), as well as on new towns evangelism (*Evangelical Strategy in the New Towns*). In all these activities Evangelicals have worked together across the denominations for limited, functional ends. And the results have served them in their several churches and societies.

On an international scale Evangelical co-operation in the last century, apart from the interdenominational missionary work already noted, took the form of bringing political pressure to bear on behalf of Protestant Christians under persecution in Muslim and Roman Catholic countries. A sharing in prayer has also been prominent since the middle of the last century, and the one strong feature of the Alliance movement on the continent of Europe has been the annual observance of a Week of Prayer in the first calendar week of the year. Originally sponsored by the Evangelical Alliance in Britain, the programme for this prayer week is now prepared by Evangelicals in different European countries in rotation and sent out from Britain to over seventy countries in the world for translation where necessary into other languages. Although the Universal (or Worldwide) Week of Prayer at the beginning of January has been in competition with the ecumenical Week of Prayer for Christian Unity in the third week of that month, and is less widely observed in Britain than it was in earlier decades, it remains a main feature of the church calendar in Germany and some other Protestant countries in Europe like Denmark.

Interdenominational Evangelical co-operation on a world scale has been complicated in recent decades by the pressures from strongly fundamentalist groups in the U.S.A., which have sought to establish their own international pressure groups. Nevertheless, attempts have been made in the World Evangelical Fellowship to provide a meeting-ground for all who share an Evangelical basis of faith and to promote services which will further the cause of the Gospel, particularly in the realms of theological education and of the relief of physical needs. The World Fellowship embraces the Alliances of a number of the European countries, with their strong state church links, as well as the active Evangelical Fellowship of India and the National Association of Evangelicals in the U.S.A. Various smaller national fellowships also belong, and the British Evangelical Alliance continues to have a major rôle in the world body. With limited objectives and considerable financial problems, the World Evangelical Fellowship remains at present a symbol of international Evangelical co-operation rather than any sort of power structure.

Interdenominational Evangelical co-operation expresses itself today not only in national organizations and in the loose international structures just described, but also in local Evangelical fellowships. These are most successful when based on a provincial city like Sheffield or Bristol, though they also exist in some London suburban areas. Often brought into being to further a particular local evangelistic purpose, such as the holding of a city-wide evangelistic campaign, they function with a loose administrative structure that brings local Evangelical leaders together on an occasional basis for particular projects. These may include the preparing of material for a local radio station, the running of a Keswick-type convention, the holding of a missionary exhibition or convention, or the running of a training course for Bible-class and Sunday school leaders. As on the international scene, the pattern of this Evangelical co-operation at the local level is uneven and somewhat untidy, and reflects local traditions (it is said that in Norfolk, for instance, the population generally is bad at co-operative effort and this is reflected in the

Evangelical world). Much depends here as elsewhere on personal leadership and the presence of a man or men with vision for what can be achieved by co-operative effort.

The picture of Evangelical co-operation that emerges is thus one of a very loose structure at every level and in every sphere. Evangelicals have tended to retain their individual freedom of action within their churches or societies—or even as individuals! They have co-operated on a functional basis as and when the need for joint action has been demonstrated. It has often needed a man of insight to show them the need to work together, and to overcome the inertia of existing patterns of work in order to achieve any united effort.

When the Rev. Ian Thomson (now Secretary of the Bible Reading Fellowship) conducted a survey of laymen in Christian mission abroad on behalf of the Conference of British Missionary Societies he noted the strikingly effective network of Christian laymen in secular work overseas who were linked by the Inter-Varsity Fellowship's Graduates' Fellowship. Contact was maintained only by means of a quarterly magazine and prayer circular and a handful of local correspondents overseas. Nevertheless, Evangelical laymen met up with one another, worked together in Christian enterprises wherever they happened to be posted, and shared a strong sense of fellowship which was reinforced by their prayer for one another. This pattern of strong interpersonal relationships, with a minimal administrative structure, is typical of the strength of Evangelical co-operation at both the local and wider levels. (It is incidentally something that Evangelicals learnt many years ago, long before it became one of the patterns that recent observers have noted in the ranks of the 'new left'.) It should be emphasized that these strong personal links can only be built because Evangelicals share a common basis of faith in a God who has spoken, who answers prayer, and, above all, who has commissioned us to proclaim a Gospel to all the world. These links *are* stronger than those between Evangelicals and non-Evangelicals in the same church or Christian society.

This brings us to the important question of the tension felt by Evangelicals in mainstream denominations (and especially by Evangelical Anglicans) between their Evangelical beliefs and the political trends within their own church structure. As already noted, the Evangelical Alliance started life partly as an expression of protest against Anglo-Catholicism in the established church, and it took an active part in the campaign against the Revised Prayer Book of 1928. Even in recent years there have been moves to use Assemblies of Evangelicals as a forum for criticizing anti-Evangelical doctrines in the Church of England, as happened over the prayers-for-the-dead controversy in 1968. (On this occasion Free Churchmen opposed the raising of the issue as it was a domestic matter for one church.) But it is much less true today than it used to be that Anglican Evangelicals look for outside help in fighting their doctrinal battles. The danger is now that they have become so bound up with the internal policies of the Church of England that they have become insensitive to the view of their non-Anglican Evangelical friends—or perhaps unaware of how out of touch they were in their respective thinking. This was particularly painfully illustrated in the controversies following the publication of *Growing Into Union*, which appeared to many Free Church Evangelicals to be an abandonment of Evangelical positions on a number of major points, including the primacy of the authority of Scripture, the nature of the sacrament, and the importance of bishops.

The controversy among Evangelicals over *Growing into Union* centred especially around the head of the Rev. Dr Jim Packer, then Principal of Tyndale Hall, the Evangelical Anglican theological college in Bristol. Dr Packer had been closely involved in a number of interdenominational enterprises, including the periodical *The Evangelical Magazine* (which carried articles on both sides of the controversy), and the Puritan Conference, an annual gathering of those interested in Puritan studies: this conference ceased after *Growing into Union* was published, but a similar conference has since been started under a purely Free Church leadership. Despite various attempts to clarify issues between Anglican and Free Church Evangelicals arising from the publication of *Growing into Union*, deep misunderstandings remain. (These misunderstandings are not confined to Free Church Evangelicals: many Anglican Evangelicals are also unhappy about parts of the book.)

Some of this controversy has merely brought into the open a basic difference in theology which has been there all the time— the difference between those who accept the situation of a church in which different doctrinal points of view live together and those who believe that the purity of the church and of its doctrine is of over-riding importance. Anglican Evangelicals have in general settled for the former position, with all that it implies in terms of accepting something less than the best (after determining what in conscience can be allowed), and being loyal to a corporate body with some parts of which one disagrees more or less strongly. Free Church Evangelicals, especially those of the more independent traditions, have in many cases been separatist in their doctrine of the church and advocated the forming of a new church when an existing one has become too corrupt. Evangelical separatists in recent years have found a rallying-point in the British Evangelical Council, which is a council of churches all of which explicitly reject the ecumenism of the World Council of Churches and its member bodies because of the ecumenical movement's inclusivist theology. The BEC urges the formation of doctrinally pure churches and seeks to co-ordinate and support the growth and development of such churches. It condemns Evangelicals who do not accept the principle of separation, and for this reason is reluctant to have any close association with an interdenominational body like the Evangelical Alliance, which advocates Evangelical co-operation in other spheres notwithstanding the age-long divisions of view over the doctrine of the Church.

By no means all Free Church Evangelicals identify themselves with the British Evangelical Council. Many, although they are themselves members of separatist churches, like the Pentecostal Churches, the Christian Brethren, individual churches and leaders in the Strict Baptist denomination, and the Fellowship of Independent Evangelical Churches, do not wish their views on church government and politics to hinder fellowship with other Evangelicals. They are concerned to work together interdenominationally in evangelism, in missionary work, in bodies like the Keswick Convention and its local counterparts, in radio work, and so on. Many other Free Church Evangelicals are themselves in 'doctrinally mixed' denominations, like the Methodist Church and the Baptist Union, whose own internal politics occupy some of their time in the same way as the internal affairs of the Church of England occupy the time of Evangelical Anglicans. At the time of writing, the Baptist Union is particularly

rent over a doctrinal controversy concerning an address on the
Deity of Christ by the principal of a denominational college which
appears in conflict with the foundation documents of the denomination. The lack of any 'disciplinary action' by the Baptist
Union Council in a case which many members of the denomination regard as clear heresy is causing several ministers to leave
the denomination and many others to consider what remedies
are open to them. In the Methodist Church, the recently formed
Conservative Evangelicals in Methodism is a body determined to
maintain the Evangelical cause *within* the structures of that
denomination.

The interest in church union schemes in recent years has of
course helped to maintain this domestic emphasis in the thinking
of Evangelicals in all denominations, and has been in competition
with the functional forms of united activity represented by the
interdenominational societies, conventions, etc. This is illustrated
by the conflict at the beginning of the year between the two prayer
weeks, the Universal Week of Prayer in the first week in January
sponsored by the Evangelical Alliance for over one hundred
years, and the Week of Prayer for Christian Unity two weeks
later, the child of the Ecumenical Movement. Few churches
manage to observe both.

The degree of involvement of a particular church in its denominational concerns, as against interdenominational Evangelical activities like conventions, prayer conferences, and joint
evangelistic efforts, depends very much on the interests of the
current leadership of that congregation. It is not difficult to
identify some nationally known Evangelical leaders who are
clearly 'interdenominational men', giving their time to Keswick
and sister conventions, to interdenominational missionary
societies, to Scripture Union, Inter-Varsity Fellowship, the Billy
Graham Association, and others. Equally there are others who
are clearly marked out as 'denominational men', active in the
affairs of their own denominational group, be it the Church of
England Evangelical Council, the Church Society, the Baptist
Revival Fellowship, the Methodist Revival Fellowship, or a
denominational missionary society. There are also of course a
few rare souls whose vision (and whose reserves of energy) can
embrace both concerns in a healthy tension.

In the last year or two new movements in the Christian world have however cast doubts on any preoccupation with ecclesiastical structures—even with interdenominational structures. The charismatic or neo-pentecostal movement has united both Evangelicals and Catholics (Roman and Anglo) through a shared experience of 'the fullness of the Spirit' and such charismatic gifts as speaking in tongues and spiritual healing. While the Evangelical leadership of this movement has been predominant, the common ground found with catholics has caused a totally new approach to the question of a spiritual unity across the denominations. The sense that an Evangelical may well find a kindred spirit in an individual member of the Roman Catholic Church, in spite of the doctrinal errors of that body, has never been far below the surface, except in the more militantly protestant among us. Now, in the charismatic revival, we see whole groups of Catholics coming together in fellowship with whole groups of Evangelicals. Small groups of Evangelical Anglican theologians have been engaged for some time in private discussion on theological questions with Roman Catholics as well as with Anglo-Catholics. In the process they have drawn closer to each other as persons and realized that some of the barriers they believed to exist between them were imagined. But the coming together in the neo-pentecostal movement is on a much wider scale and more at the grass roots of the church, and as such could be much more significant.

The other new movement, partly related to the first, is the Jesus Movement. This youth-orientated, youth-led revival could be described as an ecclesiastical expression of the generation gap that is so much a talking-point in our society in the Seventies. While the institutional church tends to be tied to its buildings, the Jesus Movement operates in the streets, using buildings as no more than a base for those operations. In America, and on the continent of Europe, we hear of separate congregations of young people and of older Christians, sometimes sharing the same complex of buildings but meeting independently. There is no doubt that the Jesus Movement is on the whole impatient of all established church structures. It is united by a Bible-based faith and a shared experience of the vitality of the new birth. Some groups within the Jesus Movement, like the Children of God who are the main group operating in Britain at the time of writing, have their own brand of fundamentalist interpretation of the New Testament as regards church order. Their communes operate like a twentieth-century monastic order, and although they include both sexes, and married couples and children, the rules regarding sexual morality as well as all other aspects of their corporate life are rigid. It is much too early to say how the Jesus Movement will affect the structures of the Christian world; and the Children of God cannot be regarded as the prototype of the Movement as a whole or of the way in which it may develop in this country. But undoubtedly it shows us that new structures, new relationships, new groupings, may well be on the way.

A common factor in both the Jesus Movement and the neo-pentecostal movement is that they are existential in their approach. It is a shared *experience* that united people, whether this is the 'baptism of the Spirit' or the 'Jesus trip'. Because of the subjective emphasis on an experience, many Evangelicals of the old school have been cautious, and in some cases openly critical, of these new movements. An emphasis on the objectivity of the Faith has of course been a feature of Calvinism from the start, and a strong strand in Evangelical thinking all down the ages. But Evangelicals have also always had a lively interest in the fellowship of shared experience, and have kept the subjective aspect of the faith in lively tension with the objective. Already some of the Evangelical leaders who have commented on the Jesus Movement have stressed the need to link the lively experience of these young people with a teaching ministry which brings them into the fullness of the 'whole counsel of God' as found in the Bible. One of the pressing issues for the charismatic revival is how it is going to relate its theology to traditional Evangelical concepts of authority and still maintain its relationships with Roman Catholics who seem unwilling to abandon those doctrines concerning the Virgin Mary and the nature of the Mass which conflict with Evangelical exegesis of the Scriptures.

An even wider spectrum of theological views is embraced in such a recent development as the Festival of Light. The aim of uniting for a political purpose with those who are not Evangelical is not of course new for Evangelicals (Shaftesbury and Wilberforce were outstanding examples in the last century), but it is comparatively new to Evangelical thinking in recent times. The main allies of the Evangelicals who led the Festival of Light were probably from the Catholic side of the Church, and the Festival could be seen as an alliance of the conservative elements in society concerning moral issues in a permissive age. The Festival of Light had another aim, which was avowedly evangelistic, and it is uncertain to what extent the way that this aim was implemented had the wholehearted support of Catholics. Yet there is no doubt that, assisted by the charismatic revival, the Festival of Light brought together, in a new form of unity in witness, both Evangelicals and those of other brands of churchmanship who however dissociated themselves from the liberal and radical wings of the established churches. As with the charismatic revival and the Jesus Movement, the unity was existential, with the slogan 'Christ is the Answer' summing this up. Prominent platform figures in the Festival included Malcolm Muggeridge (with his known Christian existentialist philosophy) and Mary Whitehouse, neither of whom is a regular church-goer yet both of whom shared with the Festival organizers a lively sense of God's over-ruling and direction in all that was being undertaken.

The conservative spirits among British Evangelicals saw in the wide platform of the Festival of Light a further demonstration of the weakness of some Evangelicals as regards co-operating in evangelism with those who do not exactly share their theology. Ever since Billy Graham started inviting establishment bishops and then Roman Catholic prelates on to his platforms there have been those in the Evangelical world who have criticized this as 'doctrinal indifferentism', or 'co-operative evangelism' (which term was given an emotively bad flavour). This conflict represents a deep-seated difference in emphasis between 'activists' who are more concerned to be up and doing, seeing the crowds drawn in, and getting the message out by all possible means, and the 'purists' who have a tender conscience about the rightness of each and every method and the orthodoxy of both the messenger and all in any way publicly associated with him. It is interesting that this difference is partly exemplified as a cultural one between the Celtic leaders, particularly from Wales and Ireland, who are strong on purity, and the English, who are strong on activism and pragmatism. This particular conflict cannot be resolved as simply a 'creative tension'; either you do have a 'doctrinally mixed' platform or you do not, and you must agree to differ and go your own ways on this point. But the existence of the other point of view can help each party to be sensitive on marginal issues. The Evangelical Alliance report 'On the Other Side' suggested some minimum criteria for evangelistic co-operation. Both sides can also have the charity to admit that God in his grace does work through a variety of channels, and in spite of human sin and weakness—even of error.

Another division of attitude within the Evangelical world has also come into the open again in connection with the Festival of Light and similar activities which have called for Christians to be involved in political and social action. This is the division between the pietists and the social activists, and, like the other emphases already discussed, it can be traced back a considerable way in the history of the Church. Earlier in this century, when Evangelicals were particularly under attack (and therefore defensive in attitude) in theological matters, a pietistic emphasis undoubtedly predominated, and any Evangelical expressing interest in social affairs was liable to be branded (adversely) as an advocate of the 'social gospel'. In recent years the younger elements in the Evangelical world have been particularly keen to become involved as 'salt' in society and to give part of their time and money to relieving human need: e.g., through TEAR Fund, through work camps run by Evangelical youth organizations, and also through secular agencies.

Achieving a right balance between 'proclamation' and 'service' is not easy, and Evangelical leadership needs to give more guidance here. From the point of view of interdenominational co-operation, however, the renewed interest among Evangelicals in social and political action, preferably in the context of the *whole* Gospel, which includes the proclamation of the Christian message to all men, has stimulated working together across denominational barriers. Effective action in society depends on proper organization, and a structure that is as broadly based as the aims of the effort allow. So we may find Evangelicals regrouping —still receiving Biblical instruction (including instruction in these social emphases) in strongly Evangelical groups like the Keswick Convention as well as in their own local churches, but coming together for social projects and political pressure in theologically looser groups where even the humanist who sympathizes with their social aims will not be unwelcome. (They will of course hope that an incidental benefit of such an alliance will be the conversion to Christ of the non-believers who join it.)

To complete the present picture, mention must be made of the development here and there of 'house churches' that are quite independent of existing church structures altogether. These are to be distinguished from the house groups linked with a local church that meet, generally midweek, for prayer and Bible-study or even just for social intercourse. Members of these independent house churches have in many cases come from existing churches, and thus the new grouping can be seen as a new form of interdenominational activity. Yet in so far as it is becoming a new, independent local congregation it is really a new 'denominational' form of independent stripe. For the purposes of our present discussion, the independent house church is significant mainly as illustrating the extreme variety and fluidity of Christian organizational structures at the moment. Experiment is the order of the day, and anything is worth trying. The Church has its share of the somewhat anarchical spirit abroad in our society, and also of the 'spirit of freedom' that *can* be the positive counterpart of anarchy. Everything in existing structures is in question. In reforming them we may accept back many of the previous elements in the structure (such as the need for the Church to find expression in a compact local group of Christians who know and care for one another and worship, study, and pray together). But flexibility and readiness to adapt to new situations (like the distinctive patterns of social life in modern suburbia) are given high priority.

The independent house church can also be seen as the epitome of the thinking of many denominational Evangelicals about ecclesiastical structures—in that, in practice if not in theory, Evangelicals often work as if the local congregation is an independent unit. They play down their denominational links if they are in a connexional church and absent themselves from denominational gatherings. They may even seek to deny their denomination funds that may be used for some ecumenical purposes that are viewed with suspicion if not actually opposed by members of the local congregation. Such Evangelicals (the heirs really of the Anabaptists) are of course strong on the doctrine of the invisible church, and they tend to support interdenominational activities run by Evangelicals (unless their independency is too strong even for that). Such interdenominational events are, after all, some expression of the invisible Church, and we all need such a visual aid sometimes. Of course, we must not over-simplify. Most Evangelicals are in fact in denominational churches, and many play a more or less active part in denominational activities. But in many minds the feeling is not far below the surface that the real unit is the local congregation, and that interdenominational Evangelical bodies are worth supporting as being partial expressions of the invisible universal Church.

What conclusions can be drawn from this short survey, which has itself illustrated the problem of defining and delineating Evangelical unity and interdenominational activity?

Evangelical unity is in many ways a vague, even a fragile thing. It is something that Evangelicals instinctively believe to be there—it is implied in the doctrine of the one true Church to which all true believers belong. But it is more than a mental proposition. More potently it is *experienced* when believers meet and rejoice together in a common faith, a common anchor in Scripture, and, above all, a common allegiance to Christ as Lord and Saviour. This experience is not however the only touchstone of Evangelical unity, and every expression of that unity, whether in the Evangelical Alliance or any other Evangelical society, is related to some objective basis of belief which is regarded as the basic minimum of theological agreement for the purposes of that particular grouping.

Evangelical unity must also be viewed negatively—as a front *against* certain forces that seem to be inimical to the growth of the true Church. These forces have varied—and regrouped. They have included, and still do include, those that would give undue authority to the institutional church, or to human reason, or to ritual, or to good works. It is, sadly, easier to unite people against an enemy than for a more far-reaching positive purpose; and there have been many well-entrenched Evangelical structures whose aims have appeared mainly negative—against catholicism, against modernism, against the secularization of Sunday, against WCC-type ecumenism, against moral permissiveness. Not that we need be ashamed of a negative thrust—it may be an essential complement to a positive one, and there are plenty of Old and New Testament examples of the need both to deny the bad and to assert the good. It can also be said that Evangelicals today are more aware of the dangers of an unduly negative emphasis, and some societies that protest too much and do not match this with more positive activity may find themselves by-passed by the ongoing Evangelical constituency.

The nub of the problem of Evangelical unity is 'What is the unit?'. We have seen how varied are Evangelical ideas on the nature of the Church and the right structural relationships between the local congregation and other Christians. Through the history of the Church, Evangelicals have had more than a fair share of the movements that have contributed to the multiplicity of denominations today. While they also pioneered the movement towards greater visible unity (in the early days of the Evangelical Alliance) they have been reluctant to identify closely with the strong trend in modern ecumenism that puts structural unity above agreement on Biblical theological fundamentals. Attempts to form a rigorously Evangelical council of churches have not been conspicuously successful. They have tended to founder on conflicts of personality among their leaders: e.g., in the International Council of Christian Churches and other American-dominated bodies led by Dr Carl McIntyre.

In Britain certainly many Evangelicals regard an overall Evangelical organizational unity as something of a pipe dream— at least while much of the strength of the Evangelical cause lies in the Anglican and Baptist Churches. Their 'unit' of the wider Church, beyond their local congregation, will vary from the vaguely discerned universal (but invisible) Church to a denominational Evangelical fellowship or an *ad hoc* service agency or interdenominational mission. For many, the approach to unity is conceived in essentially pragmatic terms—will effort in some wider body bring results in terms of either mission or effective Christian service? Thus, the picture of Evangelical co-operation and interdenominational activity has the fragmented, overlapping, and diffuse qualities that have been described earlier. This approach can also of course sit lightly to the fact that many church structures are in the melting-pot, and that flexibility and adaptability are the order of the day. If an old grouping has lost its usefulness, ditch it. Either reform the society concerned with a new set of objects, or let it die and put your effort into a new body that is a response to a current need.

I believe that this approach has much to commend it, not only in terms of the situation in which we find ourselves in British society in the Seventies, but also in terms of a Biblical understanding of the Church. The New Testament model here is the body, an organic unit that is constantly growing, reproducing, adapting, and dying, in its various parts. Parts of the body, considered in isolation, may appear in many ways quite unrelated to the whole. Yet there are channels of communication, and the observer who stands back can see how all the varied activities of the different parts of the body are in fact co-ordinated in a common purpose and plan. Again, parts of the body may seem to a casual observer to be a little 'untidy' in relation to what he conceives to be the whole structure—and this is to be expected if that whole structure is undergoing a process of continuous adjustment to changing circumstances as well as to internal growth.

There are dangers in pursuing an analogy too far, but this one of the universal Church as an organic body can be taken a little further. Just as the human body has its blemishes and its malfunctioning parts, so does the whole Church of God. Malfunction can also be a result of a breakdown of internal communication, and the Church universal needs effective 'nerves' and 'blood vessels' to keep the parts rightly related to their head and to each other, and to supply their varied needs. In an ideal world, we would expect a single organizational structure to provide within itself for these functions of communication and supply. In the world as we have it, we have to settle for a second best which involves living (at least in the short term) in a Christian society of many different denominational and interdenominational groups. But we can still approximate more closely to the ideal if we can supply these groups, and the local churches they in turn serve, with communicating and servicing structures that keep channels open through the whole Church.

This is why, I believe, there is a continuing need for some bodies whose special concern is interdenominational co-operation and the general facilitating of means of Evangelical unity. Much Evangelical effort (e.g. in missions both at home and overseas) is sadly unco-ordinated, and resembles therefore the disgusting twitching of a limb whose owner has suffered some brain damage. The linking structures need not be elaborate, but they need to be known and used by all Evangelicals.

What does this mean in practice? I believe it means that we need a body or bodies, that will be thinking strategically about mission and service from an Evangelical point of view, and also interdenominationally, so as to bring together what is going on, and what is needed, in all types of church situation. Bodies are also needed that will keep in view the various 'stresses and strains' within the Church and suggest where an emphasis is proving unhelpful to the whole or deviating too far from the clear teaching of Scripture. These bodies will have the authority of the individual leaders whose support they receive, and will be recognized for the intrinsic value of their services. They will not be hierarchical structures. But they will fulfil the increasing need in modern society for services that draw constructively from the resources of modern technology, as well as from the findings of modern academic research, both theological and sociological, and which relate these to the needs of Christians in their local situations. This may mean, for example, applying modern technical and creative skills to the production of videotapes for use with the home TV set in house meetings connected with a local church and its evangelistic efforts. The sheer financial and human resources needed to do such a job will demand a broad based, interdenominational approach, and the need to keep the 'cutting edge' of the Gospel in the finished product requires an Evangelical sponsor.

Readers will realize, no doubt, that I am here setting out some of my own vision for the rôle of my own society, the Evangelical Alliance. But I have been careful to talk about a body, or bodies, and I realize that the thesis I have been propounding itself demands the possibility of multiform co-ordinating agencies as well as multiform structures which are themselves to be co-ordinated. Existing bodies like Scripture Union, Inter-Varsity Fellowship, the Shaftesbury Project, and the Festival of Light, at present share some of the rôles I have described with the Evangelical Alliance, and there is no reason why they and others should not continue to do so in future. They are, however, exercising their co-ordinating functions in certain more narrowly defined spheres, and I believe that we need one overall co-ordinator (that may well not be the biggest or most powerful body in the field, and would have an advantage in not being, as it would then be seen not to be the wrong kind of 'big brother'). Of the existing societies, the Evangelical Alliance seems the best fitted for this overall co-ordinating and strategy-defining rôle.

Its reports on evangelism, world mission, and evangelism in new towns are recent illustrations of its usefulness in this way.

But, on the same principles, I am sure that a flexible approach and a belief that organic growth can mean the dying away of one part and the development of a new one, may mean that the Evangelical Alliance may need either to die completely or to reform in an entirely new way that we cannot at present discern. But I confidently believe that the Lord of the Church, who through his Spirit is the ultimate Controller and Director of all the processes and parts that I have been trying to describe, has his own plans and will make them known to his servants at the right time. What we can expect is that they will involve some continuing form of interdenominational co-operation among Evangelicals.

Postscript

Since I wrote my paper the editor has shown me Gervase Duffield's paper on 'Evangelical Involvement: The Doctrine of the Church'. I fear he has his facts wrong in one place where he specifically takes me to task for the content of my paper, and his conclusions are odd in another place. So I am glad of the opportunity of a brief comment.

1. My account of the founding of the Evangelical Alliance was not 'a rationalization backwards into history of a romantic idea of what (I) would like to think the Evangelical Alliance was'. It was based on the account by John W. Ewing, *Goodly Fellowship*, which was published to mark the Evangelical Alliance centenary in 1946, and even more on John Kessler's doctoral thesis *A Study of the Evangelical Alliance in Great Britain*, published in 1968. The latter work in particular makes it abundantly clear that the primary motive of the Evangelical Alliance founders was a move towards unity. The reference to a union to combat the 'three P's' of Popery, Puseyism, and Plymouth Brethrenism, is attributed to a Congregationalist minister in 1842, and Kessler is careful to point out that opposition to Plymouth Brethren is never again mentioned; indeed, a member of the founding conference of the Evangelical Alliance in 1846 was in fellowship with the Brethren. (Kessler, op. cit., p. 17). Scottish Presbyterians (staunch Calvinists) took the lead in that first conference in

asserting that the first object of the Alliance would be 'Christian union and not controversy' (op. cit., p. 25).

2. I have sought in my own paper to show the general need of interdenominational co-operation among Evangelicals, and how a body like the Evangelical Alliance is needed to facilitate overall co-ordination in a way not open to more specialized interdenominational agencies. What I find odd is Mr Duffield's claim that none of these bodies can 'do serious theology' when divided on such matters as the sacraments and the Church. The work already done in many academic and cultural fields by bodies like Inter-Varsity Fellowship, Scripture Union, and the (still very new) Shaftesbury Project, is evidence enough that better progress can often be made in many areas by those united in an Evangelical theological position than by those within a single denomination. Questions of Church and sacraments are either completely irrelevant or just marginally relevant to a whole host of apologetic, ethical, pastoral, and cultural questions, where Evangelicals are already working together across denominational boundaries.

3. As Mr Duffield has raised questions about the internal structure of certain Evangelical societies, I would be glad to make it clear that, in common with some other Evangelical interdenominational societies known to me, the Evangelical Alliance now has a governing body whose members are not allowed to stay in office for longer than about six years at a stretch (though they can be invited back if desired after a sabbatical year). The Evangelical Alliance Council also had a lay chairman and a good proportion of lay members and younger men. There is emphasis on flexibility and adapting to change, without departing from basic doctrinal standards.

11

EVANGELICAL INVOLVEMENT: THE DOCTRINE OF THE CHURCH

GERVASE E. DUFFIELD

To anyone with even a smattering of Anglican history it seems strange to have to defend the principle of Evangelical involvement in the Church of England as a whole. It is true that in early Reformation days the Reformers, the first people to be called 'evangelics',[1] were a small group; but gradually under Cranmer's wise and patient leadership the Reformation triumphed and Evangelical men shaped the Reformation Settlement which even today still largely determines the formal position of the Church of England through the Thirty-nine Articles and the Prayer Book. Yet from the middle of the nineteenth century, when battles raged between Protestants (they were not by any means all Evangelicals) and ritualists, there was a growing tendency for Evangelicals in all denominations to withdraw into interdenominational (more accurately called undenominational) societies, and into holiness movements like Keswick. The advent of radical Biblical criticism, and later modernism, accelerated the process, though some stalwart churchmen like Bishop Ryle of Liverpool stood out against the tide of withdrawal. The result was that after the First World War younger Evangelicals had largely disengaged, for all practical purposes, from the Church of England as a whole (though they still worshipped in its parish churches), while older ones were relying on a rapidly dwindling Protestant heritage to defend the Reformation Settlement, albeit in rather legalistic terms. Evangelicals were increasingly found either concentrating on local church life and ignoring the Church of England as a whole, or busy preserving 'Evangelical truth' in pure Evangelical societies like Bible Churchmen's Missionary

[1] Since I have not the space to expound terminology here, may I refer to my chapter in *Churchmen Speak* edited by P. E. Hughes, 'The Church of England: Evangelical, Catholic, Reformed and Protestant', where I sought to show the origin and meaning of the term 'Evangelical'. It is not the pietistic invention from the Evangelical Revival which some distinguished scholars imagine.

Society within the Church of England or Inter-Varsity Fellowship without it. They counted for less and less in the central councils of the Church. They had opted out, not so much by choice as by neglect. And others were keen to take their places. The main life of interwar evangelicalism was undenominational, though there always remained some who took their churchmanship seriously and urged others to do so too. The theological effect of this undenominationalism was a concentration on things that united: evangelism, personal holiness, Bible-reading, prayer; but a virtual neglect of anything that might cause differences between Evangelicals in diverse denominations baptism, communion, Church and State issues, cultural questions, and above all the doctrine of the Church.

After the war, and especially in the fifties, things began to change. A new group emerged, small in numbers but determined to take theology seriously (many earlier Evangelicals had not taken academic theology seriously and merely retreated into pietism). I think this post-war Evangelical impetus divided largely into two groups: those who wanted to do academic theology in universities, who themselves varied from a very confined Brethren-inspired concentration on things narrowly Biblical, linguistic matters, archaeology (they were slightly suspicious of Biblical theology and positively terrified of systematic theology) to a broader theological interest and a desire to apply this to the Church; and, on the other side, those who were disillusioned with the aridity of liberal-dominated academic theology under which they had been university trained, and who saw theology primarily as the servant of the Church, not a detached academic pursuit. Many of these people could have got academic jobs but they were more interested in the Church, in relating theology to church life, not spending their lives on the minutiae of Biblical archaeology, Sumerian philology or cognate Biblical languages (Evangelicals had done that in the 1880s and 1890s to little effect). They determined to take theology seriously, to take up the challenge of liberalism on the Bible but using critical methods, and in the case of the second group to apply serious theology to ecumenism and the current problems of the Church. It is not my task here to trace the rise of this new Evangelical theology, but suffice it to say that, before it became sectarian, the London Puritan Conference had considerable influence as a forum both for discussing theology generally and discovering the greatness of Reformed theology in its pastoral out-working. All of us who went admired Dr Lloyd-Jones, if not for his ecclesiology or his rather autocratic chairmanship, at least for his wealth of pastoral experience and his great concern for preaching. Also I suspect Oxford was really the academic centre of the movement, and most of the younger leaders came from Oxford. As one who studied at both Oxford and Cambridge, I was astonished at the less theological atmosphere of Cambridge, its casualness, its pietistic interdenominationalism against the more serious theological concern of Oxford; perhaps the root cause was the pressure (not always fair or even scrupulous) on Oxford Evangelicals from certain faculty members and from some college chaplains (not my own college where the chaplain was always fair and considerate) who never trusted Evangelicals and were rarely trusted by them. If you were to survive as an Evangelical, you had to know your doctrine. Some of these chaplains who have since risen to higher ecclesiastical positions had no evangelistic vision themselves, and seemed to concentrate on getting at Evangelical students. But it was noticeable that Christian unions were more effective than chaplain groups, and perhaps therein lay a cause of the trouble. At any rate most of us thought we should be better off without the chaplains, and given the way they behaved, I am not sure we were not right.

Once these new Evangelicals found their theological feet, they discovered how sadly current evangelicalism was deficient in theology, especially ecclesiology which ecumenism was dis-cussing earnestly. Single-minded enthusiasm for evangelism, prayer and Bible-reading tended to discourage, in practice if not in theory, any serious examination of sacramental, cultural or Church and State questions. But once the doctrine of the Church was rediscovered these subjects had to be treated seriously. Evangelicals had no illusions about the state of the Church of England, preoccupied with internal canon law reform, all of it away from Reformation and Biblical principles, and its establish-ment hardly sharing, indeed at times barely tolerating, Evan-gelical criticism based on the Bible.

Rediscovering ecclesiology inevitably meant church involve-ment. It went against the narrow parish pump mentality which still dominates many Evangelical clergy. It sharpened up certain differences which interdenominational activity had rather glossed over. It was the old division between Reformers and Anabaptists,[1] only now some with Anabaptist doctrines of the Church appeared within Reformed churches! There was a deep division between those who held a gathered church view, the idea that men had to covenant into membership, and those who held a multitudinous view of the Church as the company of the baptized. The Anabaptists wondered why on earth fellow Evangelicals hobnobbed with Anglo-Catholics and Liberals many of whom appeared to be very nominal Christians and some of whom actively disliked Evangelical enthusiasm. The gap widened when Anabaptist Evangelicals (really a misuse of terms)[2] felt that Anglican Evangelicals were more interested in other Anglicans than in gathered church Evangelicals. What actually happened, I think, was not that Anglican Evangelicals deserted their Anabaptist friends, but rather that in taking ecclesiology and ecumenism seriously, Evangelical Anglicans had to meet with, and indeed wanted to meet with, fellow Anglicans, and they were subsequently rather disappointed to discover that Anabaptist Evangelicals either wanted to remain in their old pietist separatist ruts, or retreat into militant independency in which they seemed to enjoy firing salvoes at their erstwhile friends whom they now assumed (without ever troubling to enquire how or why) to have forsaken them and become 'unsound'. The Evangelical Anabaptist obscurantism that greeted *Growing into Union* had to be seen to be believed. Quite responsible Evangelicals of the older outlook were strongly critical, and in discussion turned out not to have read much of the book, to be totally unaware of the previous and more large-scale Evangelical foundation-laying in *All in Each Place*,[3] and yet they charged in to attack. They obviously did not want any change and could not abide the idea of any project to meet the Anglo-Catholic except by demolishing his case. Such bigotry (I can find no other word for it, and I sat through several meetings listening to the complaints) was and is deplorable.

[1] Anabaptists. I use this here as an umbrella term to cover the gathered church, separationist approach.

[2] As I showed in the chapter mentioned in note 1 on p. 160, this term strictly applies to churchmen only, but I do not wish to quarrel about words.

[3] Edited by J. I. Packer and expounding an Evangelical open letter signed by thirty-nine Evangelical leaders. The book was published by Marcham Books in 1965. It is far more representatively Evangelical than *Growing into Union*.

The root question, I believe, is the doctrine of the Church. The Church is the company of those in all ages who are in Christ, justified by faith, born again of the Spirit. But such a Church is ultimately known to God alone, since he alone can judge the hearts of men. This Church must have a local manifestation, and since human judgement is fallible, we have to take men at their face value; in other words, the visible local Church is all the baptized, unless they openly apostatize. That is not to say that baptism makes a man a Christian, as older Evangelicals are apt to assume it is; only the Spirit of God does that, but baptism is the visible sign of the Christian, the membership badge of the Church visible. Is this Biblical? I say yes without hesitation, and the Reformers to a man (and they seem to me to have been the greatest theologians since early church days) agree. The Church, as it appears to man, will always be a mixed company, good and evil, justified and unjustified, but Jesus tells us not to usurp God's function in judging, not to pull up the tares lest we also pull up the wheat. The sheep and the goats parable shows that those who look similar (very similar in Palestine, if not in Britain) will not necessarily be so at the last day. The parable is a fearful warning to professing churchmen. But to believe in a mixed Church as I do, for theological reasons not merely pragmatic ones, means taking the membership of the Church seriously, not selecting parts of it and ignoring the rest. That is the theological basis for involvement.

What would the alternative be? To maintain a fierce independence as a few advocate would mean secession, and that is not on for a convinced churchman, save *in extremis*. Within the Church of England the alternative would be to attend only strictly Evangelical churches, ignoring or even disowning other Anglican churches, and certainly ignoring central church affairs (they would be dismissed as beyond redemption). It would mean concentrating on the local church and acting as if the rest did not exist, concentrating on evangelism in a narrow individualistic sense, working only in confessionally Evangelical groups, supporting Evangelical societies only, and forming exclusive Evangelical groups like those of the Evangelical Alliance and the Graduates' Fellowship. Trying to ignore mixed Anglican claims like central budget quotas would present thorny problems. The test in each case would be doctrinal soundness or spiritual unity, defined in a narrow Evangelical way. It would mean ignoring major differences over the sacraments, and yet to be an Evangelical means to have a high view of doctrine and its importance, and I believe it would be virtually impossible to carry out this pietistic separatism within the Church of England, certainly for a clergyman. Retreating into so-called interdenominational societies is really to withdraw from a church, and to ignore large areas of basic theology.

What happens in practice on these two views? The Evangelical who adopts this last view will eschew mixed and ecumenical gatherings and seek out the plethora of small Evangelical societies, most of them dating from Victorian times, most living on the generosity of the past, and, to be honest, few of them meeting real needs today. The committees are usually dominated by elderly clerics, since they meet at times when laity cannot be free. The general level of the secretariats is very low. A few clergy appear on a large number of these societies (presumably their curates run their parishes). The lack of calibre, vision and leadership, is piteously obvious, and the result is a drifting on in the old ways, usually with the circles of activity getting smaller and smaller. Constructive thinking would be resisted in most such bodies if it ever was allowed to appear. Some onlookers, realizing all is not well, fondly imagine that one bumper amalgamation would put everything right. That is naïve. The real problem is quality of leadership and competence of secretariats (all too often some well-meaning man who cannot make a go of his job or his parish), and the domination of elderly thinking prevents anyone different coming in. It is a vicious circle, and the less the old guard has to offer, the more it clings dearly to power. The picture is depressing indeed, but I speak from over a decade of experience.

Note the new Evangelical Anglican groups that have appeared. No one wanted extra establishments but, when the old guard refused to meet the needs of the time, there was no alternative. Latimer House was set up in Oxford as a research centre (previously the undenominational and rather narrowly Biblical centre, Tyndale House, Cambridge, was felt enough. I once worked there, and the narrowness of the academic concept there was shown by the throwing out of the church historians from membership, because their rôle was not narrowly Biblical enough for some in positions of influence). The Church of England Evangelical Council was established as a consultative body. The

Marcham Manor and Sutton Courtenay Presses were brought into being. Marcham was intended to undertake adventurous publishing, taking risks that others would not take, so it was unfettered by cumbersome committees, and since I am myself closely connected with it, I can add that it was deliberately made technically a commercial company so that it should not have a restrictive trust deed, not appeal for funds, and quickly expire when it had outlived its usefulness and viability. I am glad to add that it has to date gone from strength to strength. It has co-operated where possible with non-Evangelicals, and intends to do so more extensively in future. The Sutton Courtenay Press seeks to do likewise but works in an academic field trying to build up specialist works in areas likely to interest Evangelicals, in this case the Reformation era. Latimer House and the new presses represent 'involved' scholarship and 'involved' publishing.

What happens at the centre when an Evangelical gets involved in official Church House work? It might be revealing if some of the Anabaptist Evangelicals had to answer that question. The first thing that strikes me is that the level of staff efficiency and the calibre of committees is much higher than in the small older Evangelical bodies mentioned above (and for that matter in diocesan offices where the same absence of calibre is to be seen). Good will and devotion are evident in all these bodies, but quality and ability are not found in most of the smaller bodies, alas. It is only partly a matter of size (there are of course career structure problems); Church House can attract really able men, but mainly it is the calibre of the committee members that makes the difference. I honestly doubt if a visionary *could* do anything in the smaller societies I mentioned earlier.

But if the calibre is there at Church House, what about the policy? The trouble is that there is a certain conflict of visions, and I sometimes wonder if there is a coherent policy. If there is, it is often out of touch with the Synod and church reality; see, for instance, the inability of some at Church House and at Lambeth to see the obvious collapse of the union scheme or of Fenton Morley. If they saw it, they were singularly inept at doing anything about it, and now they talk of a lack of church credibility, which ought to be reinterpreted as lack of credibility in the persons concerned, and their leadership. Any businessman knows what a board in that position should do!

There is certainly efficiency and basic calibre in Church House, but often a conflict of policies and visions resulting in no policy or occasional muddle. At particular times particular groups gain the upper hand, but they achieve little unless they can carry the Church as a whole with them. For instance radicals have of late an exceedingly large share of the cake, witness Paul Report and Fenton Morley, but the Church as a whole rejected both, is rather suspicious of the Advisory Council for the Church's Ministry (ACCM), and in general the whole ACCM area can hardly be said to be flourishing. The message is surely clear; the Church does not want to be dominated by ACCM radicals. In the Anglican-Methodist union scheme there was clearly amongst the original team an imbalance, a dominant strand of liberal Catholic thinking with the stress on the liberal, but imbalance rarely succeeds, and the proponents could not persuade definite Catholics or definite Evangelicals. How have Evangelicals fared? Well, they were legalistically defensive on matters like vestments, and so they got a not very satisfactory measure. They were more statesmanlike on admission to communion, and argued their theology with care, so they secured after a decade of debate an open communion table. Christian statesmanship was apparent on all sides in Series Two Holy Communion and an honourable *modus vivendi* was reached on thorny matters like eucharistic sacrifice and prayer for the departed. No one thinks either is finally solved, but at least the issues were settled amicably in a temporarily satisfactory way.

I believe there is an absence of coherent policy at the centre of the Church of England, and this in a sense gives Evangelicals an opening to contribute their insights. Certain trends should be noted. Synodical Government was hailed as a great emancipation of the laity. It was nothing of the sort, and I have always feared that in reality it simply enthroned the bureaucrats and the 'platform', silencing independent criticism and drowning us all in paper at greater and greater expense. The Pastoral Measure marked a considerable change when it moved the Church Commissioners from being independent trustees (largely, at any rate) into becoming more and more Church House bureaucrats, only with vast financial power. I have never myself indulged in sniping at the commissioners, but I think the change ominous.

What does it mean for an Evangelical to be involved in this

central structure? He finds himself discussing rather different questions from traditional Evangelical ones. He does not discuss Biblical inspiration, nor do committees look at their bibles; nor do they plan evangelistic crusades or prayer meetings. The General Synod and its supporting structures handle legislation and reports. In that structure the Evangelical is in a minority and likely to be represented by laymen, since the laity make most of the contributions on the Evangelical side, there being a distinct lack of calibre in Synod on the Evangelical clerical side. That may change but it has not done so yet. This is not anticlericalism, as some clergy sometimes imagine. The leading laity regularly consult with Evangelical theologians at Latimer House (all clergy!), but it is the Evangelical laity who take the lead in almost all central Evangelical moves. Again it is a question largely of calibre. Able people naturally take leadership over from less able ones. (It may be significant that these same laity are more or less guaranteed exclusion from the plethora of small Evangelical societies by their hours of meeting and methods of behaving.)

The Evangelical will be in a minority at Church House, and that means he must work carefully with others, and he must work long term, just as Cranmer did before him. It is true that, if pressed, most Evangelicals would say that evangelicalism is the purest form of the Church of England, the most natural interpretation of the Articles and Prayer Book which are superb expressions of Biblical theology, dated to their times, of course, but the nearest things to timeless statements seen for centuries. Few Evangelicals are likely to be interested in the Anglican Communion, save through force of circumstances such as prompted the Evangelical Fellowship in the Anglican Communion, since pan-denominationalism is the very antithesis of the Biblical principle of 'all in each place', and none will stomach pan-Anglicanism, which is the acute form of the same disease. (The current ecclesiastical iconoclasm of a few younger Evangelical clergy in wanting to knock the Prayer Book and the Articles is, I think, a passing phase, partly a juvenile attempt to be 'with it', partly a pietistic attempt to break away from theology to anything new, and partly a sense of insecurity and clutching at any novelty).

If I may be personal for a moment, because some readers today will almost automatically dismiss the Reformers (or even any mention of church history) as historical fundamentalism, it was reading the major Reformers, especially Calvin, that taught me a doctrine of the Church, and made me a convinced member of the Church of England as opposed to a 'best boat to fish from' Anglican (which is the fashionable pietistic explanation— for private consumption!). The relief I experienced in getting away from arid university theology courses in which actual theology was more or less incidental, and from abstruse literary criticism of no lasting value and little importance to anyone save professional academics, to the majestic and massive Biblical theology of the Reformers, and through them of the Fathers (which the university course did encourage), was profound and has to be experienced to be fully appreciated. It was spiritually exhilarating and at last I felt I had found true theology. Men who combined great learning with a love for the Gospel and a concern for the Church (rather than intellectual fancies, literary specula- tion, and Erasmian detachment) appeal to Evangelicals.

The Evangelicals of fifty years ago, and some still today, look on other Anglicans as anything from poor misguided folk to Romanizing traitors and twisters of formularies. The new Evangelical does not. He still thinks Evangelicalism the purest form of Anglicanism, but just as all the Reformers recognized Christians within the Roman fold, even though Rome sought to destroy and often even to burn the Reformers, so Evangelicals recognize other Anglicans as fellow Christians however critical they are of Evangelicalism. Gone are the days of trying to prose- cute other Anglicans or turn them out. Instead the Evangelical wants to share with them his Biblical insights. And for any Anabaptist Evangelical reader, let me add that once a certain crude text-thumping is given up, I find a real willingness to listen to serious and informed Biblical argument, and the willingness is growing as Evangelical spokesmen show more responsibility.

The Evangelical does not imagine he knows everything and can learn nothing, but he should know his Bible and he does know where the final authority lies, even if Ecclesia Anglicana sometimes forgets that. In the last analysis all must be judged by that, and there is the first Church House rub. No one denies the Bible in Church House, but there is somehow a fear of using it, and an almost ineradicable penchant for pragmatism and expediency, cloaked in all manner of guises, when a theological problem arises and proves difficult. Here the Evangelical comes to feel with the convinced Catholic who knows what it is to believe in definite doctrine and revealed Christianity, and both feel constantly strangled by pragmatic considerations and pressure-of-events arguments. But Evangelical and Catholic keep battling away together for the primacy of theology. The Evangelical wants to test all by the Bible far more drastically than others appear to want to. He must work long term, reforming here a little and there a little, but not acting as if Evangelicals were the only people who mattered. He will take particular account of Catholic opinion as the other main theological stream in Anglicanism (one of the characteristics of Liberalism or Broad Churchmanship is that it constantly accommodates to prevailing views, so it matters rather less!), seek to learn from it, engage in friendly conversation and make decisions with it, but always on the final authority of the Bible. Some view this as selling out to 'heretics', but one can only maintain such a view from impregnable isolation and invincible ignorance. I believe that to engage in serious discussion and work with other Anglicans is to be a churchman.

Let me now look swiftly at other areas of Evangelical concern. First, devotional life. Evangelicals, and Catholics from a slightly different angle, both see this as at a low ebb, and both want to right this. It is not easy in a committee, but the priority will be high in an Evangelical mind. Second, reform and renewal. Alas, radicals have usurped these terms for their ecclesiastical iconoclasm, which bears scant resemblance to any Biblical reform, but I suspect most Evangelicals believe that far too much attention has been paid to ecclesiastical structures in ecumenism, and too little to Biblical ideas of renewal. But that is different from hailing Jesus people as an excuse to return to pietistic disinterest in the Church! Third, Evangelicals want to get the Church looking outward again to mission, away from its current obsession with internal tinkering. Looking outward does not mean an endless succession of Billy Graham campaigns. It certainly involves a permanent concern to win others for Christ, but also a concern for moral standards in the life of the nation (see Evangelical leads in Synod on pornography and broadcasting standards, etc.), a truly Gospel-orientated social involvement, and this in sharp contrast (I am bound to say) to the pathetic attempts of some radicals to substitute an almost humanistic compassion, 'caring', for the Biblical Gospel which involves real compassion,

and even more to jumping on every trendy social bandwagon
(mostly very left wing politically) as the World Council of Churches
seems to do. Turning churches into social clinics and flats is not
furthering the Gospel any more than turning them into left
wing political agitation agencies is.

In sum, involvement means meeting others regularly, explor-
ing their minds; and personally I have learnt a lot in this process.
Many of the others are fine Christians. Evangelicals, especially
those young enough not to have their minds stamped with old
ritual conflicts, find much common ground with the old-
fashioned Anglo-Catholic (not the watered down liberal Catholic)
because both understand the importance of doctrine, appreciate
the value of good church tradition, of revealed religion, of
absolute moral standards, of devotional life, of worship, and
conversion. And even to some extent one finds this with Romans,
provided they are not the *avant garde* Romans who flit round
conferences trying to impress on everyone how *avant garde* they
are. What then of Broad Churchmen? I can find considerable sympathy with the older Broad Churchman. I can admire his breadth
of vision, the large mind (mainly, I suspect, due to his historical
training, and the lack of it may be the cause of shallowness today)
of a Hensley Henson, his independence, his fearlessness, his
incisive judgement (and how often he was right even when in a
minority of one), or the wide sympathies of an H. M. Gwatkin,
the social concerns of an F. D. Maurice, or the large horizons of
a Norman Sykes, but where are their successors today? Their
more vocal radical heirs have made a few useful criticisms of
institutionalism (especially John Robinson, who strikes me as the
only one of real theological acumen), but most radicals seem just
destructive, rather pathetically trusting in reorganization schemes
and social action, with no recognizable theology in sight. Indeed
I doubt if some of them are even interested in such a thing. It
would be sad indeed if their 'theology' ever dominated the
Church of England, but it is very unlikely, and I believe their
grass roots support is almost nil. That kind of radicalism is no
gospel to preach, save to pressmen and TV! But there is a much
larger group of people who seem to regard it as their duty to
back any and every official scheme quite uncritically. They
exert the pragmatic pressures as they are largely devoid of
theology. One has the uncomfortable feeling that they would

back an opposite scheme next week if only officialdom produced some plausible reason for doing so! It is not hard to see why Evangelicals do not take to such people.

Let me now stand back and take a further look at this alternative of inter-Evangelical co-operation such as Gordon Landreth envisions for the Evangelical Alliance. Historically the issue is clearly focused in Charles Simeon's disagreement with Rowland Hill and John Berridge.[1] The last divided the clergy into 'Gospel labourers' and the main body of the clergy of whom he plainly thought very little, and, because he was pessimistic about the Church of England, Berridge felt that, with souls perishing, he should ignore church order, and he did. Simeon understood his position but did not agree. Berridge seems to have held an inadequate doctrine of baptism and of the Church, and went round insisting that admission to the Church was not baptism but conversion. As we saw earlier, this reflects a confused ecclesiology common among less theological Evangelicals. Berridge and Hill were pioneering this interdenominational Evangelical work that sat extremely light to doctrines of the Church and consequent claims of church order. Simeon and Venn did not approve.

The Evangelical Alliance was founded in 1846 to resist three things—Popery, Puseyism and Plymouth Brethrenism—but that is hardly what one would gather from Mr Landreth's account, which I think is a rationalization backwards into history of a romantic idea of what he would like to think the EA was. In its origin the EA was much more a uniting of Evangelicals across the denominations (though clearly excluding Brethren with their attacks on the ordained ministry as such; nowadays Brethren are found on the Evangelical Alliance Council) against various Romanizing threats. Support for the Exeter Hall meetings only came a decade later, and large evangelistic crusades and holiness conventions much later still. The original purpose of the EA has, as far as Anglicans are concerned, been taken over by other bodies and EA is hardly needed by Anglican Evangelicals these days. There are innumerable Evangelical agencies sponsoring various forms of evangelistic activities, so it is an open question whether the EA has a rôle there. Evangelical Anglicans regularly meet Free Church Evangelicals in other societies with clearly defined specific purposes (IVF among students, Scripture Union in

[1] See the last chapter of Charles Smyth, *Simeon and Church Order*.

Bible reading and children's work, etc.), and along with many other Anglican Evangelicals I find it very hard to see any future rôle for the EA except as a very small consultative body, and possibly a small rôle on the missionary front, but even that could well be done by the missionary societies themselves. Lest I be thought to be attacking the EA, let me add that I think exactly the same about the BCC. I find it hard to resist the argument that EA and BCC could be reduced to very small occasional consultative bodies without any loss to anyone and with considerable financial saving. These days, Christians, Evangelicals and others, have got used to doing things ecumenically and it is unnecessary to have bodies existing just to promote that. Various church groups, official or otherwise, can call in other Christians (and they frequently do) as they need them *ad hoc*. But I suspect that in practice EA and BCC both give the very small churches a rather exaggerated idea of their importance, and these are often financed by the larger bodies, to do things they otherwise could not do.

There are clear limits as to what can be done in these interdenominational Evangelical groups. I can see a rôle for specialist bodies operating in defined areas like IVF, SU, and LDOS, but general interdenominational groups have limitations. They will never be able to tackle sacramental theology, doctrines of the Church, Church and community issues, or even cultural questions. Recently some of these bodies have tried to tackle social and cultural issues, e.g., the Shaftesbury Project, but so far the results have been little more than rather wooden old-fashioned pamphleteering, and I suspect they are unlikely to get any further. One simply cannot do serious theology when there are major divides on basic matters like the sacraments and the Church. Such doctrines are bound to affect almost every cultural and ethical issue, and even such questions as family life, which Shaftesbury have sought to tackle. Indeed one could go further and ask if evangelism can really be tackled in this interdenominational Evangelical non-churchly way. One can certainly set up a campaign, but what after that, what of the converts? Billy Graham has had to face that, and more and more he has sought, quite rightly in my view, to relate converts to churches, but that in itself has caused division among Evangelicals, between the separatists and the multitudinous church Evangelicals (mainly Anglicans in England). I honestly do not think the Evangelical world would suffer if some of the smaller interdenominational or undenominational Evangelical societies, with no clear rôle and no very competent officers or councils, disappeared. The ones with clear rôles and obvious competence will survive and flourish, but I think a more fruitful method of inter-Evangelical co-operation is to tackle the matter *ad hoc* when problems arise in specific churches or specific areas of activity, and then just bring in other Evangelicals as seems prudent. Inevitably in England Anglicans will predominate, so it is likely that most things will have Anglican origins. The situation is of course different in Wales, Scotland and Ireland.

Much more important is full Evangelical involvement in the life of their own churches. Berridge kicked over the traces of church order because he despaired of most Anglican clergy. Every Evangelical accepts that there comes a point when a church is so corrupt that one simply has to leave in order to preserve the Gospel witness at all, but that point is the last extremity, only reached after every avenue has been tried to reform the corrupt church. Certainly this point is not even in sight as far as the Church of England goes, and if there has been coolness or even hostility to Evangelicals in the recent past, that is certainly changing, and it might be pertinent for Evangelicals to ask if Evangelicals have not contributed to this situation by a certain stand-offishness. I believe there is a great need for Evangelicals to be involved in central church affairs, i.e., beyond their own parishes, partly because synodical government has given so much more power to the platform and bureaucracy, and there is therefore great need for a theologically critical group to work loyally within the overall synodical structure and scrutinize proposals; and partly because, with radicals having had their fling in Fenton Morley and such-like ventures, it may well be that Evangelicals working with Catholic Anglicans can give the Church of England the clear policy it increasingly needs. If the Church of England ship is basically sound, then it behoves those within that ship to work hard and loyally to make the ship perform well. The real need is for Evangelical involvement in their churches, not retreat into exclusive Evangelical ghettos. The one development that has saddened me in recent years is that the very people in the middle of the Church of England who were so anxious to stop Evangelicals fighting Anglo-Catholics a few years back, are now saying, when Evangelicals are working with Catholics instead of attacking them, that there is an unholy alliance between them! They cannot have it both ways. I prefer to think their current criticism is really frustration that neither Evangelicals nor Catholics like particular proposals, and the criticism is a rather unthinking pragmatic reply. At least I hope it is that, for if the people who say they really value ecumenism want to stop Evangelicals and Catholics working together, then the nature of their ecumenical integrity wants careful investigation.

Finally, does such involvement in a mixed church mean compromise of Evangelical principles? This is what many of the Anabaptist Evangelicals say they fear. First, plainly one must believe the Church of England itself is fundamentally sound. John Berridge was almost totally pessimistic about it, so he went off on his own course. I am frankly not so; I know that the Church of England has many faults, but it also has many fine qualities, and in England at least has unique opportunities for furthering the Gospel. Second, one has to take a long-term view of getting the Church of England back on to a sounder course. Third, in the process one may have to accept some unsatisfactory temporary solutions, not because one believes them entirely right, but because they may be the best settlement at the moment until all concerned have had a chance for further reflection and discussion. If such solutions were permanent they would involve compromise; but if they are temporary, they do not, provided that they are honourable agreements. Fourth, in the long run, involvement tests the strength of one's own theology. I am completely confident of Evangelical theology. If there are points at which I have misunderstood the Bible, I am glad to learn from anyone where I am wrong, but if the points are truly Biblical and truly of God, then I am content to take the long view and wait till God brings fellow Christians to see them. In the last analysis it is a question of faith in God. In my Evangelical involvement I do not want some Evangelical party answer to flourish and triumph. I want God's truth and God's vision for the whole Church of England. The first would be partisan, the second is, I believe, that of a Christian seeking to serve God in the Church. And I think that is what involved Evangelicals have always striven to do, though no doubt with many failings.

12

WORLD-WIDE EVANGELICAL ANGLICANISM

JOHN STOTT

A Historical and Comtemporary Sketch[1]
Some readers will no doubt wince at the title of this chapter.
For they regard as a mistaken policy any desire to perpetuate
divisions within the Christian Church. Pan-Anglicanism is bad
enough; the fostering of a worldwide *Evangelical* Anglicanism
appears to them worse still.

In reply to this, I think Evangelical Anglicans would want to
make a distinction. Anglicanism is largely a historical phenomenon. Its death in any region or nation is not therefore to be
regretted, provided that it is followed by a resurrection in a
united church which preserves a Biblical Faith. Evangelicalism,
on the other hand, is a theological heritage. In so far as it may be
shown to embody non-Biblical traditions, it is open to reform.
But the Evangelical has no wish to be a 'party' man, owing
allegiance to any human group or set of traditions. He desires,
if he is true to his own Evangelical principles, to witness to
Biblical truth as unchanging divine revelation.

The Evangelical Fellowship in the Anglican Communion
(EFAC) was founded only in 1961. Its five stated aims are:

1. To foster fellowship between Anglican Evangelicals throughout
   the world, and to encourage the isolated and the faint-hearted,
   reminding them of the larger body to which they belong.

[1] I am very grateful to all those who have helped me to write this chapter
by supplying me with historical or contemporary information. They are too
numerous to mention by name. But they include EFAC members in Britain,
Canada, America, Australia, New Zealand, Africa and Asia, and some home-
based staff members of the Church Missionary Society (CMS), Bible Churchmen's Missionary Society (BCMS), and South American Missionary Society
(SAMS).

2. To federate regional Anglican Evangelical Fellowships and to encourage the formation of such where none exists.

3. To bear witness with courage and charity to the great Biblical and Reformation principles, so that the Evangelical voice is heard and commended, and an increasing Evangelical contribution made, throughout the Anglican Communion.

4. To formulate policy in matters of common Evangelical concern, by taking counsel together, and to make advice available to those who ask for it.

5. To exchange news so that events, projects, books, etc., important to the Evangelical cause, become known to the whole Evangelical Anglican community.

EFAC has twenty group members, namely, national or regional Evangelical Anglican Fellowships, in UK, Canada, North and South America, Africa, Asia and Australasia, and individual members in nineteen other regions of the world.

The work of EFAC is largely decentralized. Local fellowships exist for mutual encouragement and common witness, and for the study of issues facing the contemporary Church. Two central projects have been initiated, however, through the EFAC Literature Committee and the EFAC Bursary Scheme Committee.

The literary project was the publication between 1963 and 1968 of twenty-two paperbacks known as the *Christian Foundations* series. The promoters dared at first to hope that the series might do for evangelicalism in the twentieth century what the *Tracts for the Times* did for Anglo-Catholicism in the nineteenth century. They even wondered if Anglican Evangelicals might come to be known as 'foundationalists', much as the American publication of the *Christian Fundamentals* beginning in 1909 led to the coining of the term 'fundamentalists'! In the event, no great influence can be claimed for *Christian Foundations*, although some two hundred thousand copies were distributed (including complimentary copies to most of the bishops and archbishops in the Anglican Communion), and some surprise was expressed that Evangelicals were able to field an international team of authors to sustain such a series.

The Bursary Scheme seeks to serve the younger churches of Africa and Asia by giving to clergy with leadership gifts the opportunity for further theological study and pastoral experience.

12

They come to Britain for anything from a few months (in the case of parish bursars) to three years (in the case of college bursars doing a degree course). Thirty-nine have benefited from the scheme since its inception in 1965. They have come from East and West Africa, India and Pakistan.

England

The Evangelical tradition in the Church of England has a long and honourable history going back through Charles Simeon and the Wesleyan revival to the Puritans of the seventeenth and the Reformers of the sixteenth centuries. During the century leading up to the Second World War, however, it was somewhat eclipsed by the dominant Tractarian Movement. Some notable scholar-bishops like John Charles Ryle of Liverpool (consecrated 1880) and Handley Moule of Durham (consecrated 1901) did much to commend the Evangelical faith. But Evangelical clergy tended to remain in their parishes and give themselves to evangelistic and pastoral work. For the maintenance of the Gospel in the Church at large, especially in the latter part of the last century, we can now say (with the benefit of hindsight) that they made the mistake of resorting to litigation. One observer could even write: 'The Evangelical party in the Church of England . . . long before the beginning of this century was notorious for its virulence and bigotry.'[1]

And between the wars Evangelicals were such a small and struggling minority in the Church of England that the image they presented was inevitably rather negative.

The post-war resurgence of evangelicalism has not been confined to the Church of England. This was a period of rapid growth for the Inter-Varsity Fellowship, which, although an interdenominational body, has always had a number of Anglicans among its leading figures. Since the Divinity Faculties were in exclusively liberal hands, it was not done in earlier days to read theology at the university. But Dr Douglas Johnson, the first general secretary of the Inter-Varsity Fellowship (IVF), encouraged men to take theological degrees in order to equip themselves to recover a true Biblical scholarship. It is largely owing to his vision that Tyndale House and the Tyndale Fellowship for Biblical Research were founded, and that some twenty-

[1] *Roxburgh of Stowe*, Noel Annan, Longmans, 1965, p. 80.

five members of the Fellowship today occupy British university posts in Biblical, theological and related subjects.

By the mid-nineteen-fifties ecclesiastical authority became aware of the growing strength of evangelicalism, and was alarmed by it. In August 1955 Canon H. K. Luce of Durham wrote a letter to *The Times* deploring the fact that Dr Billy Graham had been invited to lead a mission in the sacred precincts of Cambridge University. Billy Graham's approach ('which pays no heed to the work of modern scholarship') would, he declared, be 'unthinkable before a University audience'. If it were made, 'it would be laughed out of court'. This provoked a long and lively correspondence, and the following verse by Timothy Dudley-Smith:

> O, hang your head for Cambridge
> Where, deluded in their youth,
> There are students who would still regard
> The Word of God as truth;
> Who in spite of current catchwords
> And the Modern Churchman's creed,
> Hold a fundamental gospel
> For a fundamental need.
> > How right that someone should reprove
> > These heresies and crimes
> > By a cannonade from Durham
> > In the columns of *The Times*.
>
> O, hang your head for Cambridge;
> She is sorely led astray
> For we know that Dr. Graham
> Will have nothing new to say.
> Let him preach his obscurantist views
> Of what salvation means
> At Wembley or at Windsor
> But not to *King's* or *Queens'*.
> > For a Sovereign and her subjects
> > He is simple and sincere;
> > But to preach to modern scholars
> > Is a laughable idea!
>
> O, hang your head for Cambridge
> That such things are now condoned
> Where the *White Horse Inn* was jeered at

And where Simeon was stoned;
Will you lay aside your learning
And demean your ancient name
To consider what the Bible said
Before the critics came?
    You cannot preach to men in gowns
    What passed with men in skins;
    You must have modern scholarship
    To save from modern sins.

In February the following year the present Archbishop of Canterbury, then Bishop of Durham, wrote an article in *The Bishoprick* (his diocesan magazine) entitled 'The menace of fundamentalism', which aroused a storm of Evangelical protest, although he had been at pains to explain that he had not been tilting at Conservative Evangelicals in the Church of England.

Despite this kind of opposition, Evangelical influence gradually spread. The Islington Clerical Conference, the *Church of England Newspaper*, and one or two additional Evangelical theological colleges, became in theological terms less 'liberal' and more 'conservative'. The Eclectic Society, first founded in 1783 by John Newton and others, was refounded in 1955 for younger Evangelical clergy, and without any attempt at promotion had grown by 1966 to a membership of about a thousand, divided into seventeen regional groups. Latimer House was founded in Oxford in 1960 as an Evangelical research centre to free one or two scholars for study and writing, and so to help re-establish the truth of the Gospel in the Church of England. And the Church of England Evangelical Council, formed the same year, and becoming the following year the English group member of EFAC, began to bring together for the debate of important contemporary issues the most representative consultation of Evangelical leaders for many years.

As Evangelicals increased in numbers, scholarship, cohesion and confidence, their desire grew to speak in some united way to the Church and the nation. So a National Evangelical Anglican Congress was held at the University of Keele in April 1967. Its nearest equivalent was the *Evangelicals Affirm* conference held in London in April 1948. A comparison between the two is instructive. A majority of the speakers at *Evangelicals Affirm* would have described themselves as 'liberal Evangelicals', and, despite the conference's title, the note of distinctively Evangelical affirmation was muted. Its concern was evangelism rather than evangelicalism. The speakers at Keele, were all conservative Evangelicals, and the 10,000-word statement which was hammered out by the delegates attempted not only to restate the Evangelical faith in clear and contemporary terms but also to relate it to some of the major social and ecclesiastical issues of the day. Keele marked our Evangelical coming of age, for there we publicly repented of our immature isolationism and resolved to take a more responsible part in the life of both the visible Church and the secular world. Keele had the unfortunate side-effect of alienating some of our non-Anglican Evangelical friends, who misinterpreted our determination to engage in ecumenical debate as a sign of theological compromise. And it is important for us to take further steps now to heal this breach and to build between Evangelicals of different churches relationships of mutual respect and confidence. But it is unlikely that Evangelical Anglicans will back-pedal from Keele. During the last five years leading Evangelical clergy and laymen have been far more active than previously in the synods and commissions of the Church (especially the Doctrine Commission, the Liturgical Commission, and the scheme for Anglican-Methodist Union), and have made important contributions (by books and pamphlets) to current debate.

It is difficult to assess the strength of Evangelical church life in the country as a whole. There are certainly areas where it still seems weak and ineffective. On the other hand, in March 1972, 285 of the 808 ordinands in the English residential theological colleges (35·2 per cent) were in the six evangelical colleges. There is, further, a welcome new 'radical conservatism' abroad among Anglican Evangelicals, who are determined both to conserve the Biblical faith itself and at the same time to subject all non-Biblical traditions—whether Catholic, Liberal or Evangelical—to a rigorous scrutiny. We are also anxious to apply the Evangelical faith in new ways to new situations. The Church in industrial areas, Christians in open youth clubs, lay training schemes, coffee-bar evangelism, liturgical composition, house groups, modern sound-strips and group-learning courses as teaching tools, music workshops, local radio Sunday schools— these are but some of a host of ways in which Evangelicals are engaging in experiment.

Scotland, Wales, and Ireland

Although episcopacy was twice restored to the Scottish Kirk (in 1610 and 1661), yet since the second disestablishment of 1689 the Church of Scotland has been firmly presbyterian. It is partly in reaction to this that the Scottish Episcopal Church has tended to be catholic in outlook. It was untouched by the Evangelical revival. It is very small, with about 50,000 communicant members concentrated largely in the south and east. In order to preserve an Evangelical Anglican witness in Scotland, St Thomas's Church, Edinburgh, and St Silas's Church, Glasgow, were built in the last century. Both were originally independent of the Scottish Episcopal Church, and were regarded as an English import, but in 1940 St Thomas's was given the official status of a 'private chapel' within the Scottish Episcopal Church, while maintaining its loyalty to the (English) Book of Common Prayer. It has a fine record of evangelism and youth work, and probably the largest Anglican congregation in the Edinburgh diocese. During the last ten years there has been a marked new openness on the part of the Scottish Episcopal Church towards Evangelicals, and several bishops have been willing to institute Evangelical clergy to churches which have had no previous Evangelical tradition. The Scottish Anglican Evangelical Fellowship was formed in 1966.

If Scotland was untouched by the Evangelical revival, Wales was deeply influenced by it. Indeed, many of the leading Welsh Evangelicals left what was then still the established Church in Wales and became nonconformists, to the lasting impoverishment of the Anglican Church. The disestablishment and disendowment of the Church in 1920 led to the formation of the Church of Wales as a separate province, and to the increasing isolation of Welsh Anglicans from the Church of England and so from English evangelicalism. The Evangelical theological colleges and patronage system, which were influential in preserving an Evangelical testimony in English parishes, had no parallel in Wales. However, the Evangelical Fellowship in the Church in Wales or Y Gymdeithas Efengylaidd yn yp Eglwys yng Nghympu (founded in 1967) now has about twenty-five clerical members and twice as many laity. Their leadership is comparatively young, as in Scotland, and they hope to gain a better hearing in the Church in future years.

The Church of Ireland was not so named until the Reformation. But Irish Evangelicals trace the origins of their Church's Evangelical tradition back to the early Celtic Christianity of St Patrick, who loved the Scriptures and relied on Christ crucified alone for salvation. After the sixteenth-century break with Rome, the Church of Ireland used the reformed prayer books of the Church of England. But when the Church was disestablished in 1870 a prayer book and canons of its own were compiled, which restricted the use of ceremonial and reflected its leaders' opposition to the Oxford Movement in England. During the century which has elapsed since then no change of importance has taken place. The Church's protestant conservatism—more 'low church' than 'Evangelical'—is no doubt due largely to its reaction to the Roman Catholic majority who form about seventy-five per cent of the population. It has been calculated, however, that more than half the clergy of the Church of Ireland are to some extent Anglo-Catholic by conviction, although this is largely hidden by the outward conformity to Protestant practice which the Church's canons require. Evangelicals complain of a lack of leadership, although some are taking an active part in the processes of Prayer Book revision. Church Society (Ireland) is affiliated to EFAC.

Before leaving Europe, two points may be mentioned about the Continent. First, the Commonwealth and Continental Church Society, which has an Evangelical constitution, continues to support Anglican Chaplaincies in several principal European cities. Secondly, one of the by-products of the European Congress on Evangelism held in Amsterdam in September 1971 has been the desire of Evangelicals within the different Confessional Churches of Europe which were formed at the Reformation— Lutheran, Reformed, and Anglican—to draw together in closer fellowship. It is hoped to publish a periodical (in German and English), to be entitled *Evangelical Confession (Bekenntnis Heute)*, 'an organ of Evangelical witness in the Confessional Churches of Europe'.

Australia and New Zealand

The first chaplains who sailed with the convict fleets to Australia for about forty years from 1787 were all Evangelicals. But the present strength of evangelicalism in the Sydney diocese seems to be due even more to the outstanding ministry of Bishop

Frederick Barker (1854–82) and Archbishop Howard Mowll (1933–58). Sydney Evangelicals have also commended their faith by their scholarship. Bishop Barker founded Moore Theological College in 1856. Today both its theological standards and its student numbers are higher than those of any other college in the country. Archdeacon T. C. Hammond (who died in 1961) and Archbishop Marcus Loane, former Principals, together with Canon Broughton Knox and Canon Donald Robinson, the present Principal and Vice-Principal, have all won a just acclaim for their Biblical, historical and liturgical expertise.

The Sydney diocese is more than a centre of theological learning, however. Its convictions are expressed in vigorous evangelistic, social and missionary activity. Its official report on evangelism entitled *Move In For Action* was published in 1971. Its Home Mission Society is responsible for some notable work in the care of children and old folk, and in a rapidly expanding counselling service. And its missionary concern expresses itself chiefly through the Bush Church Aid Society and the Church Missionary Society. Australian CMS has always sought to maintain a tradition which combines conservative theology with radical policy. Its missionaries are working in the Northern Territory among aboriginals, in New Guinea and Papua, in several Asian countries, in East Africa, and (more recently) in Peru. And its summer school in New South Wales has attracted an attendance of as many as 1,500 people.

In spite of this widespread activity, thoughtful Australian Evangelicals are not complacent. They know that Australia is by far the wealthiest country in the whole region of South East Asia and that its international policies have tended towards isolationism. They fear that Evangelicals, influenced perhaps more than they realize by the prevailing mood, have been too much preoccupied with their own domestic ecclesiastical affairs and insufficiently aroused in their conscience by the burning problems of the wider world.

Outside the Sydney diocese, evangelicalism is not so strong, although there are EFAC groups in Victoria, South Australia and Western Australia, and some individual members in Armidale, Queensland, and Tasmania. Canon Leon Morris, Principal of Ridley (Theological) College in Melbourne, has gained an international reputation as a New Testament scholar.

In August, 1971, 550 delegates from all over the country assembled at Monash University in Melbourne for a National Evangelical Anglican Congress. The theme was 'Christ Calls us to a new Obedience'. And the Congress Statement, which began with a summary of 'the authentic Gospel', went on to refer bravely to new moral problems, a new strategy for the secular city, new patterns of ministry, new structures of worship, and questions of spiritual gifts, church unity and mission. Although the delegates gloried in their Evangelical inheritance, 'they saw it as a springboard for new advance and new approaches, not as a confining straitjacket' (Leon Morris). They gave 'clear evidence of a radical restlessness urging reform, not in doctrine but in methods, to match the times' (Lance Shilton).

Samuel Marsden, who was the second chaplain to sail for Australia, later went on to New Zealand (1814) and with the help of CMS missionaries began to evangelize the Maoris. George Selwyn was consecrated the first Bishop of New Zealand in 1841 at the age of thirty-three, and has been described as 'one of the greatest bishops in the whole history of the church'. Although Marsden was an Evangelical and Selwyn a Tractarian, they were agreed in their loyalty to the Prayer Book and Articles of the Church, and these were written into the constitution of 1857. Remote from the Biblical criticism and ritualism controversies which were rocking the Church of England in the latter half of the nineteenth century, the New Zealand Church retained its 'low church' conservatism unchanged until the 1920s.

The patron saint of recent evangelicalism in New Zealand (although he would not have relished this designation) is William Orange, who, as Vicar of Sumner near Christchurch in the 1930s, led a Sunday afternoon Bible class for young men. His method was systematic verse-by-verse Biblical exposition, spending three years (it is said) on the first three chapters of Genesis. From this group more than forty men—familiarly known as 'Orange pips'—went into the ministry or on to the mission field. Several are church leaders today. William Orange continued to exercise a faithful Biblical ministry as a Canon of Christchurch Cathedral, and after his death his library of nearly 15,000 books was made the nucleus of a new Biblical research foundation, known as Latimer House.

The Evangelical Churchmen's Fellowship was formed in

1945, became a founder member of EFAC in 1961, and changed its name in 1967 to the Anglican Evangelical Fellowship of New Zealand. Its major support still comes from Christchurch, although there has also been strong evangelical influence in the Nelson diocese (which has had a long association with Sydney), and there are smaller Evangelical groups in Wellington and elsewhere. The Anglican Evangelical Fellowship now has a membership of about five hundred, including nearly one hundred clergy. Its own Spring School and the CMS Spring School alternate, and draw from the same constituency. It publishes a quarterly journal entitled *Latimer*. Lively interdenominational evangelical work—Inter-Varsity Fellowship, Scripture Union and the Crusader movement—has contributed much to its strength.

Despite its comparative isolation, New Zealand has not escaped the cross-currents of change in which the rest of the Church is caught. In the onslaught upon traditional orthodoxy led by the radical Professor Lloyd Geering, formerly Principal of Knox (Presbyterian) College, in the very different challenge of neo-pentecostalism, and in the controversial questions of prayer book revision, intercommunion and church union, the Anglican Evangelical Fellowship (AEF), has been, for Anglican Evangelicals, a valuable focus of unity and forum for debate. It is not only in ecclesiastical politics that New Zealand Evangelicals spend their energies, however. In pulpit and parish, in inner city and youth centre, they are giving evidence of a virile and growing leadership in the Church, and the recent appointment of Dr Francis Andersen as Principal of St John's (Theological) College in Auckland augurs well for the future of Biblical scholarship in New Zealand.

North America

It was in 1534 that the French seaman Jacques Cartier planted a huge thirty-foot cross on Canadian soil near the mouth of the St Laurence River. For the next three centuries Canada was a mission field. Many of the missionaries were Roman Catholics, especially from France, and Quebec was founded in 1608. But others were men of Evangelical conviction.

The history of the indigenous churches of Canada may be said to date from 1867, when the British North America Act became law and the provinces of Ontario, Quebec, New Brunswick and

Nova Scotia were formed into the confederation of Canada. Of those Canadians who claim any church membership today, about eighty per cent belong to the three largest churches. Nearly fifty per cent are Roman Catholics, mostly in Quebec, about twenty per cent belong to the United Church (a union formed in 1925 of Methodists, Congregationalists and some sixty per cent of the Presbyterians), and about thirteen per cent are Anglicans.

Evangelicalism has never been strong in the Anglican Church of Canada. In 1877 an English clergyman called W. H. Rainsford led a remarkable preaching mission in St James' Cathedral, Toronto, during which large numbers were converted. It was to train for the Anglican ministry men won during this mission that Wycliffe College, Toronto, was founded. Evangelical Professors like Dyson Hague and Griffith Thomas are still well-remembered names at Wycliffe, and the college maintains a tradition of Evangelical scholarship today.

As in other countries, especially of the Commonwealth, the fortunes of Evangelical Anglicanism in Canada are linked with the work of both the Inter-Varsity Christian Fellowship and the Scripture Union. God used the visit of a young medical student called Howard Guinness in 1928–29 to establish 'Inter-Varsity' right across Canada. The ministry of Gerald Gregson is also well remembered for its effectiveness, first as a chaplain in the 'Empire Air Training Scheme' during the Second World War and then as General Secretary of the Scripture Union until 1951.

The Koinonia Youth Fellowship was widely influential in Toronto and Montreal in the Fifties, and in 1961 the Canadian Anglican Evangelical Fellowship became a founder member of EFAC.

Anything savouring of 'party spirit' has always been strongly deprecated in the Anglican Church of Canada, and some have for this reason been reluctant to call themselves 'Evangelical'. It is becoming more widely understood now, however, that 'Evangelical' is not necessarily a synonym either for 'divisive' or for 'emotional'; and Evangelical Anglicans are being heeded as never before. They see Canada's need of Christ and are anxious to take a lead in Christian witness.

Although the Protestant Episcopal Church of the USA (PECUSA) is today largely 'liberal catholic', it has not always been so. On the contrary, its origins were Evangelical. The first 132 pages of E. C. Chorley's *Men and Movements in the American Episcopal Church* (Scrivener, 1946) are devoted to an account of the early Evangelicals, their leaders, doctrines and activities. 'The Evangelical Movement in the American Church', he begins, 'sprang to life in Virginia about the middle of the eighteenth century'. Indeed, 'Virginia was the nursery of Evangelical religion' (p. 55). But the formation of the Methodist Episcopal Church in 1784 led to many secessions, and a consequent weakening of the Protestant Episcopal Church.

It is true that, after the Episcopal Church won its autonomy following the War of Independence, its first bishop (Samuel Seabury of Connecticut) was a Society for the Propagation of the Gospel (SPG) missionary and received his episcopal consecration in 1784 at the hand of Scottish bishops in Aberdeen. He took back with him to America the Scottish Communion Office of 1764, whose Prayer of Consecration contained several distinctively 'catholic' traditions and was incorporated (with one emendation) into the first American liturgy of 1789. At the same time, the young Episcopal Church had been profoundly affected by the great Evangelical awakening, and this influence remained. 'The golden age for the Evangelicals', writes E. C. Chorley 'was in the eighteen thirties and forties' (p. 132). He mentions that thirteen strong bishops at that time were men of definite Evangelical persuasion, 'with not a few presbyters of like mind'. One observer estimated that in 1841 two-thirds of the clerical deputies to the General Convention were Evangelicals.

The promise of those years was never fulfilled, however. The early High Church and later Tractarian movements, the secession of the Reformed Episcopal Church in 1873, the spread of deism and liberalism, and the reaction of cultured men against emotional revivalism were some of the factors which contributed to the dwindling of Evangelical influence in the Protestant Episcopal Church of the USA. Phillips Brooks (1835–93), for example, a leading bishop and dynamic preacher, turned away from his Evangelical upbringing and became a key figure in the Broad Church tradition.

During the first half of this century there seems to have been no distinctively Evangelical witness in the American Episcopal Church. Some of the organizations founded in the previous century continued to exist. The most influential was (and is) the Evangelical Education Society, which was founded in 1862 by Phillips Brooks (though he later resigned from the Board) to educate young men for the ministry and distribute Evangelical literature. It publishes *The Protestant Episcopal Standard*. With it were merged in 1949 the Protestant Episcopal Society for the Promotion of Evangelical Knowledge (founded in 1847 to combat Tractarianism), and in 1961 the Episcopal Evangelical Society (founded in 1813 to deepen its members' spiritual life). The Evangelical Education Society claims to have helped 2,000 men in their ministerial training. But these are no longer required to express their sympathy with the Society's original 'Distinctive Principles' which concerned the Bible as the sole rule of faith, justification by faith only, the exclusive priesthood of Christ, etc. Indeed, the epithet 'Evangelical' has come to mean for many in PECUSA little more than 'low church liberal'.

Today several fairly new movements are bringing hope of fresh life to the Episcopal Church, through prayer, fellowship groups and lay witness. Such are 'The Anglican Fellowship of Prayer' (founded by Sam Shoemaker and continued by Helen his widow); 'Faith Alive' (which has evolved from 'the Brotherhood of St Andrew'); 'Faith At Work' (an interdenominational group with strong episcopal connections); a new 'Episcopal Centre for Evangelism' in Miami; and the small American branch of EFAC called 'the Fellowship of Witness'.

Contemporary churchmen of decidedly Evangelical conviction are a small, scattered and disorganized minority. Yet there are signs of growth, as an increasing number of lay people become disenchanted with liberalism and hungry for the Biblical faith, a tiny group of Evangelical clergy take seriously the need for a theological 'defence and confirmation of the gospel', and some promising young men are offering for the ordained ministry.

Latin America

It is not an exaggeration to say that in the republics of Central America and the islands of the Caribbean there is virtually no Evangelical Anglicanism. In the British West Indies missionary work was largely pioneered by SPG (the few CMS missionaries had all been withdrawn by 1848), while the American Episcopal Church has work in both Central America and the northern part of South America. The Brazilian Episcopal Church became autonomous in 1965 and boasts some 25,000 members with over eighty ordained Brazilian clergy.

In six republics of South America, however—Argentina, Bolivia, Chile, Paraguay, Peru, and Uruguay—the Anglican Church, though comparatively small, is entirely Evangelical, with the exception of a few English-speaking urban chaplaincies. This is due to the notable work of the South American Missionary Society.

SAMS was founded by Captain Allen Gardiner when he settled in the Falkland Islands in 1844, although until 1864 it was called the Patagonia Missionary Society. He and six fellow missionaries died of exposure and starvation in 1851 in Tierra del Fuego, having won no converts, but having 'lit a fire which has never been put out'.

Waite Stirling, consecrated the first Bishop of the Falkland Islands in 1869, a missionary bishop of rugged courage, common sense and godliness, travelled all over South America until he resigned in 1900, and may be said to have established the Church over a wide area.

It is significant that at the World Missionary Conference in Edinburgh in 1910, since attendance was limited to agencies working in 'pagan countries' and since Latin America was regarded as a Roman Catholic preserve in which 'proselytism' was frowned upon, there were no missionary representatives from the whole Continent. But the Panama Congress, held in 1916 to consider Latin America's unique problems and attended by 304 delegates (mostly American), recognized that Latin America was a mission field. So did the Roman Catholic Chimbote (Peru) Conference in 1953, accepting that nominally Christian Latin America like contemporary France needed to be re-Christianized. These varied assessments of South America hardly affected SAMS, however, as the society's work has (until recently) been exclusively among Indian tribespeople.

The Lambeth Conferences of 1958 and 1968 both called for a strengthening and extension of Anglican missionary work on the continent, and during the last decade the work of SAMS has grown by leaps and bounds. Their thirty-six missionaries in 1959 had more than trebled to 114 in 1969. Meanwhile in 1960 an important policy decision had been taken to train and ordain national pastors. There are now sixteen in Chile, together with twenty-six presbyters and ten deacons in the diocese of Paraguay and Northern Argentina.

A recent investigation by SAMS into the role of Anglicanism in South America entitled *Towards a More Certain Call* (1971) contains some fresh and radical thinking. In the long term they look forward, even if it is a distant goal, to 'the formation of national churches, which, while being true to Scripture, unite progressively more denominations and bear a more effective witness to the republics they represent'. Meanwhile, they see a distinctive rôle for the Anglican Church, offering a truly Biblical theology to Roman Catholics who want it and Pentecostals who lack it, and seeking the right kind of Christian political and social action between the extremes of Pentecostal disengagement and Roman Catholic manœuvring.

In addition, the Anglican Church is feeling for new ways of adapting traditional structures. Here are some examples: an episcopal jurisdiction made more meaningful and manageable by being restricted to a single region or ethnic group; a living liturgy which adds spontaneity to uniformity; training for the ministry by an 'apprenticeship' system; ministerial dress which combines variety according to climate and culture with some common symbol; training other church leaders by means of 'theological education by extension'; and a larger vision of winning South America for Christ by urban penetration as well as primary rural evangelism.

Africa

The first Anglican Evangelical missionary enterprise in Equatorial Africa was in Sierra Leone. Here a settlement was founded in 1787 for freed slaves from England, and another ('Freetown') in 1792 for slaves from Nova Scotia. Here in 1806 the first of all CMS missionaries arrived, seven years after the formation of the Society, and here in the so-called 'white man's grave' many of the first missionaries died. Here too in 1816 CMS built tropical Africa's first college of higher education, Fourah Bay College, originally for the training of clergy, catechists, and teachers, but now the University of Sierra Leone.

CMS missionaries came to Nigeria in the 1840s. Expeditions up the River Niger were organized in 1841, 1854 and 1857, and a member of each of them was a remarkable African who came later to be known as Samuel Crowther. When he was a small boy of eleven, Adjai had been first kidnapped by slave traders and then rescued. After being educated at Fourah Bay College and in England, he was in 1864 consecrated the first Bishop of the Niger. He was a simple Evangelical believer. 'If I am to be told no longer to hold up Jesus Christ as a propitiation for sin,' he said, 'what am I to offer the African in place of his sacrifices of goats, fowls and pigeons?' His keen intellect and tireless energy were wholly devoted to the service of his people, until he died in 1891. He dreamed of an indigenous native church, and to that end ordained several African clergy, and himself translated the Prayer Book and parts of the Bible into Yoruba.

The Christian Church in West Africa has made its own contribution to the movements towards national independence, not least through its mission schools in which many of each country's leaders have been educated. The Church is almost entirely Africanized, although the Anglican Church's theological complexion reflects the outlook of the pioneering mission, SPG in Ghana, CMS in Sierra Leone and Nigeria. Of these last two countries Evangelical strength is more evident in Nigeria, partly because of the influence of Immanuel College, Ibadan, where most of its Anglican clergy are trained. A promising means of renewal in the churches of West Africa (and elsewhere) is 'New Life For All', an interdenominational evangelistic project, patterned after Latin America's 'Evangelism in Depth', which seeks to mobilize all the churches to co-operate in gospel witness. And both Scripture Union and the Pan-African Fellowship of Evangelical Students are having an increasing influence on West African youth.

The foundation and growth of the Christian Church in East and Central Africa could not be described without mentioning the name of David Livingstone. His intrepid explorations between 1840 and 1873 brought Africa to the attention of Europe. A year after his death his young friend and admirer, H. M. Stanley, after visiting Uganda and hearing Mtesa King of the Baganda profess faith in Christ, wrote to England appealing for missionaries. CMS heeded the appeal, and in 1876 the first missionaries sailed. Another group sailed in 1882, led by James Hannington, who in 1884, after returning to England, was consecrated the first Bishop of Eastern Equatorial Africa. He landed again in Mombasa in January 1885, and nine months later was murdered on the borders of Uganda, the country he had come to serve. In those years at least 150 of the first Ugandan converts were also martyred.

The third bishop was Alfred Tucker, an unusual combination of artist and athlete, who was consecrated and sailed for Mombasa in 1890. For more than two decades he sought to guide the young Church according to indigenous principles. Perhaps he had learned them from one of the official CMS statements issued in about 1850. In these Henry Venn described the ultimate object of a mission as the creation of 'a Native Church under Native Pastors upon a self-supporting, self-governing and self-extending system'. When this goal is reached, he went on, 'the Mission will have attained its *euthanasia*'. Certainly Bishop Tucker wanted an African Church with an African Bible and an African ministry, supported by African money. In 1909 the 'Uganda Native African Church' was established, and by the time Tucker retired in 1911 the number of Ugandan Christians had grown from 200 to about 75,000.

One of the most notable features of the East African Church in this century is the revival movement which began in the early 1930s in what are now the countries of Rwanda and Burundi (where the Anglican Church is entirely Evangelical), but has since deeply affected church life in Uganda, Kenya, Tanzania, and Southern Sudan. The *balokole* (or 'saved ones') lay stress on the Christian's three relationships. First, with Christ himself. 'Revival is Jesus', they say. For Jesus Christ is willing to fill with his Spirit every heart his blood has cleansed. The resultant Christian life is one of 'brokenness'. Secondly, Christians are to 'walk in the light', in open fellowship with God and with each other. The fellowship groups of the revival movement, uniting Africans and Europeans and members of different African tribes, have exhibited Christ's power to conquer racial and tribal prejudice even in the days of Mau Mau. Thirdly, the *balokole* are keen evangelists. Individually and in teams they bear witness to Christ and seek to win unbelievers to his allegiance. Of course the Movement has its weaknesses. It has tended to despise theology (and so to lose East Africa's young intelligentsia from the Church), and to avoid involvement in the social and political life of the nation. Yet it has been an evident work of

God, has stayed within the Church, and continues unabated today after forty years.

Mention must now be made of the Bible Churchmen's Missionary Society (BCMS), founded in 1922 'for the word of God and for the testimony of Jesus Christ'. They have been working in four African territories. The first is the dry and rugged terrain round the southern tip of Lake Rudolf, where, since 1929 they have been seeking to serve nearly a quarter of a million primitive nomads from several tribal groups. The second is in Central Tanganyika, at the request of Australian and New Zealand CMS. During the notable episcopate of Alfred Stanway (1950–71) the Church's growth has been phenomenal: approximately one new church has been planted every week. The third BCMS field has been North Africa, where during the Roman Empire there had been flourishing Christian churches until they were obliterated first by the Vandals in the fifth century and then by Moslem Arab invaders at the end of the seventh. BCMS began work in Morocco in 1929, and in 1936 a Diocese of North Africa was formed, comprising Morocco, Algeria, and Tunisia. But nearly all missionaries have now had to withdraw from these Moslem strongholds.

The fourth African territory in which BCMS are serving is Ethiopia. Their work there introduces us to an important missionary principle which CMS, BCMS, and the Church's Ministry among the Jews (CMJ), have all adopted towards the ancient Orthodox Churches of that country and of Egypt. When CMS sent Samuel Gobat first to Egypt (1825) and then to Abyssinia (1830)—he became the second Bishop in Jerusalem in 1846—they counselled moderation and caution towards 'a benighted and corrupted Oriental Church'. Rather than ignore and abandon it, however, their policy has been to spread Bibles and Christian literature, and to work for the reform and renewal of the Church. So they established in Cairo a seminary in which to train priests for Egypt's Coptic Church. In Ethiopia too both BCMS and CMJ are seeking to be the means of reviving the Ethiopian Orthodox Church, and of arousing its members to evangelize the Moslems and pagans of their own country.

In South Africa, Christianity has had an involved history. When the British seized the Cape in 1795, they found Dutch settlers and the Dutch Reformed Church. At first the Anglican

Church limited its responsibility to chaplaincies for the garrison, but by 1847 the number of Anglican immigrants had grown sufficiently for a bishop to be appointed to shepherd them. The first Bishop of Cape Town, who subsequently became the first Metropolitan of South Africa, was Robert Gray, a man of Tractarian views and autocratic temper, who confessed himself determined to establish a Church in South Africa, rid of 'the bonds and fetters of the Reformation'.

The first bishop of Natal, John Colenso, was consecrated in 1853. He had a great love for the Zulus and translated the New Testament into their language. He also had a more seemly view of episcopacy than Gray, and, in sacramental terms, was a 'low' churchman. But theologically he was a universalist and a modernist. So in 1863 Gray brought him to trial as a heretic and had him deposed. Two years later, however, the Privy Council's Judicial Committee declared his condemnation null (on technical not theological grounds), which decided Colenso to remain in his diocese. Gray proceeded to excommunicate him and consecrate his successor, although the civil courts ruled that he was the rightful possessor of the diocesan churches and schools. Thus the country was treated to the scandalous spectacle of rival and competing bishops. Ironically, this was a major reason for the summoning of the first Lambeth Conference in 1867.

In 1870 Gray's provincial synod adopted the canons and constitution of 'The Church of the Province of South Africa', while a small minority of Evangelical churches determined to remain loyal to the 'Mother Church', the Church of England. The history of the succeeding century is sad and complicated.

A series of legal judgments, by ruling that the Church of the Province had separated itself from the Church of England, recognized the existence of two Churches in South Africa, the Church of the Province of South Africa (CPSA), and the Church of England in South Africa (CESA). Various solutions to this anomaly were proposed. At first the CPSA bishops exercised a dual ministry to both Churches. Next a few CESA churches made private contracts with CPSA, agreeing to accept that church's episcopal jurisdiction and ministry in return for a guarantee of their evangelical continuity. Then in 1933 the 'Silvertrees Agreement' nearly succeeded. It would have brought the two Churches into communion with each other, while recognizing

13*

the independence of CESA and granting them their own bishop(s) under the Archbishop of Cape Town, together with the right to maintain their evangelicalism and to expand. CESA accepted these terms, but regrettably CPSA repudiated them. Finally in 1953 Archbishop Fisher sent Canon J. P. Hickinbotham to mediate. But the 'Thirteen Points' he submitted were interpreted by most members of CESA both as a non-negotiable ultimatum and as an erosion of their position, and were rejected.

So in 1955 CESA took the decisive step of electing Fred Morris (previously Bishop in North Africa and then Rector of their leading church in Johannesburg) as their Bishop. Archbishop Fisher responded—with extremely questionable authority—by declaring that Bishop Morris had 'put himself out of communion with the See of Canterbury and outside the fellowship of the Anglican Communion'. In 1959 and 1961 Bishop Morris proceeded to consecrate Bishop Stephen Bradley and Bishop Peter Chamane, the latter to care for CESA's growing work among the Zulus.

It is a tragic story of a century of misunderstanding and mistrust. Probably neither Church has been wholly free from blame. Certainly each accuses the other of schism. One may feel that CESA have resorted too often to litigation. On the other hand, their historical and legal case is very strong, and their loyalty to the Evangelical doctrine of the Church of England is beyond question.

Meanwhile, there is a small and struggling Evangelical minority in the Church of the Province. Their position is extremely difficult, for CPSA is an almost monochrome, Anglo-Catholic Church. Promotion is virtually denied them, unless they are prepared to compromise their convictions. For Holy Communion they are forced to choose between the 1662 service (which they find too English and too archaic) and the South African liturgy (which they cannot use with a good conscience). The policy of CPSA towards them appears to be one of containment, tolerating an Evangelical remnant but giving it little or no opportunity to expand.

In 1961 the Council of EFAC decided to admit to group membership the Evangelical fellowship of both Churches. The relationship between these two groups, itself tenuous, is the only remaining bridge between the two churches. EFAC hope it will be fostered. Both Evangelical fellowships maintain through their members some flourishing youth work and evangelism. In addition, *Africa Enterprise*, an independent evangelistic project led by a young layman, Michael Cassidy, bears a brave and effective testimony to Jesus Christ across the barriers of both race and denomination.

Asia

It is impossible in a few paragraphs to attempt more than the briefest sketch of Evangelical Anglicanism in Asia.

In the Middle East the Anglican churches are tiny. But the work of CMJ missionaries in Israel, and of CMS missionaries in Egypt, Jordan and Iran, has helped to preserve an Evangelical testimony in these countries. The Anglican Church in Jordan is still called 'the Evangelical Episcopal Community'; about a sixth of Jordan's Christians belong to it.

The first Anglican missionary to India—in distinction to chaplains of the East India Company—was the scholar-saint Henry Martyn. He sailed in 1805, and later went on to Persia, where he died in 1812 at the early age of thirty-two. The first Bishop of Calcutta (whose original diocese extended as far as Australia and South Africa!) was consecrated in 1814, and the fifth bishop was that vigorous Evangelical leader Daniel Wilson. That he was a man of strong conviction may be judged from his edict that in the Church 'caste must be abandoned decidedly, immediately, finally'. For a quarter of a century he led his vast diocese with immense energy and devotion. Between 1814 and 1840 CMS sent a hundred missionaries to India, including a number of Lutherans, and established centres in the south (Madras) and West (Bombay) as well as in the North-east (Calcutta). SPG also had missionaries in Bengal and the South. Later the diocese of Lahore covered the whole of the west of the subcontinent, until it became part of Pakistan. Here British, Australian and New Zealand CMS have co-operated in city and tribal work.

CMS missionaries have played a prominent part in the negotiations which led to the formation of the Church of South India (1947), the Church of North India (1971), and the Church of Pakistan (1971). Probably more than fifty per cent of CSI members are, at least in general terms, 'Evangelical'. No EFAC group has been formed in India, however, largely because of the strength of the interdenominational Evangelical Fellowship of India, which is affiliated to the World Evangelical Fellowship.

The first CMS missionaries reached Ceylon in 1817, and in 1840 the first missionaries of SPG. As a result, the Evangelical and Catholic traditions of Anglicanism have enjoyed an uneasy coexistence. Christ Church Galle Face has been a kind of evangelical centre in Colombo since it was dedicated in 1853, and the Ceylon Anglican Evangelical Fellowship includes some gifted younger clergy who are calling the church to Biblical exposition and evangelism.

Burma has been a pioneer BCMS mission field since A. T. Houghton opened up work among the Kachins (or Jinghpaws) of Upper Burma in 1923. BCMS took over a School for Deaf and Dumb children in Rangoon in 1929, and later began missionary work on the western coastal strip of Arakan. The Japanese occupation scattered the Christian communities, but after the war the Church consolidated and grew, and in the newly independent and largely Catholic province of Burma, without the aid of any foreign missionaries, the Burma Anglican Evangelical Fellowship is seeking to maintain its witness to the truth of the Gospel.

A major problem facing the Church in all these countries which were previously included in 'the Church of India, Pakistan, Burma and Ceylon' is the relation of the Christian faith to other faiths. True, the situation is very different in Moslem Pakistan, Hindu India, and Buddhist Burma and Ceylon. Yet in each case the Church is called to witness within an alien culture and is tempted to surrender the uniqueness of Christ to the contemporary mood of syncretism.

By far the largest and most densely populated Asian country is, of course, China. But after the Communist takeover in 1949 all missionaries were obliged to leave the country. Of China's brave little underground Church not much is known. What is known, however, is that the withdrawal of missionaries from China led to their re-deployment in many countries of South East Asia, especially but not exclusively among the Chinese dispersion. They have helped to strengthen the Christian Church in Singapore (whose first small mission to Asians began in 1856, and whose first Asian bishop was consecrated 110 years later); in

Malaysia (in both towns and new villages); in Sabah (where Australian CMS are serving, and British CMS give a grant to indigenous evangelists under their *Fontier Fund*); in Hong Kong (which became a CMS station in 1862, and where one of the first women to be ordained to the presbyterate is a CMS missionary); and in Japan (which was entirely closed to the Gospel for about two and a half centuries until the 1858 treaty with Britain, and whose Christians today form less than one per cent of the population, including the little indigenous Anglican Church, the Nippon Sei Ko Kai). It will be seen that the Anglican Church is small in these countries, and the Evangelical constituency smaller still.

Conclusion

One conclusion which may seem to emerge from this brief survey of world-wide Anglican Evangelicalism is that Evangelicals are better at evangelism than at consolidation. Evangelical chaplains and missionaries had a large share in the planting of Christianity in Britain's colonies and in foreign lands. The origins of the national churches of many countries were Evangelical. But the early momentum has not always been maintained. Of many possible reasons perhaps the chief are our tendencies to be anti-intellectual, pietistic and internally divisive.

We seem, however, to be learning some of the lessons which history teaches. International Evangelical youth movements like the Scripture Union and the International Fellowship of Evangelical Students, in whose work Evangelical Anglicans have shared from the beginning, are increasingly concerned not only to evangelize but also to teach and train young Christians, and to encourage them to become responsible members of both Church and community. Missionary societies have been turning their attention from rural areas to the teeming cities. Theological colleges are taking more seriously the task of training men to be Christian communicators, and to expound Scripture relevantly as well as faithfully. All of us see more clearly the need to become involved in the life of our church and nation; to stand together for the fundamental truths of the Gospel, and not to allow ourselves to be divided by secondary matters; and, above all, under God and in the power of his Spirit, to defend and commend the Evangelical faith by a sound Biblical scholarship.

13

WHAT I HOPE FROM EVANGELICALS

JOHN LAWRENCE

I am asked what I hope for from Evangelicals in the next few years. I hope above all that they will help to lead us back to the Bible, that they will help us to live by justification through faith, and that they will help to restore the Church's sense of mission.

I have my points of difference with some Evangelicals, as I have with some who call themselves Catholic, Liberal, or Radical. I am not a strict or conservative Evangelical and I do not generally spell the word with a capital E but I claim to have as good a right as anyone else to call myself evangelical. However, I do not regard such labels as very important. When Temple Gairdner of Cairo was asked whether he was high church or low church, he used to answer 'I hope I am deep church.' That is my own position. About many things I agree more deeply with conservative Evangelicals than with many who call themselves liberal. I see full well why Gervase Duffield was repelled by so much Oxbridge theology. We live in an age when professional theologians give us more stones than bread. When was it not so? Yet there must be theology; even now, some of it is concerned with the bread of heaven; and I am myself fully orthodox and catholic, if I understand what those words mean. So I start with some fairly sharp criticism of some conservative Evangelical positions but with more sympathy than criticism.

I agree with some other contributors to this volume that in the recent past Evangelicals have been too defensive about the Bible. But these same contributions show how far some Evangelicals have already moved. I want to see them move farther, but not in the direction of a 'liberal' interpretation, if I may use that word for shorthand. Evangelicals have kept their awe before the record of God's mighty acts in Scripture. They see the Bible for what it is, a divine book, where many scholars and translators have tried to reduce it to a human level. When I read up-to-date books about the Bible, I often get the feeling that the peaks are being eroded and the deep places filled up. I am being given a picture where the bright colours are toned down, a Bible in which there is neither height nor depth, neither angel, nor demon, no fall of man and therefore no salvation, no wrath of the Father and no deep love, no heaven or hell, no providence, no prophecy, and finally no Cross. No one will, I hope, think that I want to take an excessively simple view of any of these matters. I see the traps in some traditional views of prophecy or the last judgement, to take the most obvious cases, and I am not convinced by some of what is written in this symposium; but the writers do at least start from a position where they are open to the Truth from outside that shatters our limited human structures of understanding. They are not deaf to the words 'Thus saith the Lord.'

I do not think that Evangelicals have a monopoly of understanding love for Scripture. I think of R. H. Lightfoot, Temple, and Westcott, on St John's Gospel and Epistles, and Austin Farrer and Maycock on St. John's Apocalypse; yes, I do link these works and suppose them all to emanate from the beloved disciple, for reasons which I could give, but which would not interest anyone; I am not a scholar, though I am an interested spectator of scholarship. I only mention this here to show that on some important points I am in agreement with the conservatives against a great volume of contrary opinion. But I would like to see Evangelical scholars give less attention to defending the traditional authorship of Biblical writing and more attention to bringing us back to aspects of the Bible that tend to be forgotten in this age.

Rob Pearman's understanding of metaphor and symbol encourages me to hope that there will soon be Evangelical scholars who can fill out the fragmentary and one-sided work on the Book of Revelation done by the two Anglo-Catholics referred to above. I am conscious of needing more help than I have got for reading the prophetical parts of the Bible. I have no great hope of getting this help from Oxbridge, Tübingen or Yale, as they now are. I do not want a merely historical analysis of Scriptural prediction, though I do not want to see history neglected. Biblical prophecy contains a predictive element, but this is hardly the most important element in it. Anyway, some of the things shown to us in prophecy are presumably outside time. The difficulty is that understanding of some of the more important things in the Bible takes one outside the common material of scholarship. Writers on the Bible need to be scholars, but they also need to be much more than scholars.

Biblical scholarship, if it is to be true to the Bible's own pattern, needs less argument and more insight. The Bible gives us images more often than argument. The Body, the Vine, the Bread of Heaven, the Water of Life, the Good Shepherd, the Heavenly City. 'What seest thou, Jeremiah?' It is truly said that this age is tired of words. But we cannot do without words. I am writing now. In the next century more people will be converted by pictures, symbols, Biblical images—call them what you will—than by the words of sermons. I hope therefore that the Evangelical concern for mission will lead Evangelicals to a bolder use of Biblical imagery.

I know the reasons, some good and some less good, which have in the past made Evangelicals over-careful, as I think, in their use of some visual and imaginative elements in Biblical worship. I hope that their concern for the souls of men will now make them bolder to use all that the Bible gives us. This will mean, among other things, an evangelicalism that is more sacramental than much of what we have known in the past. Here Colin Buchanan's excellent contribution to this volume fills me with hope.

I hope next that Evangelicals will show us how to live according to justification by faith. It is easier to talk about this doctrine than to live by it. evangelicals have a reputation—not always undeserved—for a moralism that can become a substitute for faith, and a belief in once-for-all conversion that can hinder moral and spiritual growth after conversion. I do not want Evangelicals to turn permissive, and I do not think they will do so; but I want to see more faith in Faith, which in turn will lead to a less cramped morality.

Here I am touching on the most difficult question in human life, and no one will expect me to say the last word on it. I can only point to the paradox that a proclaimed belief in justification by faith often leads to an excessive emphasis on correct conduct—I do not say 'on works' because that word has a technical meaning that may not altogether fit the present context.

The age of half-faith has passed. We live in an age when there is a choice between a full faith and a state when life seems 'absurd' in the existential sense. Full faith involves a moral and intellectual openness that has not always gone with Evangelical convictions. But if Evangelicals will really live by their belief in justification, they will bring many people to a moral life that has lost all traces of Pharisaism.

The Church is always losing the spirit of mission and then finding it again. The pattern recurs but the reasons are not the same. At one time there was not much mission, because there were no people within shouting distance who did not claim to be Christian. Today the reason is that a confused world is inclined to think that all opinions are relative, uncertain, and a matter of personal choice. Western European individualism, both Protestant and Catholic, must bear some of the blame for this. And the cure for unbridled individualism is a renewed feeling for the Communion of Saints, a doctrine which we recite in the Creed but then forget. A sense of belonging to each other, of the oneness of the Church in heaven and on earth, and of being one with the Lord, will, in the Evangelical context, lead to a renewed sense of an objective truth in matters of conduct, which ought to be combined with a renewed concern for those who are not one with us in the faith, though they are our brothers in the body of humanity.

Evangelicals do for the most part care for mission. It must, I think, be admitted that this care has sometimes been nurtured by a presumptuous limiting of God's mercy to those who are without, and an ignorant contempt for those who differ from us in religion. It may not be easy to say why it makes all the difference to know the Lord, or rather to say it without caricaturing those who think otherwise. Yet it does make all the difference; and Evangelicals can be trusted to remember this, even when they have come right out of their beleagured fortress, as, please God, they will. We do not know what God intends for his Church in the next century, but surely he is preparing some great thing. It is not right to assume anything about Christian numbers in the future. There may be fewer of us in the future or there may be far more than in the past. In either case we are to proclaim the

Gospel with equal boldness, and to proclaim 'the whole Gospel for the whole man'; but this involves commitment to some this-worldly causes which Evangelicals have sometimes thought comparatively unimportant. It does not, therefore, involve the neglect of the things of the other world; and in the hands of Evangelicals it will not do so. They are unlikely to fall for what I have elsewhere called the heresy of 'justification by the works of renewal', but it is good that some Evangelicals are now increasingly concerned for a renewal that has a this-worldly consequence.

The serious criticism that I do want to make of some of the contributions in this symposium is not so much that they put forward any views that I cannot accept, but that sometimes they distort the views of those who disagree with them. I would claim for myself some of the appellations which seem to be used in this book as 'boo words'. But I do not recognize either myself or my acquaintances in some of the descriptions that are given.

This brings me to my final hope for Evangelicals. I hope they will be less and less moved by party considerations and that old grievances will be forgotten. Evangelicals have not had a monopoly of party spirit in the injurious sense of the phrase. None of us is immune from that. Personally I specially dislike the arrogant self-righteousness of progressive thinkers; perhaps I see myself in the mirror and do not like what I see.

The whole Church needs the Evangelicals, but they are not the whole Church; and it makes it harder for others to accept what they have to give, if even a few of them appear to speak as if they had the whole counsel of God, and they alone had it. The Revelation we have in Jesus Christ is full and final, but we understand only a part of what we have been given, and, when we understand more, it may modify our previous understanding in ways that we do not yet foresee. So I want to see Evangelicals who are fully open to all truth. I make no judgement about how many of them are so already. But I want to see an Open Evangelicalism playing a greater part than before in the life of the Church. I do not want to see Evangelical principles diluted. I do want to see them applied with breadth of understanding.